TRANSACTIONAL ANALYSIS IN
CONTEMPORARY PSYCHOTHERAPY

TRANSACTIONAL ANALYSIS IN CONTEMPORARY PSYCHOTHERAPY

Edited by
Richard G. Erskine

KARNAC

First published in 2016 by
Karnac Books Ltd
118 Finchley Road
London NW3 5HT

British Library Cataloguing in Publication Data

A C.I.P. for this book is available from the British Library

ISBN-13: 978-1-78220-263-9

Typeset by V Publishing Solutions Pvt Ltd., Chennai, India

Printed in Great Britain

www.karnacbooks.com

CONTENTS

FOREWORD

James R. Allen

When Richard Erskine asked me to write a foreword to this book, I accepted with some reluctance. After almost sixty years of practice, I had recently retired and, for now at least, had turned my attention elsewhere. However, I am now delighted that I accepted the invitation. The chapters are interesting descriptions of how the authors have used and shaped what they understood as Transactional Analysis and often how they themselves in turn have been reshaped in the process.

Reading this book has been like looking at a geological cross section: there are veins of Berne, the Gouldings, Erskine, and a variety of relational perspectives, all separating, combining, and then separating and combining again. It has been a retrospective on my own therapeutic development and has opened vistas of possible futures. However, in addition to Eric Berne, there are two important precursors whose contributions have been largely neglected: Fritz Perls (Perls, Hefferline, & Goodman, 1951) and Virginia Satir (1983).

Perls was important in that 1960s hotbed of psychotherapy between San Francisco and Big Sur, the location of the Esalen Institute which was the first "growth center" in the USA and Perls's then home. All knew each other personally and the work of one another. Indeed, in personal conversations in the early 1960s, Bob Goulding told me he saw himself as combining Berne's ideas of pathological script outcomes with Perls's techniques, including imaginary two-chair dialogues. Behind Perls, however, stood such giants as Wilhelm Reich and the director Max Reinhardt—to say nothing of Perls's wife, Laura, and the Weimar and New York Gestalt groups.

Erskine asked me to write a combination of personal reactions, associations, critiques, and questions for potential readers. So, let us proceed.

First is Erskine's paper on the treatment of obsessing and repetitive fantasising. The first section of this chapter is a masterful condensation of theory as it subserves integrative psychotherapy. His diagram of the script system is especially helpful. It may be difficult for first-time readers to appreciate fully its subtlety and implications. However, you will find help in the detailed description of long-term therapy conducted by this mindful therapist. I was impressed by his six-faceted conceptualisation. Young and not-so-young therapists will find much to emulate. This includes noticing and acknowledging our own therapeutic errors.

A second version of a two-person relational approach is Ray Little's description of a transference-countertransference focused Transactional Analysis. He conceptualises psychopathology in terms of activation of predominantly unconscious defensive/maladaptive Child–Parent, or self-other relational units. Both of these need to be addressed. For example, in dealing with the after-effects of abuse, the therapist needs to address both victim and abuser representations. Little's approach entails the working through of old object relationships and the development of new ones; as he writes, the therapist is both magnet and architect. He gives us admirable examples of mindfulness, a therapist's efforts to understand his own internal workings and motivations as well as those of the patient and the resulting constructed interpersonal matrix. He reminds us of the necessity of careful exploration of how the patient may interpret the therapist's behaviour, whether the latter coincides with the patient's projections or whether the patient's interpretation varies considerably from the therapist's actual experience.

These papers remind me of the importance of non-verbal behaviour, and especially of the role of the "smart" vagus in social engagement. Out of our awareness, it influences our muscles of facial expression and even what we are able to hear (Porges, 1995).

John McNeel provides a very clear description of the redecision work of the Gouldings as they actually practised as well as his own explorations and elaborations of it. Although he went to California to train with the Gouldings about three years later than I did, he captures the zeitgeist that I remember, as well as the Gouldings' generosity, and even their prejudices. By the time he arrived, the Gouldings had diverged somewhat from Berne and David Kupfer, whose contributions included "rubber bands" and with whom they had shared offices in the Carmel Institute of Transactional Analysis. By the time McNeel arrived, they had set up the Western Institute of Group and Family Therapy at Mt. Madonna outside Watsonville, California.

McNeel's doctoral dissertation focused on a Goulding weekend workshop and a follow-up of the involved patients. Among other things, it showed that, at least at three months, participants had been redirected in their life course. Another important piece of research at that time, Lieberman, Yalom, and Miles's 1973 study of seventeen different groups, showed that of all the groups, that of the Gouldings had the most improvements and no casualties. The second "best" group was a Gestalt one, but it had casualties.

In his chapter, McNeel reports his explanations of and his current conceptualisations of injunctions. He now calls them "injunctive messages". He also recounts how he came to reject Mary Goulding's belief that anyone who saw patients for more than one year was "ripping them off". He has concluded that, although the redecision process was helpful as a building block in a larger therapeutic process, patients needed more extensive reprogramming—and he has proceeded to elaborate just what that involves.

And now for something entirely different! If what matters most in therapy is the therapist's passionate curiosity in the service of the patient's self-inquiry, then William Cornell provides an excellent example! His relentless self-inquiring, willingness to face unknowing, and his active searches remind me of the journey described by the turn-of-the-century mystic Gurdjieff (1963) and his meetings with remarkable men.

Cornell extends Berne's idea of first-, second-, and third-degree games to scripts. I am filled with admiration as I follow him in learning what not to "do" in working with those deep issues not amenable to insight which characterise third-degree scripts. He does not try to "fix" these patients, but listens and lives the countertransference rather than acting it out in interpretations or self-disclosures. He does not to try to make the unconscious conscious but rather to think of enriching both the patient's and his own conscious experience with the vitality of unconscious processes. I am reminded how often therapists think of unconscious processes (or even the unconscious as a structure) in terms only of the unwanted, the feared, and repressed rather than as a source of vitality! His paper is a needed antidote.

I feel lucky that early in my career I was influenced by Milton Erickson (Erickson, Rossi, & Rossi, 1976). He explicitly treated the unconscious as a creative resource. Then, in the back room of the Haight Ashbury Free Medical Clinic in 1967, the heralded "Summer of Love", I guided people in turning "bad trips" into "good" ones. Today, we are beginning to understand that daydreaming, trance, meditation, and psychedelics calm down the default network of the brain (Baird et al., 2012; Buckner, Andrews-Hanna, & Schacter, 2008). It stretches between the cortex and deep structures, and its calming is associated with the blurring of self and object and the release of previously inhibited brain connections. I suspect that Cornell's approach works in a similar manner.

We need to remember that although Berne himself continued to see a few patients in psychoanalysis, TA originally dealt only with conscious processes. This approach has remained strong in some San Francisco groups. As Cornell discovered, working with the conscious alone often is sufficient for first- and second-degree scripts, but usually not for those of third-degree. Today, I conceptualise work with third-degree scripts in terms of dealing with early experiences encoded in the implicit memory system and so not directly available to consciousness. However, we may all need to be reminded that although people may espouse the idea of the unconscious intellectually, they may not really "believe" it emotionally. One of the most helpful, and most shocking things my analyst said to me was, "Well Jim, did you think you had no unconscious?" I had to conclude the answer was no, at least as applied to me—although I already was well into my psychiatric training.

For those of you who are moving from a traditional one-person psychology involving therapeutic impenetrability and "doing" psychotherapy to a two-person approach involving keeping mutuality, and feeling one's way along—and struggling with the accompanying self-scrutiny, self-doubt, and mourning—Elana Leigh's paper will be a comfort. It has been for me.

Leigh's paper is both a model of and a source of permission to explore what relational approaches fit best for us personally, our clients, and our shared situation, and to make it our own, integrating who we were with who we are becoming.

Leigh proposes that Freud needed to exclude subjectivity from his theories and practice because of his need to gain acceptance and recognition from the scientists of the time, and perhaps also as a reaction-formation to protect his own narcissism. Yet, after the therapeutic session, he sometimes did have coffee and cakes with his patients. I did some of my training with Anna Freud at the Hampstead Child Therapy Clinic. Working with children, she taught that with this age group the therapist is required to be a real person, and sometimes a kind of substitute parent as well as a therapist. Children will not permit anything else.

In case conferences, Miss Freud usually took an explorative view, and usually a few of the assembled would then object, quoting her father from various periods and, if this did not work, then quoting her own writings back to her. This seems to support Leigh's view of theory as both a map and a protection, and also a restraint. As I recall, Miss Freud also had the courage to take a position of not knowing and devoted a great deal of conference time to the examination of therapeutic failures.

At the Carmel Institute of Transactional Analysis, an office was reserved for Virginia Satir (1983, 1993), then probably the most respected and certainly the most charismatic family therapist in the USA. She clarified communication, had a system's view of family based on the concept of "I count, you count and context counts" and had a multi-generational psychodramatic approach to family therapy she called "family reconstruction". All these have been taken up, often without acknowledgement, and publicised by others.

Still, family dynamics and transgenerational family dynamics have rarely—and then only fleetingly—been acknowledged in Transactional Analysis. It has remained for Gloria Noriega Gayol (2009) to do significant research in this area. Here, she describes her clinical approach. It is an exciting integrated one in which the patient is presented with a banquet of ideas and experiences in carefully sequenced courses. She draws from many traditions. Indeed, this paper might well be used as a basic text in TA training. She is also one of the few authors in this book to acknowledge incorporating non-TA concepts into her practice. It is of note that, at a purely biological level, the new field of epigenetics (Craig & Wong, 2011) also encourages us to look at generational interactions. For example, whether or not a man develops diabetes may depend on whether his grandfather was born in a time of famine or in a time of harvest.

While Noriega's approach combines one- and two-person psychologies, it seems largely one-person. Erskine and Mauriz-Etxabe return us to the two-person relational realm. They describe the sensitive use of age-regression to deal with the fixated relational patterns that constitute the core of a life-script as well as the integration of earlier ego states into an Adult ego.

The case history of Maria is an instructive example of the power of implicit memory. It causes people to repeat past actions and experience past sensations and past emotions as if they related only to the current situation. This paper describes facilitating the translations of these subsymbolic and often fragmentary memories into words and explicit memory while simultaneously promoting new endings. The later may be through the therapist's presence or the patient's making physical movements to protect herself, or finding some new perspective on the experience. They wisely write that "talk is not enough." Impressive is these authors careful attention to the patient's developmental level and window of affect-toleration. I have been amazed to see therapists who seem to think it is enough to get a "trauma narrative"—all the details— and, mistaking the resulting retraumatization for a corrective emotional experience, then wonder why the patient did not improve!

Expanding on the work of the Gouldings, Tony White describes his work with suicidal patients, and working with the ambivalence caused by Free Child—Adaptive Child conflicts. To better understand a puzzling group of patients who generally seem "normal" but who engage in high-risk behaviour, including having poor health habits, he introduces the concept of the death wish as a drive of the Free Child. This formulation destigmatises these people, but does not gloss over their destructiveness.

In the USA at least, the death instinct is not much talked about. In part, this may be because such a conceptualisation is seen as harking back to a drive psychology and did not fit with the American emphasis on ego psychology. However, the box office popularity of such movies as *Fifty Shades of Gray* and Mel Gibson's *The Passion of the Christ* give a different picture. The death wish also does not easily lend itself to interventions. However, the Hampstead Metapsychological Profile developed by Anna Freud (1965) and colleagues insisted on a description of the strength, quality, and direction of the aggressive drive—to say nothing of the writings and practice of Melanie Klein (1987)! It seems relevant to note that in the USA, psychoanalysis met with some resistance because libido had been mistranslated as sexual drive and Freud was therefore seen as a "dirty old man". In contrast, I understand that after the Bolshevik revolution, psychoanalysis in Russia was suppressed at least in part because of the death instinct; Freud was seen as a warmonger! Pavlov seemed a more suitable model for the New Soviet Man.

In the early Eighties, there were many publications on closing escape hatches, including "no suicide contracts". This work soon became distorted. In the mistaken hope of preventing lawsuits, a number of psychiatric hospitals and emergency rooms in the USA presented patients with preprinted "no suicide contract" forms. These generally read something like, "I promise not to kill myself while in the hospital"! At the very least, these invited resistance and transference, actually gave patients permission to kill themselves after they left the hospital— and completely missed the need for the contract to be used within a sensitive and careful therapeutic relationship. Not surprisingly, the American Psychiatric Association issued a condemnation of the practice. It is good that White brings us back to the Gouldings' original intention (Drye, Goulding, & Goulding, 1973).

Through a riveting case history of a patient with borderline dynamics, Moniek Thunnissen describes her work in a three-month hospital setting. She has previously published research on the therapeutic outcomes (2001a). Here, however, she describes a coherent, reflective milieu based on TA principles, and which takes advantage of the metaphoric use of puppetry and archery, as well as the practice-ground of residential living. This is a paper which will be useful to anyone thinking of setting up a residential treatment programme.

In contrast, I remember the first group treatment I saw Berne conduct in a regular psychiatric unit at St. Mary's Hospital in San Francisco. He began by addressing a new patient, a nun, with "Well, Sister, who gave you your crazy license?"

However, he had also set up a very productive therapeutic structure. For the first hour, we trainees sat in a circle outside the therapeutic group. Then we changed places and became the inner circle, discussing what we had observed, while the patients formed the outside group, observing us. Finally, we changed places again and the patients commented on our observations and interpretations—and on us.

One psychotic patient, who had talked to a presence others could not see during the therapy group, began the same behaviour in the outside group. Another patient immediately stopped him, saying, "This is not the time for that!" Another patient commented on how much less depressed one of the female trainees looked since attending the group and expressed her hope that, now that the trainee was looking more attractive, she would find a "good boyfriend"! Today, we could see these as precursors of a reflective chorus and even of a nascent relational approach.

In their well titled and carefully sequenced paper, Karen Minikin and Keith Tudor show how various TA traditions can be fruitfully combined, each reinforcing the other. Gender offers a beautiful example, as they point out, of the social construction of identity and the sequence of becoming, being, and belonging in the matrix of individual, interpersonal, organisational, and cultural processes. They describe the process of their male patients developing a sense of themselves as full human beings. Perhaps in another paper, they might explore this subgroup whose presence is finally being recognised.

Every day, we can read of problems of alienation, especially among the disadvantaged and marginal. Relational dynamics with its emphasis on self-awareness, contactful presence, and engagement are, as the therapeutic vignettes here demonstrate, a powerful antidote. Indeed, in programmes to prevent the recruitment of people to ISIS, mentoring is turning out to be one of the most powerful interventions.

To what degree can concepts derived from analysis of society be applied to individual treatment? For example, I have trouble in conceptualising the consequences of an absent father as "oppression", except perhaps in a very metaphorical way. However, the absence of a father is a fact in some groups, including a disproportionately large number of British prime ministers and US presidents. Conversely, how far are Transactional Analysis concepts applicable to analyses of social processes? Most of us do not have the appropriate understanding of the complexities of historical, economic, sociological, and political interactions. Yet, we surely can use our specific knowledge to examine political spin and contribute to the analysis of social issues and interventions. Seeking to understand just such cultural processes Berne did much foreign travel—until a suspicious government took away his passport.

Long ago, TA therapists prided ourselves on how we might change the world. Everyone only needed to learn TA! Some even calculated how many years this would take! Today, we are wiser and humbler and much of our social psychiatry has been reduced to "doing good" with disadvantaged groups. Berne himself set the example: he had the International Transactional Analysis Association support "our orphan George" in Crete. To me, social psychiatry seems the most disappointing aspect of Transactional Analysis. It promised too much and we were too hopeful and too naïve.

The book *Games People Play* (1964) first brought major national and international attention to Berne. I doubt that anyone, including Berne, really understood its implications. Now, Charlotte Sills and Jo Stuthridge offer us a beautifully written relational perspective.

They describe three levels of games from an interpersonal point of view. This differs from but complements William Cornell's intrapsychic conceptualisation in the fourth chapter. Briefly, they conceptualise first-degree games as nameable, and responsive to phenomenological inquiry and objective analysis. Second-degree games involve action/inaction and leave the therapist with a sense of unease or disorientation. These may be explored in images and associations. Third-degree games, on the other hand, leave the therapist overwhelmed and destabilised. These seem associated with early unresolved trauma and neglect (This work begs correlation with Ainsworth, Blehar, Waters, and Wall's (1978) and Main's (1995) attachment research).

The chapter's vignettes are informative. They are also riveting. Early in the chapter, the authors write that games in the therapy room are the most vibrant experience—near revelation of the client's "unspoken truth"—and often also the therapist's. By the end of the chapter, they have shown games to be isomorphic with script and third-degree games as a royal road to key unconscious processes.

For most readers, probably the most difficult chapter will be Maria Teresa Tosi's on the social-cognitive approach. Yet, this paper will very much repay careful reading and consideration.

It is important for several reasons. It is grounded in research. It bridges TA and cognitive psychology. It offers clear, operational definitions which can help us make more refined and nuanced descriptions of ego states, transactions, and our interventions. To add to this, Tosi's paper provides clear examples of the sensitive use of this approach in clinical practice.

Although social-cognitive TA may be unfamiliar to many, it actually has an active forty year history. Its originator, Pio Scilligo (2011), was a priest with a curious, scientific, wide-ranging mind. The last time I saw him, over a delightful relaxed dinner, we discussed factor analysis, the special priests the Roman Catholic Church approved to address paranormal phenomena, and his excitement about completing the first and only dictionary of the language of the mountain valley where he grew up in the north of Italy. The last living speaker of this language, he had left the area at the age of fourteen.

I value this work because, although it is grounded in research, it does not sacrifice the subjective to universatism. It embraces basic TA assumptions but adds many other levels to them, including the evolutionary (existence, survival, and continuation of the species). It treats ego states as the processes or functions of constantly evolving schemas. It conceptualises the Self as a composite of several Self-ego states, each with its own history. These Self-ego states encompass how we experience and treat ourselves. They are developed in relationship to and in tandem with ongoing relational transactions.

You may find it difficult to follow the labelling of ego states. Based on my current understanding, I humbly offer the following sequence:

1.1. Decide the relational positions of each person in the relevant dyad of interest to you (e.g., Relational Parent position and Relational Child position).

1.2. Determine the involved developmental ego states of each (e.g., Parent, Adult, Child) and the corresponding Self-ego state (P/A/C) based on the quality of the processes they manifest. For example, regulating emotions suggests Developmental Adult while dealing with exploration/attachment suggests Developmental Child (Figure 3 in Chapter Eleven). In doing this stage, it is important to look at the quality of the process. Do not use other definitions or your intuition.

1.3. Determine whether the ego state interaction you are interested in involves giving power to self (being free or rebellious) or taking power away from others (e.g., being protective or critical). This corresponds with the "activity-passivity dimension" depicted in Figure 4 (Chapter Eleven).

Giving power to oneself correlates with being free or rebellious (e.g., FC, FA, FP, and RC, RA, RP), while taking power away from oneself correlates with being protective or critical (PC, PA, PP, and CC, CA,

CP), depending on the friendly or hostile affectivity, in Relational Child, and Self.

Taking power away from others correlates with protective or critical Relational Parent (e.g., Protective or Critical Parent, Protective or Critical Adult, Protective or Critical Child), depending on whether the affect is friendly or hostile (see Figure 2). Giving power to others correlates with Free and Rebellious Relational Parent (e.g. Free or Rebellious Parent, Free or Rebellious Adult, Free or Rebellious Child), depending on the friendly or the hostile affectivity (see Figure 2).

Good luck in titrating your descriptions of transactions and interventions. It can be exciting!

And now?

Now, that we have gone through the book, what have you found useful, interesting? Have any of your hopes/expectations been disappointed?

Although the book is indeed an admirable summary of TA practice and development in 2015, I have been somewhat disappointed by the lack of emphasis on research, although many of the authors have been engaged in it. In part, this may be because much of TA practice now is long term, and multifaceted, aspects that do not easily lend themselves to empirical research. In part, this may be because most of us see ourselves as therapists, and have to earn a living. I have also been struck that, while at least as presented in the bibliographies, we are highly knowledgeable of the TA literature and certain aspects of psychoanalysis, we also seem to live in intellectual silos. While the reference list resembles a library catalogue, there is only passing reference to relevant biological foundations, and relatively little on the complexities of economic, cultural, social, and political interactions. Still, as Richard Erskine hopefully points out in his first chapter, the development of Transactional Analysis is not complete.

Erskine has written that one of the things he likes about current TA is that it gives the therapist a rich variety of options. Let me invite you to think of one of your patients. How are you currently conceptualising your work together? What might happen if you switched models? What becomes available, what is lost? Is there a difference that makes a difference?

Happy explorations!

PREFACE

Richard G. Erskine

The Transactional Analysis community of psychotherapists and counsellors is, and has always been, flexible and willing to integrate diverse ideas into the core of TA theory and practice. This book reflects that openness and integration by presenting new concepts and perspectives that are integrated with the theories and methods of Eric Berne—truly a collection for contemporary Transactional Analysis.

The idea for this book began during a psychotherapy and counselling symposium entitled "Therapeutic Methods in Transactional Analysis: Current Perspectives and Emerging Developments" at the World Congress of Transactional Analysis in San Francisco, August 7–10, 2014. The symposium consisted of formal presentations, a round table conversation, a large group discussion, and a series of workshops conducted by the symposium faculty. Several Transactional Analysts from various countries were invited to talk about what they currently think about theory and therapeutic practice and how they have developed professionally. Each of the symposium faculty members presented a renewed and unique perspective on how they use Transactional Analysis with their clients.

In the more than fifty years since Eric Berne published his most significant work, *Transactional Analysis in Psychotherapy* (1961), countless numbers of psychotherapists and counsellors have applied Berne's theories in their therapeutic practice of TA. Berne's original theories have been an inspiration to many. They have provided the theoretical foundation for understanding clients' behaviours and phenomenological experiences, interpersonal transactions, re-enactments of childhood neglects and traumas, and the unconscious relational patterns that form a life script. Berne's writings have stimulated the development of a variety of methods—cognitive, behavioural, affective, physiological, relational, and social/cultural/political—that lead to significant changes in clients' lives.

Over the years Berne's original theories have been preserved by some authors and expanded, challenged, altered, simplified, or radically changed by other authors. A reading of the *Transactional Analysis Journal* from 1972 until now will reveal that many writers are describing an array of theories and methods, all within the rubric of Transactional Analysis. Some authors have remained consistent with Berne's original theories, some have developed and expanded Berne's concepts, while others are inconsistent with or contradict Berne. Yet, all the publications seem to be influenced in some way by either Berne's publications or those writers who were among the first generation of Transactional Analysts.

How does this altering of theory and practice occur? One possible answer is that all these authors have had a combination of professional and personal experience that influences how they understand theory and the nature of their therapeutic practice. They are writing about what is either personally or professionally meaningful to them and their clients. Clinical practice and psychotherapy theory push and pull each other, constantly challenging and augmenting both our concepts and what we actually do with clients. The group of experienced Transactional Analysts who have contributed to this book have certainly been pushed and pulled professionally over a number of years. They have struggled to understand what each client required in his or her psychotherapy. They have thought about the advantages and disadvantages of a particular theory or therapeutic stance. They have explored various ways of being fully present in the therapeutic relationship, the dialectic of being both authentic and therapeutic. Now we are each sharing our current ideas and clinical experience with you. Therefore, this book presents the rich diversity of TA theory and methods in contemporary psychotherapy.

As I wrote my chapter on the "Transactional Analysis of obsession" I realised how I have remained consistent with the Transactional Analysis I first studied more than four decades ago while, at the same time, I have developed new perspectives on various theories and methods of psychotherapy. How I practise Transactional Analysis today is the result of years of blending the theories of TA with what I have gained from listening to my clients—learnings that have helped me appreciate the richness of some of Eric Berne's original ideas. The changes that I have made in my clinical practice have been influenced mostly by my clients' reactions and feedback, what I have discovered from the many errors I have made, and the quality of involvement that my clients required from me.

All the authors in this book, in their unique way, also portray how they have been shaped and modelled through their therapeutic involvement with clients. Each author has experienced a personal metamorphosis in professional development as a Transactional Analyst. William Cornell's (USA) and Elana Leigh's (Australia) chapters both vividly describe how they think, embody, and perceive the process of psychotherapy. Such contemplation often necessitates a change in therapeutic perspective and interpersonal contact. Cornell articulates how psychoanalytic supervision led him to a new understanding of Eric Berne's theory. He describes the importance of unconscious experience of both client and psychotherapist. Reading Cornell's chapter is like looking into his heart. Elana Leigh describes her dilemma between embracing a new two-person, interpersonal perspective and holding on to a familiar perspective that maintains a therapeutic neutrality. Her journey reflects what many of us experience as we grapple with how to integrate new ideas with the old, what to keep and what to discard, to what extent is self-disclosure therapeutic for our client, and the interplay between being "for" and "with" our clients.

Other authors, such as Ray Little (Scotland) and John McNeil (USA), explicitly describe a new perspective on an older theory. Ray Little defines specific forms of transference that unconsciously express ego state relational units. He expands on Berne's original theory of ego states and clearly demonstrates how Child and Parent ego states are always intertwined and expressed through transference. John McNeil describes the history of redecision therapy. He elaborates on the concept of injunctive messages in his clients' lives, messages that are combined with both "despairing" and "defiant decisions". McNeil has formed a unique taxonomy that distinguishes five categories of injunctive messages: survival, attachment, identity, competence, and security. Both Little's and McNeel's writings bring revitalisation to the theory and practice of classical Transactional Analysis.

Jo Stuthridge (New Zealand) and Charlotte Sills (UK) have written a refreshingly new perspective on Eric Berne's theory of games— a perspective that entails a careful consideration of both the client's and the therapist's unconscious stories. They have provided us with a new understanding of the sub-symbolic dynamics involved in confusing and conflictual interpersonal relationships by looking at such dynamics from three levels of unconscious process. Their revised theory provides us with a humanistic understanding of the transference/ countertransference enactments central to games. Sills and Stuthridge's revision of theory may well change the way many psychotherapists use the concept of games in their therapeutic practice.

Karen Minikin (UK) and Keith Tudor (New Zealand) remind us that the radical psychiatry perspective that Claude Steiner, Hogie Wyckoff, and others brought to Transactional Analysis in the early 1970s is still a central and meaningful perspective in TA psychotherapy. Their presentation of "gender psychopolitics" takes into account the cultural, economic, and social pressures that shape the life script of men and is expressed through their relationship to their masculinity. They clearly describe how men, as potential oppressors, are oppressed themselves through alienation, social and cultural scripting. This chapter is refreshing in that it expresses the sometimes forgotten social aspects of Transactional Analysis: the significance of psychopolitics in considering our society's attitudes about different social identities.

Gloria Noriega Gayol's (Mexico) chapter on transgenerational scripts expands on Berne's ideas about life script and how emotional and interpersonal conflicts are passed on from one generation to another. She provides us with a theory that helps in understanding the unconscious influences in our clients' lives.

Tony White (Australia) brings his years of expertise to his discussion of the psychotherapy of potential suicide and his work with self-destructive individuals. He reminds us to think about the forces of Eros and Thanatos in our clients' lives. Moniek Thunnissen also writes about her experience with patients who engage in self-destructive behaviour and what they need in a protective therapeutic community. She describes the Transactional Analysis-based treatment facility that she developed in the Netherlands to treat patients with personality disorder.

Maria Teresa Tosi (Italy) introduces us to a new development in TA theory and practice called social-cognitive Transactional Analysis. Her explanations of ego states integrate the social/cognitive/interpersonal perspectives offering a model that facilitates research on the psychotherapeutic processes. She proposes the relational approach in a way that diverges from other chapters; instead she focuses on the ongoing process of ego states development and the reciprocal use of transference in the patient-therapist dyad.

Finally, Amaia Mauriz-Etxabe (Spain) and I have written a chapter entitled "Inference, re-experiencing, and regression: psychotherapy of Child ego states". In his 1961 book *Transactional Analysis in Psychotherapy* Eric Berne wrote about age regression and his explorations in providing psychotherapy for his traumatised clients' Child ego states. He suggests that Child ego state therapy is essential for script cure. However, Berne did not articulate the methods and protections that are necessary for a reparative age regression therapy. In this chapter we describe the value of working with therapeutic inference, sub-symbolic memory, and the importance of a relational focused, supported age regression in the healing of trauma and cumulative neglect.

I am a Transactional Analyst because TA offers an array of theories and methods that guide us in providing psychotherapy and counselling at the cognitive, behavioural, affective, physiological, and relational levels of the client's development. This book reflects the vastness of Transactional Analysis. I trust that you, the reader, will find the range of ideas in this book interesting and useful, and that you will be enriched by reading this variety of theories and perspectives. Each of the authors in this book has influenced my thinking about psychotherapy. In studying these chapters I feel blessed to have had the opportunity to think about different aspects of psychotherapy by viewing my therapeutic involvements through the various authors' perspectives. I have had some new insights that have both challenged and affirmed how I practise Transactional Analysis in psychotherapy. Come join me in the adventure of discovering contemporary perspectives on Transactional Analysis in psychotherapy.

ABOUT THE EDITOR AND CONTRIBUTORS

James R. Allen, MD, MPH., is a graduate of the University of Toronto, McGill University, and Harvard. In 1967 he began his training in Transactional Analysis with Eric Berne, David Kupfer, and the Gouldings at the Carmel Institute of Transactional Analysis. He is a co-recipient of the Eric Berne Memorial Award for his contributions to the development of Transactional Analysis theory and practice. In 2014, he retired as professor of psychiatry and behavioural sciences and Rainbolt Family Chair in child psychiatry at the University of Oklahoma Health Sciences Center, Oklahoma City, OK, USA.

William F. Cornell, MA, TSTA-P, studied behavioural psychology at Reed College in Portland, Oregon and phenomenological psychology at Duquesne University in Pittsburgh, Pennsylvania. He followed his graduate studies with training in Transactional Analysis and body-centred psychotherapy. Since those trainings, Bill has studied with several mentors and consultants within psychoanalytic perspectives. A co-editor of the *Transactional Analysis Journal*, Bill is the author of *Explorations in Transactional Analysis: The Meech Lake Papers* and *Somatic*

Experience in Psychoanalysis and Psychotherapy: In the Expressive Language of the Living, and is a contributing author to the forthcoming *Into TA*. He is a recipient of the Eric Berne Memorial Award.

Richard G. Erskine, PhD has been practising Transactional Analysis in psychotherapy since 1969. He is a licensed psychologist and psychoanalyst. He has been a university professor, worked with emotionally disturbed and socially maladjusted children, conducted a therapeutic community in a maximum security prison, and since 1976 has served as the training director of the Institute for Integrative Psychotherapy (New York City and Vancouver, Canada) where he has specialised in the psychotherapy of acute and cumulative trauma. He has twice received the Eric Berne Memorial Award for advances in the theory and methods of TA. He may be reached at www.IntegrativePsychotherapy.com.

Elana Leigh gained her BSc in social work from the University of Cape Town, and an MSc In integrative psychotherapy at Middlesex University, London. She is a certified Transactional Analyst and training and supervising Transactional Analyst (ITAA). She lives in Sydney, Australia where she works as a psychotherapist, supervisor, and trainer. She has worked across a range of cultures and her passion lies in integration and diversity in both theory and application.

Ray Little, CTA, UKCP registered psychotherapist, is a relational TA psychotherapist, supervisor, and visiting tutor, working both in the UK and in Europe. He is a founding member of the International Association for Relational Transactional Analysis (IARTA). Ray works as an adult psychotherapist in private practice and has been working with individuals, couples, and groups for thirty years. His published articles in the *Transactional Analysis Journal* reflect his interest in integrating psychodynamic concepts into relational Transactional Analysis, with an emphasis on working with primitive states of mind.

Gloria Noriega Gayol, PhD, is the director of Instituto Mexicano de Análisis Transaccional in Mexico City, and a clinical psychologist, psychotherapist, and teaching and supervising Transactional Analyst; she is a former president of the International Transactional Analysis Association (ITAA); a recipient of the Eric Berne Memorial Award in 2008; author of several articles, chapters, and the book *Codependence Script in*

Couple Relationships: Diagnosis and Treatment (Manual Moderno, 2013). She speaks and trains in Europe and Latin America.

Amaia Mauriz-Etxabe, is a licensed clinical psychologist, trainer and supervisor in Transactional Analysis, and a certified European psychotherapist who specialises in the psychotherapy of adults, adolescents, families, and groups. Since 1988 she has served as the director of the Institute Bios, Psicólogos in Bilbao (Spain) where she conducts training programmes in Transactional Analysis. Throughout her professional life she has been an involved member in several professional associations including serving as a delegate to the European Association of Transactional Analysis.

Karen Minikin works in East Sussex, UK, as a psychotherapist, supervisor, and trainer. Previously, she edited the race and culture column for the BACP journal and she contributed a chapter on "The Politics and Psychology of Alienation" in *Relational TA: Principles in Practice*, edited by Fowlie and Sills (2011). She teaches psychotherapy at a number of training institutes within the UK and has presented workshops at national and international conferences. She has a particular interest in social identity and integrating humanistic and relational psychoanalytical approaches within Transactional Analysis.

John McNeel, has been a student of redecision therapy for over forty-five years. He makes his home in Palo Alto, CA where he conducts a private practice in psychology. He was a member of the faculty of the Western Institute for Group and Family Therapy in Watsonville, CA and is currently a certified teaching member of the International Transactional Analysis Association. He is a former editor of the *Transactional Analysis Journal* and is a recipient of the Eric Berne Memorial Award. He holds a master's degree in divinity from the Louisville Presbyterian Theological Seminary and a PhD in psychology from the California School of Professional Psychology.

Charlotte Sills is a teaching and supervising Transactional Analyst and a UK registered psychotherapist. She works in private practice and is also a faculty member at Metanoia Institute, London and Ashridge Business School, UK, and a visiting professor at Middlesex University, London. Her publications include *An Introduction to*

Transactional Analysis (with Phil Lapworth, Sage), *Relational Transactional Analysis—Principles in Practice* (edited, with Heather Fowlie, Karnac), and *Transactional Analysis: A Relational Perspective* (with Helena Hargaden, Routledge), chapters of which were awarded the Eric Berne Memorial Award in 2007.

Jo Stuthridge, MSc, NZAP is a teaching and supervising Transactional Analyst (psychotherapy) and a registered psychotherapist in New Zealand. She maintains a private psychotherapy practice in Dunedin and is director of the Physis Institute, which offers training in TA. She has published several articles and book chapters on Transactional Analysis and psychotherapy. Jo is a teaching and research associate with the Department of Psychotherapy and Counselling at Auckland University of Technology. She is also a current co-editor for the *Transactional Analysis Journal*.

Moniek Thunnissen, MD, PhD, is TSTA in psychotherapy. She is a psychiatrist working in her own company for treatment, supervision, consultation and training. Through the Transactional Analysis Academy in Soesterberg, Netherlands she developed a TA psychotherapy training programme. Her PhD research described the long-term results of a TA programme for patients with personality disorders. She is the author of seven books and numerous articles on TA, psychotherapy, and psychiatry. She was vice president of research and innovation of the ITAA and is part of the editorial board of the *Transactional Analysis Journal*. moniek@ta-academie.nl.

Maria Teresa Tosi is a licensed psychotherapist and a teaching and supervising Transactional Analyst in the field of psychotherapy. She lives and works in Rome as a psychotherapist and supervisor. She is also a trainer in the Salesian University School for Specialisation in Clinical Psychology and in the Institute of Training and Research for Educators and Psychotherapists, in Rome. In 2013 she was awarded the EATA Gold Medal "for outstanding services to Transactional Analysis in Europe". Her publications focus on the dialogue between Transactional Analysis theory and practice and contemporary scientific studies.

Keith Tudor is a Transactional Analyst (CTA(P), TSTA(P)), and Professor of Psychotherapy at Auckland University of Technology,

New Zealand. His interest in working with men dates back to the mid/late 1980s, influenced by feminism and the gender politics of Big Flame, as well as some involvement in the men's movement in which he had contact with influential figures such as John Rowan, Michael Meade, and Robert Bly. He writes: "My own development as a man has been hugely influenced by my own personal therapy, and, as a therapist, I have always worked with men, including running a long-term men's psychotherapy group."

Tony White is a teaching and supervising Transactional Analyst and psychologist in private practice in Australia. He has been practising and teaching for thirty-five years in psychotherapy and training psychotherapists. In 2011 he wrote a book—*Working with Suicidal Individuals*—which won a high commendation at the 2011 British Medical Association medical book awards in the category of psychiatry. He has specialised in the area of suicide for over twenty-five years.

CHAPTER ONE

A Transactional Analysis of obsession: integrating diverse concepts and methods

Richard G. Erskine

"Worry, worry, worry. That's all I do," despaired my first client on Monday morning. She had been worrying for most of her life and was convinced that she would never stop worrying. She was like many of the clients I was scheduled to work with that week: habitual worrying and repetitive fantasising absorbed much of their mental activity and interfered with their capacity for spontaneity, intimacy, and living joyfully in the present. I knew that I would be attending, at least some of the time, to aspects of obsession with several of my clients throughout the week no matter what other issues we might be addressing.

Psychological problems such as repetitive fantasising, habitual worrying, and obsessing appear to be on the rise over the last few years among people seeking psychotherapy. These types of problems seem to cut across many psychological diagnoses and include some clients who would not necessarily receive a confirmed DSM-IV or DSM-V diagnosis (American Psychiatric Association, 1994, 2013). Obsessing and habitual worrying may be among the major treatment issues of our time, reflective of the lifestyle and career pressures, developmental experiences, deficits in interpersonal relationships, and issues of life script (McAdams & Pals, 2006). Obsessing, repetitive fantasising, and habitual worrying are so common, and often so private, that these issues may go unreported in therapy. When addressed in psychotherapy such rumination may receive only cursory attention or may not seem pertinent to issues of life script (Berne, 1972).

The psychotherapy of obsessing and repetitive fantasising was briefly addressed through clinical case examples in a few previous *Transactional Analysis Journal* articles (Allen, 2003; Erskine, 2001, 2003, 2008; Nolan, 2008; Novellino, 2006; Schaeffer, 2009). Yet the Transactional Analysis psychotherapy of habitual worrying, repetitive fantasising, and obsessing has not received adequate attention in the clinical literature. Neither theoretical conceptualisations for understanding these problems nor a description of various methods have been published. This chapter fills that deficit by presenting a six point treatment perspective for the psychotherapy of obsessing, habitual worrying, and repetitive fantasising.

This chapter is the outcome of a qualitative multiple case study which has identified six major facets of psychotherapy that integrate both an understanding of the psychological dynamics of obsessing, repetitive fantasising, and habitual worrying and an integration of psychotherapy methods that are effective in maintaining permanent change to such dynamics (Erskine et al., 2001). In describing human personality characteristics, such as obsessing and worrying, Kluckholm & Murray (1953) wrote that every person is like all other persons, like some other persons, and like no other person, therefore we can often take clinical data from a few individuals and effectively generalise our knowledge to a larger population provided that we constantly monitor and also inquire into the unique, phenomenological experience of each client. This chapter is a compilation of the Transactional Analysis methods that were significantly effective with some clients and suggest that these methods may be equally effective with a wide variety of clients in Transactional Analysis psychotherapy.

The *Psychodynamic Diagnostic Manual* describes obsessions as relatively common symptoms wherein obsession is an attempt to disavow affect and engage in intellectualisation rather than to feel emotions, especially among more cerebral and perfectionistic individuals. Obsessing, habitual worrying, and repetitive fantasising often indicate a person's reluctance to feel emotions associated with either being "overwhelmed" or "out of control" (PDM Task Force, 2006, p. 58). Freud (1913i) described obsession and worry as originating in early child–parent dyadic struggles. He related the stubborn, punctilious, and hoarding tendencies of the adult with obsessional neurosis to childhood battles over toilet training. However, current client narratives indicate the significance of power struggles between child and parents around rigid standards of behaviour, eating, school work, sexuality, and general obedience as the childhood conflicts that underlie many obsessions and repetitive worries. In essence, growing up with relational discord is central for people who engage in habitual worrying, repetitive fantasies, and obsession.

Many such clients report that their childhood attempts at expressions of subjectivity and affect were labelled as bad or immature or not rational. As a result, many clients are absorbed with repetitive fantasies or reoccurring obsessions; they are out of touch with their emotions and are more preoccupied with self-definition or making an impact than interpersonal relationships. They appear to be internally compelled by their rumination and often fear their own feelings and thoughts, especially if they are aggressive. "Living machines" was the term used by William Reich in *Character Analysis* (1933) to describe such obsessive people. Obsessive thoughts are an attempt to counteract phenomenological experience that is feared to be overwhelming. As a result, such clients have trouble relaxing, joking, being intimate, and living in the now. Obsessive people are chronically "in their heads": thinking, reasoning, judging, doubting (Fisher & Greenberg, 1985; Salzman, 1980; Shapiro, 1965 as cited in PDM Task Force, 2006).

Transactional Analysis in psychotherapy

The treatments identified as empirically supported therapies are behavioural or cognitive-behavioural in nature, reflecting the greater formal or empirical research activity of psychotherapy outcome researchers of that orientation (Chambless, 2005). However, addressing and resolving the clients' underlying loneliness, resolving unconscious longing for meaningful relationship, appreciating and reorienting the homeostatic functions of obsessing, dissolving archaic script beliefs and introjections, and enriching their emotional lives requires considerable time— time with an involved psychotherapist who is willing to help them explore emotional memories and express phenomenological experiences that they otherwise spend an inordinate amount of time and energy to avoid.

An in-depth psychotherapy of this nature is a profoundly co-creative process that does not lend itself to empirical research (Summers & Tudor, 2000; Tudor, 2011b). As of the time of writing there are no outcome studies of the use of Transactional Analysis in the psychotherapy of obsession, habitual worry, or repetitive fantasising. Yet clinical discussions among experienced colleagues have clarified several therapeutic facets that seem to be effective with a number of clients.

As an overview I want to briefly describe how I organise the psychotherapy of obsession along six distinct facets. I use the word "facets" rather than "stages" because the psychotherapy is not linear. Our therapeutic dialogues cycle from one facet to another in response to what is emerging in the intersubjective process. The client and I may address one or two of these facets in a particular session or series of sessions, then move on to another facet for a while, eventually returning to a previous facet. In due course we interweave all six facets to form a comprehensive psychotherapy. For the reader interested in further case examples or an elaboration of the theoretical concepts mentioned in this chapter I will reference several publications that will cover the various ideas more thoroughly. A careful reading of these primary sources may illuminate the comprehensiveness of Transactional Analysis in contemporary psychotherapy.

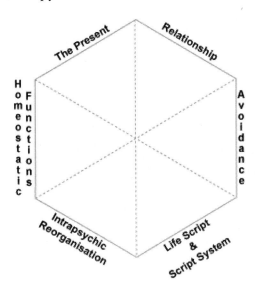

Figure 1. Integration of six therapeutic facets.

Relationship: The therapeutic relationship is central no matter what methods or other perspectives we may use. My clinical experience has shown that clients who are habitually worrying are unconsciously longing for a meaningful relationship. They are lonely, yet they often carry a fear of repeating the disruptions and failures of past relationships. As a result they avoid full interpersonal contact and fill the emptiness with internal dialogue, fantasy, or anticipations.

In this facet the therapeutic focus is on establishing and maintaining the client's sense of relational security, self-definition, and interpersonal agency and efficacy (Erskine & Trautmann, 1996; Erskine, 2003a). This is accomplished, in part, by the psychotherapist's transactions of respect, acceptance, kindness, clarity, and patience. At the same time, the therapeutic focus is on inquiring about the client's current relational needs, his unrequited archaic needs, how he coped with previous relational disruptions, and the unconscious story encoded in the emotional transference of previous relational experiences—transference both with the psychotherapist and with others (Erskine, 1991, 2010a; R. Little, 2011a; Moiso, 1985; Novellino, 1984).

Avoidance: The second facet involves discovering what is being avoided through the repetitive fantasising or obsessing. The anxiety associated with obsessing or fantasising is often about avoiding one's feelings, thoughts, and/or memories (Erskine, 2001, 2003a, 2008). This concept is an elaboration of the Transactional Analysis notion of "rackets" as a substitute feeling, a distraction from what one may authentically experience (such as shame, despair, or loneliness) if there was no interfering alternative or substitute (Berne, 1972; English, 1971, 1972).

I may ask, "What would you be feeling if you were not feeling the fear in your fantasy?" or "What would you be experiencing right now if you were not distracted by what you are saying?" Some clients are clear in answering these questions and others are initially confused by them. These are the types of questions to which I often return throughout the psychotherapy. The client's answers are often surprising and lead us to other facets of the psychotherapy, to new levels of discovery and awareness.

Life script and the script system: The third facet requires uncovering and dissolving the client's life script. Life scripts are a creative and accommodating strategy to manage the psychological stress, or even the shock, of repetitive, problematic relationships (Erskine, 2010b).

I usually work with the script system (previously called racket system) to help the client identify his accommodating strategies—the core beliefs about self, others, and the quality of life. Script system work often begins with identifying the behaviours or fantasies that generate reinforcing memories that, in turn, maintain the script beliefs (Erskine, 2015; Erskine & Zalcman, 1979; Gildebrand & Shivanath, 2011; O'Reilly-Knapp & Erskine, 2010). Life scripts keep people within a closed system composed of archaic feelings and needs, childhood conclusions and decisions, egocentric fantasies, and related body-tensions. This closed system interrupts both internal sensitivity to current relational needs and the capacity for full interpersonal contact (Erskine, 2010b). The therapeutic resolution of a life script involves an affective/cognitive reorganisation of core beliefs about self-in-relationship. Such an intra-psychic reorganisation both precedes and maintains changes in behaviour and fantasy.

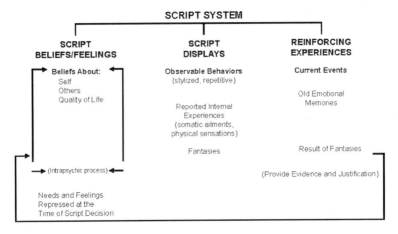

Figure 2. The script system.

Intrapsychic reorganisation: The fourth facet of the psychotherapy encompasses working with the client's archaic experiences via a developmental perspective, therapeutic inference, and a secure relationship that allows the client to have a supported and restorative regression. The therapeutic focus is on the client's processes of archaic self-stabilisation and self-protection, his restrictions in physiology and affect, as well as decoding the client's enactments of implicit and procedural memories. This is where the therapy is concentrated on the feelings, needs, and reactions of a young child and the qualities of a reparative relationship that the client requires. This work may include:

- *Deconfusion of the Child ego states* (Berne, 1961; B. D. Clark, 1991; Clarkson & Fish, 1988; Cornell & Olio, 1992; Erskine, Moursund, & Trautmann, 1999; Hargaden & Sills, 2001, 2002; R. Little, 2005; Moursund & Erskine, 2003; Novellino, 1990; Stuthridge, 2006, 2012).
- *Redecision work* (Allen, 2010; Campos, 1995; Goulding & Goulding, 1979; Masse, 1995; McNeel, 1977; Thunnissen, 2010).
- *Deep emotional/physiological expression and intrapsychic reorganisation referred to as "disconnecting rubber bands"* (Childs-Gowell, 2000; Erskine, 1974; Erskine & Moursund, 1988; R. Little, 2001).
- *Psychotherapy of the Parent ego states* (Dashiell, 1978; Erskine, 2003b; Erskine & Trautmann, 2003; R. Little, 2006; McNeel, 1976; Mellor & Andrewartha, 1980).
- *Working with the retroflections and inhibitions in the body* (Cassius, 1977, 1980; Child-Gowell & Kinnaman, 1978; Cornell, 1975, 1997; Cornell & Landaiche, 2007; Erskine, 2014b; Hawkes, 2003; Ligabue, 1991; Uma Priya, 2007; Waldekranz-Piselli, 1999).

Whether the psychotherapy is with a Child or Parent ego state, the aim of such intrapsychic work is to provide a reorganisation of sub-symbolic experience and archaic homeostatic functions that interfere with the client's current life (Erskine, 2015). In-depth psychotherapy, when done according to the client's needs and rhythm, facilitates a physiological/affective reorganisaation that involves a neurological realignment of the amygdala-hippocampus-adrenal system of a nuclear sense of self (Cozolino, 2006; Damasio, 1999). For a further elaboration on psychotherapy with the Child ego states please see Chapter Seven by Erskine and Mauriz-Etxabe in this book.

Homeostatic functions: The fifth facet, homeostatic functions, contributes an understanding and appreciation of affect and physiological equilibrium—a homeostasis that maintains external behaviours as well as internal processes such as script beliefs, habitual worrying, or repetitive fantasies, and emotionally laden habits. Obsessing, habitual worrying, and repetitive fantasising are each creative strategies to maintain an emotional balance and to manage the psychological stress, or even the shock, of repetitive, problematic relationships. These accommodating strategies are a desperate attempt at either self-reparation or self-stabilisation.

There are several possible psychological functions. Some examples include *self-regulation, compensation, self-protection, orientation,* and *insurance against shock* of further disruptions in relationship. The repetitive behavioural patterns and internal rumination may also function to maintain *a sense of integrity*—a continuity of the struggle to define and value one's self within a variety of relationships. These examples of psychological functions reflect the person's outmoded attempts to generate and maintain a sense of psychological equilibrium following affectively overwhelming disruptions in significant relationships. They are homeostatic strategies that provide predictability, identity, consistency, and stability (Erskine, 2015; Erskine, Moursund, & Trautmann, 1999).

A frequently used way to stop obsessing and worrying is to say to one's self, "Stop!" Such an exhortation may work temporarily; however, a more effective way to permanently stop obsessing is to identify and maintain awareness of the archaic homeostatic functions that perpetuate the obsession and to transform those archaic functions into mature functions.

Underpinning any emotional or behavioural change, I find it essential to work collaboratively with clients in uncovering the various archaic functions of obsessing and habitual worrying and then to transpose those archaic functions to mature forms of self-regulation and self-enhancement (Kohut, 1977; Wolf, 1988).

The present: The sixth facet focuses on helping the obsessing client live in the present moment rather than ruminating about the past or fearfully anticipating the future. Habitual worries and fantasies or repetitive uncomfortable memories are each an attempt to influence either the past or the future; they serve as a distraction from living in the now. Paradoxically these habitual worries and fantasies are a sign of hopefulness in that they serve as an insurance against emotional shock if something were to go wrong.

Awareness of what is currently occurring both internally and externally is a central point in the psychotherapy of obsessing. I often have the client look back over time and examine the wasted energy and lost opportunities for enjoyment, spontaneity, creativity, or adventure that may have occurred if he were not obsessing. In this facet of therapy we focus on fostering the client's sense of "OK-ness" through discovering and maintaining self-awareness, accepting the uncertainties of life, living in the "now", and perhaps developing a sense of universal connectedness or spirituality. As an alternative to habitual worrying I may work with the client to develop a motto such as, "No matter what the outcome, I will learn and grow from the experience" (Erskine, 1980). A principal focus in the psychotherapy of obsession is helping the client to develop present centred mindfulness (Allen, 2011; Trautmann, 2003; Verney, 2009; Žvelc, Černetič, & Košak, 2011).

An elaborative case

Bobby's wife had insisted that he seek psychotherapy because his obsessive worries and behaviours were interfering with both their marriage and the relationship with his two young children. He was not certain that he "needed psychotherapy" or that he even had "a problem". "I only worry a bit," he said. His body squirmed and tensed as he complained about his wife not understanding him, how hard he worked, and how some of the other men at work were "not taking responsibility". Although he expressed some concern about his marriage he was primarily worried about his firm's success and his future career. My reaction in this first session, and during the next few, was to relax and listen—to listen with a sensitive ear, not only to his current distress, but to the stories he was unconsciously telling, to the interpersonal conflicts he had endured, to how he had coped, and for his unarticulated developmental and relational needs.

Bobby at the age of thirty-six was an executive in a growing firm and proud of his responsible position. In the first few sessions he described how he had a reputation for being "on top of things", always anticipating that "something will go wrong". He proudly described how the phrase, "something will go wrong" had become his motto for success both as a university student and on the job. The other men at work, his only male companions, teased him about being "Mr. Doom and Gloom". Yet they also expressed their appreciation for how he anticipated problems in securing materials and production.

Although I customarily inquire about each client's subjective experience, I sensed that Bobby needed me, in these first several weeks, to simply listen attentively to what he was telling me, even though he was repetitive. I concentrated on acknowledging each thing he was saying, sometimes with words and most often with my body language. I wanted Bobby to feel secure with me. It seemed crucial that he be the one to set both the rhythm and interpersonal stage for our work together. I had the impression that Bobby, like most clients who engage in obsessing and habitual worrying, was deeply lonely—a loneliness that had been with him so long that he did not distinguish that sensation from other affects.

A relational Transactional Analysis perspective (Cornell, 2008; Fowlie & Sills, 2011) and the use of phenomenological and historical inquiry, validation, and normalisation would become central in our therapeutic dialogue (Erskine, Moursund, & Trautmann, 1999; Erskine & Trautmann, 1996). For now it was apparent that he needed my undivided attention to, and acknowledgment of, the little nuances of emotion and patterns of attachment, or non-attachment, encoded in his stories (Erskine, 2009). Eric Berne outlined eight "therapeutic operations" that he used in psychotherapy and suggested the use of "interrogation" and "specification" as the initial step in gathering information (1966, pp. 233–247). I have repeatedly discovered that Berne's information gathering methods are disconcerting to many clients. Instead of revealing their affectively entrenched narrative in their own rhythm, with their own examples and metaphors, they focus instead on providing factual information and lose contact with a deeper subjective experience. I have stopped using such strident methods in our initial sessions and instead have relied on interpersonal contact to build a secure therapeutic relationship (Moursund & Erskine, 2003).

In our individual psychotherapy sessions over the next month Bobby described in detail how he had received several promotions because he could anticipate what would go wrong in his firm. What the men at work did not know was that Bobby could not sleep at night. He hesitantly told me how he would lie awake and worry about the various aspects of his job. Sleeping pills did not work to ease worrying. Slowly he came around to telling me that his obsessing propelled him to get up during the night to work on his computer or to stay late at the office. He was reluctant to tell his wife about the full extent of his constant worries and his feeling of exhaustion. The tentative way in which he was beginning to reveal his personal story prompted me to inquire about his sense of shame.

Talking about shame, even thinking about it, was painful for Bobby. He repeatedly avoided my initial attempts to bring his possible experience of shame into our therapeutic dialogue. For the next couple of months I took some time in each session to address his avoidance and to inquire about possible sadness at not having been accepted as he was or fear of being rejected for who he is (Erskine, 1994). For the first time in our therapy relationship he began having fragments of memory about feeling ashamed of his family when other kids at school were talking about their family activities. This provided us with several opportunities to talk about how habitual worry was an attempt to avoid emotionally laden memory. Throughout the three years of our work together we often returned to investigating what feelings, memories, or thoughts he was possibly avoiding, particularly when he wanted to tell me about current events or the happenings at work.

I knew from experience with clients who habitually worry that they not only avoid their feelings and memories but that they are often lonely; they fill the relational gap with mental activity. I wondered about his possible loneliness. I speculated about the nature of the relationships and qualities of life for the little boy and adolescent that he once was. I hypothesised about how he had managed, and how the relational experiences of that child affected his life today. I could see that his chest was concave; he described the tension in his shoulders and upper back. I wondered if these muscle constrictions were a "script signal" (Berne, 1972, p. 315) reflecting very early physiological and sub-symbolic survival reactions, the "protocol" and "palimpsests" of a life script (Berne, 1961, pp. 116–126).

I was reminded of Eric Berne's descriptions of how Child ego states are formed from early relational traumas that are mentally registered as internal confusions, restrictions, and fears (Berne, 1961). I could feel an internal pull to be fully present with Bobby, to remain sensitive to his slightest affect, to follow his body movements, to be completely with him. I searched internally to ascertain if my feeling sorry for him and desiring contact with him was a *reactive* or *responsive countertransference*. My introspective sense was that my feelings were an emotional response to what he needed in a therapeutic relationship and that my sensations would become central in our work together.

Over the next few months it became increasingly clear that Bobby was deeply lonely. As a young boy, Bobby sat in the window most Sundays waiting for his father to pick him up for their one day a week together. His father would often be hours late or on occasion he would not show up at all; he would not even telephone. Bobby began to anticipate disappointment. He protected himself from the emotional pain of his father's broken promises by predicting that "something will go wrong". He grew up being a "loner"; he had no close friends at school.

As a child Bobby never told his mother or the children at school about his deep disappointment in his father. He keep all the disappointments to himself, "held back the tears", and imagined various ways to avoid further disappointment.

Bobby's mother never inquired about his feelings or what he experienced on the many Sundays when his father would be hours late or not show up. He could not remember any conversations with his mother; it seemed to him that they had never talked together. Bobby's only memory of conversation with his mother was about school work or her complaints about her ex-husband's "irresponsibility" in their marriage. Bobby said that he would "tune her out" when his mother would complain about his father or criticise him for being like his father. At an early age Bobby figured out that he could not rely on any parental relationship for emotional stabilisation or regulation. He learned to stabilise and regulate himself through fantasy.

At this point in the psychotherapy it was time for me to increase the use of phenomenological inquiry—a respectful inquiry aimed at increasing his awareness of internal processes of affect, body sensations, associations, fantasy, and memory. Phenomenological inquiry is particularly effective in stimulating the retrieval of implicit and procedural memories, converting those sub-symbolic memories from affect and body sensations to narrative, and encouraging personal introspection (Erskine, 1993).

Loneliness and the absence of a meaningful relationship become a core issue for clients who engage in obsessing, habitual worrying, and repetitive fantasising. The worries and fantasies divert the awareness of the need for relationship. Berne stated that "a hunger for human contact" was one of the three motivations for all human behaviour (1970, p. 208). When *relationship hunger* is repeatedly not satisfied the person may overcompensate through increased absorption in the biological imperatives for *stimulus* and/or *structure* (Erskine, 1997). I based my therapy with Bobby on the premise that obsessing is a response to increased internal stimulus and a compensating reliance on structure—a displacement of the "sensations that can only be supplied by another human being" (Berne, 1972, p. 21). One result of this displacement is the intense anxiety and rumination associated with obsessing and habitual worrying, what Winnicott called "overactivity of mental functioning" (1949, p. 246).

Based on this theoretical premise and many clinical observations, I approached this first year of therapy with a relational perspective on Transactional Analysis (Cornell, 2008; Cornell & Hargaden, 2005; Erskine, Moursund, & Trautmann, 1999; Eusden, 2011; Fowlie & Sills, 2011; Hargaden & Sills, 2002; R. Little, 2013; Novak, 2013; Moursund & Erskine, 2003; Trautmann & Erskine, 1999). I emphasised our mutual dialogue, although he often did much of the talking. I maintained an attitude of acceptance, respect, kindness, and patience—the manifestations of the Transactional Analysis philosophy of *I'm OK—You're OK* (Harris, 1967). As the therapy progressed I used more and more phenomenological inquiry, coupled with an increased historical inquiry into his relationship with his mother and father, as well as an inquiry about his various strategies of coping with conflict, stress, and disappointment. These inquiries were paired with my active acknowledgement, my validation of his affect, and my normalisation of his reactions and ways of coping with relational neglect (Erskine & Trautmann, 1996).

From time to time I worked with Bobby's transference on other people (such as the men at work) and within the transference/ countertransference interchanges of our emerging relationship (Cornell & Landaiche, 2006; Erskine, 1991; Hargaden & Sills, 2001; R. Little, 2006, 2011a; Moiso, 1985; Novellino, 1984, 1985). Space in this chapter does not allow me to describe the many subtle transferential enactments that ensued throughout our work. Briefly, there were many occasions wherein Bobby assumed that I was not listening to him, that I would not be in the office when he arrived, or that I would belittle him. He periodically anticipated that I would "outright reject" him.

Bobby and I examined our interpersonal communication transaction by transaction (Berne, 1961, 1966, 1972) to uncover what he and I both brought to our interpersonal encounter (Stolorow, Brandschaft, & Atwood, 1987). These occasions required me to soul search and make an internal evaluation of my relational style, attitudes, and feeling. I was continually mindful that my various affects and behaviour may have an adverse as well as beneficial impact on him so I often inquired about how he experienced both my behaviour and our relationship. We compared and contrasted our mutual transactions with the qualities of the relationships he previously had with his father, mother, and others.

I made several therapeutic errors in my work with Bobby. He never commented on or complained about my various misattunements but he would turn his eyes away, change the subject, or launch into one of his catastrophic fantasies. At these crucial moments I surmised that I had been the first to disrupt our interpersonal contact. It was up to me to take responsibility by acknowledging that I had missed him in some important way, to identify my error, and to find a way to correct my error.

These important error-correcting transactions were significant in the ongoing development of a secure therapeutic relationship (Guistolese, 1996). Near the end of Bobby's psychotherapy he talked about a few of the occasions when I took responsibility for "misunderstanding" or "pushing" him. He said that each event was significant in that "no one", neither of his parents or any teacher, had ever "owned-up" to their errors and that when I made it my "fault", "something happened inside"; he felt "honoured and cared for in a new way".

On several occasions he described what Freud termed the "transference of everyday life": he feared that the men at work would laugh at him if they ever knew about his worries, fears, or family history (Freud, 1912b). Each of these transferential stories provided an opportunity for us to explore together both the current and historical context of his relationships with his fellow workers and with family members. The Transactional Analysis of our conversations and an analysis of his enactments with family members and co-workers provided the stimulus to recall explicit memories as well as sensations and emotions that I assumed were significant memories, albeit implicit and procedural. This approach to understanding transferential enactments is based on the biological, developmental, and existential dynamics of interpersonal relating, what Berne referred to as "advantages" of games (Bary & Hufford, 1990; Berne, 1964, pp. 56–58).

When Eric Berne wrote about the script protocol (1972) and the "primal dramas of childhood" he was writing about unconscious infantile attachment patterns that formed an "extensive unconscious life plan" (1961, p. 123), a concept similar to Bowlby's "internal working models" (1969, 1973, 1980). Through our transference/countertransference work it became increasingly evident that Bobby dismissed the significance of relationship and avoided intimacy; he inhibited his emotional expression, he insisted on the importance of self-reliance, and he was not conscious of his needs for interpersonal connection. Bobby avoided vulnerability. I concluded that his life script was based on an *avoidant attachment pattern* (Erskine, 2009; Horowitz,

Rosenberg & Bartholomew, 1993; Kobak & Sceery, 1988; Main, 1990, 1995). It was clear to me that Bobby needed my investment in him, my involvement and presence—a responsive countertransference—if he were to heal from his avoidant attachment pattern, obsessive coping style, and lifelong feelings of loneliness.

A relational psychotherapy was essential throughout Bobby's psychotherapy, not only in this first year of therapy, but as the foundation to which we returned in every session, even when our attention was on cognitive understanding, behavioural change, or deep emotional work. I was always mindful of the little boy's loneliness and his need for a healing relationship. The contactful quality of the relationship between us provided the secure foundation on which all the other facets of therapy relied.

In the second half of this first year I increased my use of three other therapeutic operations: explanation, confrontation, and illustration (Berne, 1966, pp. 233–247). Over the years I have modified how and when I use these three therapeutic operations: Berne used them to decontaminate and strengthen the Adult ego state; I use these methods to stimulate the client's awareness of implicit and procedural memories of early family dynamics, childhood vulnerabilities, sensitivities, and developmental needs. I am always thinking developmentally and my explanations and illustrations are based on an understanding of child development. I frequently ask myself questions such as: What is the psychological age(s) of my client? How does a child of that age achieve validation, influence others, and define him or herself? What does a child of that age need in a healing relationship? How will a young child make sense of what I am saying?

I kept in mind that confrontation is only effective when done respectfully and when the client has the conviction that "This therapist is invested in my welfare". By this point in our work together I assessed that our therapeutic relationship was sufficiently secure that I could periodically confront Bobby's obsessions. My aim was to bring his attention to how he was avoiding uncomfortable sensations and memories. I accompanied these confrontations with extensive use of phenomenological and historical inquiry to activate his internal contact with feelings, needs, associations, and memories. I also focused on how he managed the relational disruptions of his early life and how he still relied on old patterns of coping with neglect and disappointment. He responded with ever increasing memories of his father's neglect, his mother's ridicule and coldness, his constant childhood loneliness, and how he tried to restore and stabilise himself with fantasy. He was beginning to differentiate sadness from loneliness, withdrawal from anger, and how he often disavowed the fear underlying his script belief, "No one is there for me". These were the very sensations and memories that he avoided through obsessive fantasy.

In many sessions I used explanation or illustration to communicate to Bobby that every child needs validation, companionship, and someone steady to rely on; his stories revealed that his normal relational needs for security, self-definition, and agency seemed to be ignored by his parents (Erskine & Trautmann, 1996). Bobby's range of emotions and detail of memories increased with our sessions. The building of a secure therapeutic relationship and our attentions to his avoidance of affect, body sensation, and memory had the effect of lessening his obsessing. It was now time to concentrate on his script system and how it reinforced his life script.

Although we had addressed his script system in previous sessions, during this second year we again returned to examining his script system in finer detail (Erskine, 2015; O'Reilly-Knapp & Erskine, 2010). Interwoven with our relational psychotherapy and our focus on the avoidance of feelings and memories in Bobby's obsessions, we spent several sessions writing a description of his overt behaviours and how they were linked to other people's behaviour which Bobby in turn used as a reinforcing experience to confirm his script beliefs. We paid particular attention to how each fantasy also became another reinforcing experience, the imagined evidence to support the script conclusions he had made in childhood: *"I don't need anything from anyone"; "I'm the only responsible one"; "No one is there for me"; "People are only interested in themselves";* and, *"Life is full of disappointments".*

Throughout this period of time in our therapy I used a combination of phenomenological inquiry, explanation, confrontation, and illustration as the impetus for a "systematic experiential discomfirmation" of Bobby's script beliefs (Widdowson, 2014, p. 202). As part of the overall therapy these cognitively and behaviourally focused sessions had several purposes:

- To stimulate Bobby's awareness of how his childhood reactions, fantasies, and conclusions continued to affect him as an adult.
- To gather additional information about how Bobby's life script was being lived out day by day.

- To help him understand and transform the homeostatic functions of his script system.
- To assess his willingness or reluctance to relinquish his old script beliefs, and;
- To set a more secure base for doing any reparative age-regression therapy that may be necessary.

There were occasions when Bobby talked about his intense hurt as a result of the criticisms from the men at work or his anger at his wife's "demands" for more pleasurable time together. Although his description of these events had many of the elements that Eric Berne (1964) described as constituting a "game", I found it more effective to address his experience as an emotional enactment of his primary relationships as a child. Rather than confront his playing a game we sensitively explored how his experience fitted the "con" and "gimmick" of Berne's game formula (Berne, 1972, pp. 23–25).

We defined the con as his unrequited developmental and relational needs and the gimmick as his archaic self-stabilising and self-protective facade. The "cross-up" in the game occurred when other people did not display a suitable empathy and understanding that he was needing in the relationship. We investigated how his hurt or angry feelings (Berne's "game payoff") were a replay of what he felt as a boy with his mother's criticism, neglect, and demands, and his father's disregard of what he needed. We clarified how these enactments became a reinforcing experience that once again confirmed his script beliefs.

In the midst of working with the script system Bobby told me that his mother would often tell him that his father "lacked any true emotion", that he was "irresponsible", "without morals". Bobby remembered promising himself that he would have his mother's love if he were responsible and moral. I could see the tension in his body so I asked him to close his eyes and imagine his mother sitting in front of him. I encouraged him to move his tight shoulders and say whatever came to him.

He began to shout at the internal image of his mother and tell her about his anger at her degrading comments about his father. He went on to express his anger at her "coldness" and "control". Then he shouted, *"You were never there for me."* He repeated these words a few times and then added, *"... and that is how I live, mom, believing that no one will ever be there for me."* At this moment he burst into tears and sobbed for a few minutes. At several points in this work I encouraged him to keep talking to her, to tell her his truth, to tell her what he had never said. He then softly cried, *"I am always so afraid … I'm afraid, mom, that I won't be responsible and then you will never love me."*

I encouraged him to repeat what he was saying and to do it louder. He shouted it again and then said, *"I have lived my whole life in fear that you would not love me if I weren't the responsible one. You are always cold, mom. You were never there for me. You are always interested only in yourself. I have lived my whole life believing that no one was there for me and that I had to be the responsible one. Martha and Robie and Sheila* [his wife and children] *are there for me, mom, not you. I am loved by them and I need them. With you I learned to never need … but I do need them. I am changing that, mom. I don't have to always be the responsible one. I need my family."* With these final words he took several deep breaths. Bobby was disconnecting the emotional "rubber band" and making a "redecision" (Erskine, 1974, 2011; Erskine & Moursund, 1988; Goulding & Goulding, 1979). This therapy session involved much more than a cognitive redecision, it generated a physiological and affective reorganisation leading to a new sense of self.

In our weekly individual psychotherapy sessions, over the next year and a half, I often addressed the relationally neglected boy—a child of several different ages—who lacked the opportunities to express himself, who unconsciously yearned for validation and companionship, and who needed someone to help him put his emotional experiences into words. Like Eric Berne's description of working with Child ego states, I talked to the boy that Bobby once was (Berne, 1961). If someone were to analyse our transactions during this phase of the therapy it would often appear as though I was a benevolent father helping a vulnerable and bewildered child to understand and articulate his feelings, needs, and aspirations (B. D. Clark, 1991). On many occasions I could feel the fatherliness of my relationship with Bobby. I acquired a love for him and he was slowly allowing himself to be emotionally attached to me. This new style of attachment was evident in his "longing to talk" to me when there were holiday breaks in our scheduled appointments or when I was travelling.

Early in our therapy together I invited Bobby to join a weekly therapy group. I assumed that the relational group process of the ongoing therapy group would augment our individual sessions and help to address and resolve his shame and loneliness (Erskine, 2013). He repeatedly refused. However, after the deep emotional/redecisional work with the internal image of his mother, he agreed to attend a weekend marathon therapy session. These sessions, which met from Friday evening until Sunday afternoon, were a combination of relational group psychotherapy, supported regression and redecision therapy, and some body psychotherapy (Erskine, 2014b; Erskine & Moursund, 1988).

In his first therapy marathon Bobby did another piece of redecision therapy similar to what he had spontaneously done in his individual session. This time we focused on his mother's criticism of him. He was angry at her self-centredness which he connected to his script conclusion that all "people are only interested in themselves". As he expressed his anger he had several insights about his relationship with his mother and how he re-enacted that relationship with his wife. This intensive session involved an affect/cognitive reorganisation leading to an important realisation about how he avoided intimate involvement with people and operated as a "loner". The group was caring and supportive of Bobby's experimenting with new ways of being in relationship. Bobby was able to talk to the group members about his shame and loneliness. In addition to our weekly therapy sessions, Bobby eventually attended a series of three more weekend therapy marathons.

In the second marathon he focused on the absence of his father. He cried deeply, calling for his father while his body convulsed with emotion. He was reliving being a little boy and crying out, "Daddy where are you? Daddy you are not there for me." He reached out, grabbed my shirt, and pulled himself into my arms and continued to weep for many minutes. He then nestled his head onto my chest and put his ear to my heart. The latter part of this therapy was without words; it was a mixture of sounds, movement, and tender touch—an affect/physiological reorganisation. In our debriefing later that day Bobby said that "something had shifted inside", that he felt "much more present and adult". "My chest is much more open."

Several months later, in his individual psychotherapy Bobby talked at length about his self-criticism, as though it was his own voice chastising him with "I'm not being good enough". We used a two-chair method to create a dialogue between his own voice as the "criticiser" and his felt sense of being "criticised". Bobby realised that he had learned to criticise himself to make sure that no one else would ever criticise him. This therapy work had some positive effect in reducing the intensity of the internal criticism. Weeks later, at his third marathon therapy group he talked about the internal criticism that remained. I again began with a two-chair dialogue (Erskine & Moursund, 1988; Goulding & Goulding, 1979; Moursund & Erskine, 2003) but soon discovered that the "criticiser" was no longer talking in a first-person voice, "I am ...", but was now talking in a second person voice, such as, "You are useless". I began a dialogue with Bobby's critical voice; after a couple of minutes it was as though Bobby was talking in his mother's voice.

I continued the conversation and inquired about her life, the kind of family in which she had grown up, her marriage and divorce, and the stresses and fears she felt as a single parent. Our therapeutic dialogue focused first on the neglect and criticism that she received as a child from her mother. Then I turned the discussion to how she had neglected Bobby's relational needs when he was a young boy. My inquiry was guided in part by Noriega Gayol's description of transgenerational scripts (Noriega Gayol, 2004, 2009, 2010). She talked about her disappointment in her marriage, how she never wanted to have a child, and her anger at her former husband. She then confessed that she criticised Bobby because she was angry at his father, whom she described as "useless". She cried when she talked about how she had "mistreated" Bobby. In response to my inquiring and empathically responding, just as though she was my own client, Bobby's introjected mother (his Parent ego state) was expressing the emotionally charged story of her own life script.

Near the end of our hour long session, she told Bobby that he was a "fine son", "never any trouble", and that she was proud of him. I then asked Bobby to change chairs and respond to his internal image of his mother. He told her about his "emptiness" and "loneliness" and how she was never there for him in the ways he needed her. He cried. His body relaxed.

Several hours later Bobby said, "I feel as though there is a giant load off my back." Weeks later he reported that he had spent several weeks of living without any internal criticism. The absence of any internal criticism reflects the affect/cognitive/physiological reorganisation that therapy of the Parent ego state can provide for a client (Erskine, 2003b; Erskine & Trautmann, 2003).

An investigation of possible archaic homeostatic functions was woven throughout many of our sessions. From our early sessions onward, I was often silently hypothesising about the various functions underlying Bobby's habitual worrying. Periodically I used these hypotheses to form some of my inquiries. From clinical experience I was fairly certain that Bobby would not totally stop his obsessing as

Script Beliefs >>>	Script Manifestations >>>	Reinforcing Experiences
Self:	**Overt behavior:**	**Current:**
I don't need anyting from anyone.	No meaningful relationships. Self-protective facade. No talk about emotions. No close friends, a loner. Silenced by shame.	Others don't inquire. Others tease. People show no personal interest. Hurt by criticism.
I'm the only responsible one.	Takes all the responibility. Complains about others not taking responsibility.	Notices others not taking responsibility. Appreciation from men at work. Promotions.
Others:		
No one is there for me.	Awake at night, on computer.	Wife complains about his getting up at night and not coming home in evenings. Wife withdraws.
People are only interested in themselves.	Reacts to wife as though she were his mother.	
	Physiological:	
	Chest concave, tension in shouldrs & back. Sense of "emptiness".	Body & sub-symbolic memories.
Quality of life:		**Old memories:**
Life is full of disappointments. Something will go wrong.		Waiting for father. Absent father.
	Fantasy:	Mother is cold.
	Worry about work and career. Catastrophic fantasies of something going wrong. Richard will belittle me or not listen. Richard will not be there for me. Richard will reject me. "I will get mother's love if I'm responsible". Mother will never love me as I am.	Mother's; neglect. Criticism, demands, self-centeredness, & lack of validation. Mother never asks about feelings. Mother says father has no morals, irresponsible. Mother says: "You are useless".

Repressed Feelings & Needs
Loneliness, anger, emotional pain.
Need for security-in-relationship, validation, someone to rely on,
companionship, to define self, to make an imapact, to give and
receive intimacy.

Figure 3. Bobby's script system.

long as his fantasies and related script beliefs served archaic homeo-static functions such as predictability, identity, continuity, or stability (Erskine, 2015; Erskine, Moursund, & Trautmann, 1999).

I periodically inquired about Bobby's subjective experiences with the realisation that he would eventually discover and appreciate his internal urge for a familiar sense of equilibrium—the homeostatic stabilisation—that maintained his habits of worrying and obsessing. Fairly early in the psychotherapy I asked Bobby if he could describe the purpose of his fantasies about "something will go wrong". He immediately exclaimed, "To know what will happen!" This led us into several memories where he described his internal urge for predictability and his intense fear when he could not predict the outcome of events. We further explored how his fantasies served to reinforce his script beliefs and, at the same time, functioned to provide insurance against the shock of disappointments.

Through my consistent phenomenological inquiry Bobby became aware of three other homeostatic functions:

- That his script belief "I don't need anything from anyone" and his related fantasies of being "totally independent of anyone" were a childhood form of identity.
- That many of his fantasies and their accompanying script belief "no one is there for me" served as an orientation in his relationships with others, and;
- That his habitual worrying provided a sense of continuity throughout his life.

Each of these homeostatic functions were a childlike attempt at self-reparation and provided a synthetic stabilisation of his intense affect—a self-stabilisation necessary to reduce the strong emotional reactions that occurred as a result of the absence of need fulfilling contact with significant others, either in actuality in his current life, as fantasy, or as traces of implicit memory (Kohut, 1977; Wolf, 1988).

However, to relinquish archaic insecure attachment patterns and the homeostatic functions that both constitute and maintain a life script, clients such as Bobby have to shift the archaic functions to mature functions (Erskine, 2015). This shift often involves experimenting with and temporarily allowing the therapeutic relationship to provide such psychological functions as stabilisation, predictability, or a new identity-in-relationship. Over the three years of his psychotherapy Bobby did a lot of experimenting and testing of my honesty, consistency, reliability, and dependability.

During this phase of the psychotherapy I repeatedly used the method of *relational inquiry* to ascertain how Bobby experienced me, to define our intersubjective processes, and to contrast the difference in the qualities of our relationship with the various other relationships in his life. When doing this sort of relational inquiry we were cycling back to the relational phase of our work together and simultaneously relying on what we had discovered about Bobby's life script and his script system. Each phase of our psychotherapy became interfaced with the other phases. I periodically had the perception that we were working in a hologram of therapeutic concepts and methods.

Gradually throughout his psychotherapy I fostered the transferring of Bobby's archaic homeostatic functions into a reliance on the consistency and dependability of our therapeutic relationship. My aim was to provide a secure relational base as an alternative to his previous avoidant attachment patterns and to provide a transitional phase in the establishment of mature homeostatic functions. Gradually Bobby's out-of-date identity was replaced with a new sense of identity, an identity based in the current contexts of his life—a mature identity that included an intimate relationship with his wife and children and a more open and contactful relationship with the men at work. Through our psychotherapy together he was developing new and mature forms of affect stabilisation and intersubjective regulation.

During the second and third year we periodically focused on the sixth facet of our psychotherapy, the concept of "living in the now". A year earlier in our therapy Bobby disregarded my attempts to introduce awareness exercises. He did not like the concept of living in the present and argued with me that "worrying about the future was good insurance". I talked about how his worrying was a sign of hopefulness—that he could protect himself from the surprise and shock that "something will go wrong". In a number of sessions I reiterated the stories he had told me about various hurts and disappointments and explained how it would be normal in those situations to emotionally stabilise and regulate himself by predicting the worst. In several sessions we talked about his struggle to control the future. Hope and control was a theme to which we returned for some minutes during several sessions.

During our psychotherapy sessions, while I continued to make use of phenomenological inquiry and our intersubjective experiences, I began to introduce some awareness and grounding exercises and requested that he practise them at home. Over time we created two new mottos, "I don't know yet" and "What I am now worried about will pass", to replace his script belief, "Something will go wrong". During the second year I suggested that he attend a meditation weekend. At first he was uncomfortable with the experience but I was pleasantly surprised when he continued in an ongoing meditation programme.

In the final year of the therapy I suggested that he join a twice a week yoga class, which he did. After a few weeks Bobby was pleased with how his body was changing. He was committed to continuing the yoga and meditation; they were both providing mature forms of self-stabilisation and self-regulation. His reliance on me was now much less than in the previous year. He involved himself in family activities as he had never done before. And he was delighted that he was no longer obsessing and was enjoying a full night's sleep. When things were uncertain he focused on what he was experiencing within his body in the present moment.

Bobby was out of the city when one of his children had a severe accident; he stabilised his anxiety with "I do not have enough information to be worried". When his wife was having complications with a new pregnancy he taught her to use the motto, "I don't know yet. We will solve the problem if it ever happens". He was living spontaneously in the present: in touch with his vulnerability, aware of the functions of his previous obsessions, and intimate in his relationships. When we terminated our psychotherapy sessions he planned to continue with both his meditation and yoga.

Conclusion

The story of Bobby's psychotherapy provides a collection of concepts, therapeutic facets, and methods that merge together to inform you, the reader, about the use of Transactional Analysis in contemporary psychotherapy. I have chosen to present a case involving the psychotherapy of obsessing, habitual worrying, and repetitive fantasising because the psychotherapy of such clients illustrates the use of both Eric Berne's theories and the newer concepts and methods of contemporary clinical Transactional Analysis such as:

- Psychotherapy from a relational perspective—respectful, non-pathological, and co-constructive.
- Psychotherapy from a developmental framework, informed by current knowledge of neurobiology and the developmental and relational needs of children.

- The significance of re-enactments (what Berne called "games") and transference as the communication of unconscious experience and the interplay between a reactive and responsive countertransference.
- Child and Parent ego states and the reciprocal relationship between ego states.
- The affect/physiological/cognitive reorganisation that can result from the deconfusion of Child ego states, a therapeutically supportive regression, and the decommissioning of a Parent ego state.
- The identification of the script system and the interchange between script beliefs, behaviour and fantasy, and script reinforcing experience.
- The homeostatic functions of behaviour, repetitive fantasies, and script beliefs and the importance of transferring the client's habitual use of archaic functions to mature functions, and;
- The mature stabilisation and regulation of living in the present moment.

The Transactional Analysis psychotherapy of obsessing, habitual worrying, and repetitive fantasising is complex and requires a multifaceted approach that addresses and resolves the client's underlying loneliness and unconscious longing for meaningful relationship, thereby reorienting the client's archaic homeostatic functions of obsessing to mature function, dissolving archaic script beliefs and introjections, facilitating a physiological/affective/cognitive reorganisation, and enriching the client's emotional life via intimacy and living in the present moment.

Eric Berne laid the theoretical foundation for Transactional Analysis psychotherapy, and other insightful and creative clinicians contributed a multitude of concepts and methods—contemporary Transactional Analysis abounds with effective methods—but the development of Transactional Analysis in psychotherapy is not complete. This chapter has outlined a six-faceted approach that associates of the Institute for Integrative Psychotherapy and I found effective in our work with clients who are immersed in obsessing, repetitive fantasising, and habitual worrying. More exploration and clinical research may reveal other therapeutic facets effective in the psychotherapy of obsession. For now these six facets (relationship, avoidance, script and script system, intrapsychic reorganisation, homeostatic functions, and living in the present) each form a useful orientation in the practice of Transactional Analysis in contemporary psychotherapy.

CHAPTER TWO

Transference-countertransference focused Transactional Analysis

Ray Little

Many of the problems that our clients present have their roots in their experience of earlier relationships, particularly with their primary caregivers. A variation of these difficulties is often then perpetuated in their current relationships. Therefore, I believe a relationship has the potential for transforming their difficulties, and thereby creating a narrative with different meanings. The particular principles and concepts that influence my approach to Transactional Analysis psychotherapy include aspects of both the psychodynamic and humanistic traditions.

I see that human development occurs within a "relational matrix" (Burke & Tansy, 1991, p. 370), with the mind made up of relational schemas (R. Little, 2011a, 2011b). My clinical focus is to attend to these schemas within the transference-countertransference relationship. During therapy the client and therapist create a unique coupling. This engagement offers the opportunity for the client to meet the new object (Cooper & Levit, 1998; Greenberg, 1986), working through (Greenson, 1965) the old object relationship, and reclaim the self. In this process I position myself to be used as both the longed-for and feared, old and co-created new object.

When we choose to address the transference-countertransference processes I suggest that there are broadly speaking two options (R. Little, 2011a, 2006, adapted from Gomez, 2004). First, working *with* the transference, alongside the client, to support change and transformation: this may include using expressive techniques (Erskine & Moursund, 1988; Goulding & Goulding, 1979; Ohlsson, 1998). Second, working *within* the transference-countertransference dyad to facilitate transformation and integration.

In in-depth psychotherapy I choose to work *within* the transference-countertransference matrix. This entails working with the ego state relational units that are manifest in the therapeutic dyad; a here-and-now approach.

The choice the therapist makes may be influenced by the context or circumstances of the therapy. I am aware that some therapists move between the two approaches. However, I think this may be difficult to manage for both client and therapist.

In working within the transference-countertransference I am working with the client's past and present simultaneously. Although Child–Parent ego state relational units (R. Little, 2006) are underdeveloped fixated archaic structures, working with the past in the present entails treating them as if they were a direct response to the present.

What I will focus on here are the *theory* and *methods* that I use to facilitate clients in individual long-term, in-depth transference-countertransference focused Transactional Analysis psychotherapy. I believe that the *therapeutic action* involved in these processes is dependent upon how we conceive of four elements: psychological development, psychopathology, the nature of the therapeutic relationship (both conscious and unconscious aspects), and the role and stance of the therapist.

In terms of *psychological development* I focus upon the mind as consisting of self-other relational schemas, adaptive *and* defensive (Zvelc, 2009). I consider the developmental notion of moving from dependency through to separation and individuation; from psychic unintegration (Winnicott, 1965, p. 44) to psychic integration.

Psychopathology involves the activation of various dissociated, largely unconscious, defensive Child–Parent ego state relational units, and their involvement in psychological games, enactments, and re-enactments. A re-enactment is where the therapist remains reflective and an enactment is where the therapist has joined the client in an unconscious and mutual script bound process (Stuthridge, 2012). This, coupled with ego state relational units, represents an addition to Berne's categories of pathology, that is, exclusion and contamination (1961).

The *therapeutic relationship* involves engagement in the transference-countertransference matrix from the perspective of a two-person psychology (Stark, 1999), consisting of a focus on the relationship between therapist and client, including the acknowledgement of a mutual unconscious interaction (Ehrenberg, 2010). From this perspective the client and therapist are seen as participating either defensively or adaptively in a co-constructed relationship. Engagement in this process offers the opportunity to explore what transpires between them, therefore offering/creating an opportunity to transform the implicit relational expectations. Corrective experiences emerge out of the relationship that has been forged and are not deliberately structured for the client's benefit; an intersubjective two person psychology.

The *therapeutic stance* involves what I have described as the therapeutically required relationship (R. Little, 2011b), and entails working with and responding to both the repeated and needed relationships (S. Stern, 1994), *and* the old while co-creating the new. Several TA authors (Barr, 1987; Clarkson, 2003) have listed various relationships that occur within the therapeutic dyad. My particular focus is on the transference-countertransference matrix.

Working in the present with the past

A version of the past is alive in the present, and as Riesenberg-Malcolm states, "[T]ransference is an 'alloy' of past and present" (1986, p. 52). The resolution of the client's conflicts and deficits are achieved by addressing the client's relationship with the therapist; that is, addressing the transference-countertransference matrix directly. It is this total picture that may be tentatively presented to the client as my understanding and is offered in terms of the present moment.

For example, Mark describes feeling tired, needing a holiday. Having been caring for his dying mother, and feeling resentful that his siblings don't acknowledge his hard work, he tells me he feels uncared for. Whilst I listen to his words, feel and observe his behaviour, I see myself as occupying a stance of inquiry and clarification. I examine my reactions to him and try to understand the impact his behaviour is having on me, what this might have to do with our relationship, and about the impact of my behaviour and communications on him. I wonder in what way the experience he is describing might relate to what is going on between us here and now.

I am aware that I had recently been unwell and he may have felt overlooked and uncared for at that time. I believe his feelings to be a mixture of past and present. His sense of not being cared for is both historical and current.

An aspect of the therapist's behaviour may often coincide with the client's projection, even if the client is interpreting my behaviour differently to the way I intend and different to the way I experience myself. The part of Mark that felt uncared for as a child may be responding to my lower than usual energy level, for example.

I may then draw the process into the therapeutic relationship, and towards myself, the therapist. The act of staying within the process and responding counter to the unconscious expectations of the client offers the possibility of a "new bad object" (Cooper, 2010) relationship experience. The client is responding to the presence of the therapist, whether it is like the past or not.

Merton Gill (1982) is another author who describes the transference as a combination of past and present. He suggested that what activates the transference is the client's attempt to make sense of the various cues he may be picking up from the therapist's behaviour. In turn this triggers various templates in the client's mind. For example, I seemed more caring than Mark was used to, then not so much so.

Riesenberg-Malcolm suggests that "Generally the patient perceives what we say in (at least) two ways. If it makes sense to him, he may feel relief and think about it. But at the same time, the interpretation interferes with the client's usual way of reacting, and this can either loosen the defences or bring out further defensive behaviour" (1986, p. 434). As she suggests, we are disturbing the client and this continuous shift in the contact of the client with the therapist gradually reveals the defensive relational units. In Mark's case, he may acknowledge that he had been disappointed in my seeming lack of care, and relieved that I had noticed and responded. He may be scared to have been seen so clearly.

Structure of the mind: relational schemas and ego states

"Every human being is born into a powerful relationship with a primary caretaker which sets up a very powerful influence on the architecture of the mind" (Shmueli, 2014).

I have previously described how infants and children internalise their experiences with significant others and their environment as relational schemas (R. Little, 2011b). Various authors support the notion that it is relationships that are internalised as self-other configurations (Beebe & Lachmann, 1988; Loewald, 1970), and that these representations subsequently influence the child's behaviour (Horner as cited in Schore, 1997). These early internalisations are laid down in implicit memory, consisting of procedural knowledge of relationships and the rules of how to be with someone, established through trial and error.

When we examine the nature of these internalised relational schemas, we can distinguish between those tolerable experiences that have been integrated and those that remain unintegrated. Internalisations that consist of the tolerable non-defensive experiences are an aspect of the integrating Adult ego state, and represent autonomous, here-and-now functioning from an open system (R. Little, 2006, 2011b), with the capacity for assimilation and accommodation (Piaget, 1952; Zvelc, 2010).

If the growing child experiences insufficient holding and containment or experiences trauma, or if there is a predominance of all-bad, aggressive internalisations, then the child may not be able to integrate his experiences, and these will remain as a dissociated structure. These structures constitute defensive, or maladaptive, schemas (Eagle, 2011; Zvelc, 2010). From a transactional analysis perspective, I describe these as ego state relational units. Although we internalise both the tolerable and intolerable experiences, it is the intolerable that have not been integrated, and constitute the Child–Parent ego state relational units (R. Little, 2006). These unintegrated schemas result in a closed script system, located in unconscious, implicit memory, forming the foundation for characterological structure and defences.

The therapeutic relationship is likely to stir the defensive aspects of early attachment patterns, which will then manifest as the transference of ego state relational units. For example, when a child has experienced violent abuse, and internalises those experiences, the nature of the ego state units that result is that the Child ego state can often appear as a victim while the Parent manifests as a persecutor or abuser. Anna Freud (1968) describes one of the ways an individual may manage this process is by identifying with the aggressor, to avoid feeling like a victim.

Several clients I have worked with who were sexually abused as children have defended themselves later by identifying with the abuser in some way and on occasions have disavowed their sexuality. In their minds it is easier to identify with the abusers rather than identifying with the victims. It is better to be a persecutor, powerful and strong than be a victim and helpless. I believe that when working with these issues we need to eventually work with both the victim *and* internalised abuser in the client. In my view, to see the client as solely a victim is a betrayal. The client will have internalised the persecutor as part of a Child–Parent ego state relational unit and both aspects will need to be addressed. The encounter with the internalised persecutor is a daunting one for the therapist, whether as a confrontation, or even scarier as identification. A successful challenge brings great relief to the victimised part(s) of the self (Davies & Frawley, 1994).

Olive: fighting back

An emerging theme in my work with Olive was her struggle with her sexuality. She began one session by speaking of envying a woman who appeared very feminine. Olive described how she dressed down to conceal her own femininity. I responded by saying, "So sitting here right now with me you are restraining your femininity and power. You are afraid of me criticising and humiliating you or being seductive." My use of the words "criticising", "humiliating" and "seductive" was based on what I knew of her history with her father and a youth worker in her past.

Olive said that at the last session she had heard me say that she should be more feminine. This was a projection of her mother's expectations and a painful experience of not being allowed to be herself. She mentioned that this morning she had thought of putting a dress on but had "refused". She said she had fought against the impulse. Olive seemed to believe that I had told her what to wear. In the transference I appeared to be a mother telling her how to behave, or the abuser.

In a following session she spoke of her clothes and appearance as masculine, protecting her from being vulnerable and what she saw as the tyranny of having to be a perfect female. She saw herself as rebelling against her mother. I also saw her as protecting herself from sexual attack.

I went on to say to her, "You see me as forcing you to be a certain way and you are fighting back against me." I felt uncomfortable in experiencing the sense of forcing her to be a particular way. I wanted to step aside from being seen as cruel and nasty.

Her ego state relational unit consisted of her defensive rebellious position against an imposing, perfectionist, and inhibiting mother/other. I wondered whether my desire to object to her perception of me echoed her desire to rebel.

It was a more feminine presentation that was attractive to Olive's abuser, and Olive had described how her abuser would dress her. A further aspect consisted of her disidentification with her femaleness in the face of this internalised female sexual abuser. This led to a defensive identification with a more masculine presentation. This served, in her mind, as a protection from further sexual attack. In this re-enactment I was able to maintain a reflective stance and avoid overidentification, and thus becoming either Rescuer or Persecutor (Karpman, 1968).

Transference-countertransference matrix

Transference is ubiquitous. When we engage with people we unconsciously attempt to make sense of the various cues and behaviours that we encounter in the other. Sometimes we may respond to others in adaptive ways from relational schemas that can assimilate and accommodate what we are experiencing/encountering.

Occasionally we respond to others' behaviours more defensively. This is often the case in the therapeutic dyad, since due to the nature of the relationship and the therapeutic frame, early attachment patterns will be activated, as will our defensive systems. These defensive relational schemas, which entail Child–Parent ego state relational units, will assimilate the encounter into archaic structures and schemas without accommodation.

I see the transference-countertransference matrix as a dynamic living relationship, and everything of importance in the client's internal world will probably, sooner or later, be lived out in some way in this matrix. Additionally, everything that the psychotherapist is or says is likely to be responded to according to the client's internal structure (or script), rather than the therapist's intentions and the meaning she gives to what has been said (Joseph, 1985). By understanding and interpreting the transference-countertransference in the here-and-now the therapist is dealing with the client's early conflicts and deficits, which can only be understood and integrated when lived through in the present with the therapist (Riesenberg-Malcolm, 1986).

Both the integrating Adult and the Child–Parent relational units are responding to cues and transferring onto the other, but the Adult is able to respond flexibly and adaptively, while the Child–Parent unit responds more rigidly and defensively. This rigid response by the various Child–Parent units is what most people would describe as transference, and what I will be referring to as transference in the remainder of this chapter.

Erskine (1991) has previously discussed four aspects of the psychotherapy of transference and he described how it demonstrates the thwarted developmental needs, and the unaware enactment of childhood experience (p. 73). The way I would describe these processes is that transference involves the client unconsciously inviting the therapist to repeat old experiences but longing to be exposed to the needed experiences. The therapist will seem like someone from the past and at other times, someone new; this is the nature of psychological games. We need to hold in mind that both client *and* therapist enter the therapeutic relationship with the capacity to act, think, and feel transferentially.

At any given moment, the client and therapist may be struggling to make sense of what is happening in the therapeutic relationship. The transference is often triggered by the client's interpretation of the therapist's behaviour (Gill, 1982). The experience and behaviour of the client and therapist alike will unavoidably be shaped unconsciously both by (a) who they are, independent of the therapeutic dyad, and (b) who they are in response to each other (Wallin, 2007, p. 271).

For a recent overview of various Transactional Analysis authors' explorations of the relevance and significance of transference for transactional analysts, I refer readers to Scilligo (2011), as well as Erskine's (1991) exploration of transference and transactions.

Andros and the fear of aliveness: the false self vs. the real self

Andros is a single man in his late twenties who lives in a flat that he shares with another man who only occupies it during the week. He is not there at weekends, much to Andros's relief. Both Andros's parents emigrated from Greece when he was quite young, locating themselves in a poor part of a big city. He was an only child and reported that he didn't have many friends. At school he would not be seen playing with the other children but would be found on his own, reading comics. As a child he mentioned being ashamed of his parents who could only speak "basic" English with a Greek accent.

Andros's job involves working with computers for local government. He is very good with computers but his employer has given him a warning that his relations with his fellow employees needs to improve otherwise he might face disciplinary action.

Andros's presentation is "android-like", with a rather emotionless expression. I have come across this kind of presentation on several occasions in various clients with schizoid structures. In working with Andros, I was aware of containing my "aliveness" with him. During the beginning phase of therapy, this resulted in our communication having an intellectual, stilted quality, although I would experience a variety of emotions in reaction to him, all of which I would keep to myself.

Andros had retreated into the isolation of his "castle" (R. Little, 2001; O'Reilly-Knapp, 2001) many years ago. Paul Simon's (1966) song "I am a rock" comes to mind when I think of Andros. In the song Simon sings "I've built walls, a fortress, steep and mighty, that none may penetrate. I have no need of friendship, friendship causes pain. It's laughter and it's loving I disdain."

Andros had withdrawn from ordinary social relations, leaving himself alone in the world but longing for connection with others. He did engage with the world, but from what might be described as a defensive "false self" position (Winnicott, 1965). He had a way of managing the world while keeping his vulnerability hidden away deep in his internal castle. Andros appears quite attractive, looking like Paul Newman, a film actor from earlier times (At this point there is a hint of an erotic stirring in my countertransference). Andros described how he would struggle in relations with women, and having occasional contact with prostitutes. These encounters would make his loneliness and isolation more bearable. Initially, I had not realised that these relationships were engaged with by a part of him that was playing a role, as if he was a film actor. In addition to seeing prostitutes he had occasional sexual relationships with other women. With them, while he was having sex, he would run "pornographic" films in his head as guides as to how to "perform". After a time the women would complain that something was missing and leave. When I think of Andros in relation to women, the next verse of Simon's song comes to mind. "Don't talk of love, well,

I've heard the words before. It's sleeping in my memory and I won't disturb the slumber of feelings that have died. If I never loved, I never would have cried."

Early in our work I would sit with Andros and feel controlled by him. I would feel held by his gaze, unable to look away. I came to understand my countertransference reaction as my fear of attack and humiliation in his presence; we had been keeping our vulnerabilities and vitality out of the relationship, as if it was dangerous to do otherwise. I was identifying with his "self" in the relational unit, a concordant identification (Racker, 1957), while we both projected the attacking object outwards. As a result, it was as if there was a sadistic "other" in the room terrorising both of us with the potential to humiliate us, an historical experience that was not unknown to each of us.

Vitality and aliveness might provoke such a vicious, sadistic attack. For Andros, this resulted in a defensive, android-like stance. At times he would appear quietly aggressive and threatening, as if he was the bodyguard for some criminal boss. His vulnerability remained hidden away in isolation, out of fear of humiliation and attack, but at the same time he longed for kind and loving relationships. This process represented an emerging impasse within the transference-countertransference dyad between the needed and repeated relationships (R. Little, 2011b). The final verse from Simon's song now comes to mind: "I am shielded in my armour, hiding in my room. Safe within my womb, I touch no one and no one touches me."

I mention Simon's song as an expression of an aspect of my countertransference association and reaction to Andros. I take notice of what comes to mind, no matter how bizarre it might seem, and then wonder how it might relate to the therapeutic relationship. The trigger for the associations is my *emotional* experience of the client, which needs to be tolerated to enable me to be mindful of it.

The progress with Andros seemed very slow at times, and sometimes it was as if we were going nowhere, remaining entrenched in this intellectual, emotionless engagement. I knew that nothing would shift until we could bring more of our vulnerability to the relationship, and that this would take time. As the work progressed, he came to see and experience my feelings and vulnerability. This occurred when he saw me moved by his stories of brutality, inflicted upon him by his father. Sitting with him in those moments was uncomfortable, because I was aware that I was feeling something and he was sitting opposite, his critical defensive self, rejecting me as a "wimp" for having feelings.

For Andros, the presence of aliveness in himself or others arouses the fear of ending up trapped in the "hell of other people" (Sartre, 1976, p. 199), with its judgements and violence. In Jean-Paul Sartre's play entitled *No Exit*, first performed in 1944, three people are trapped together in hell. In the play Sartre conveys the notion that *"hell is other people"*. What Sartre said he meant was that "If relations with someone else are twisted, vitiated, then that other person can only be hell." He went onto say, "We judge ourselves with the means other people have—and have given us for judging ourselves. Which means that if my relations are bad … then I am indeed in hell" (ibid.).

I would suggest that what Sartre is referring to is that, in psychological development, a person introjects the judgements and behaviours from others, usually our primary caregivers and attachment figures, and subsequently projects them outward, onto others, and then feels victimised by the perception of those judgements and expectations. My association to Sartre's play and philosophy is another aspect of my countertransference reaction to Andros.

Andros often seemed trapped by his fears of me and others, and his defence was to deaden his emotions. The "true self" (Winnicott, 1965) experience, with its vitality and creativity, may be both a sought after and a feared process.

I believe that being consistent, reliable, and impacted by his emotions enabled Andros to experience me as being more than the transference expectation of the sadistic other, and for me to see him as more than "android-like".

On one occasion, before I was due to see Andros, I had received some news about a friend who had been involved in a car accident. I felt concerned and angry about what had happened. When Andros arrived, I was still feeling stirred by my friend's circumstances, although I thought I was reasonably contained.

Whenever I opened the door to him, Andros would examine me carefully to ascertain my mood. He would notice if my behaviour was in any way different or inconsistent from previous weeks. The image that came to mind as I reflected on this was that he appeared like a boy returning home, watching his father to check his mood. This became apparent after we had spoken of this process.

On this occasion he had noticed that I was not my usual self. Initially he did not say anything. However, eventually our conversation got round to how I was and what he had noticed at the door. He pointed out that I was clearly different. We explored his experience of me and my behaviour, and he ended up by saying, "Why didn't you say when I came in. You could have cancelled the session." This was said in a frustrated and irritated manner. I found myself thrown by his response and felt attacked. Normally my mood and appearance were consistent, which had probably been important to him, creating a reliable and stable environment. I realised that, as we sat down, Andros was feeling afraid of me and I was experienced as dangerous. What became apparent was that he was uncomfortable being in my presence whilst I was experiencing my emotions. He had a desire to leave.

As I thought about how I felt and his response to me, I wondered, "What is it that is so problematic or dangerous about my feelings and my behaviour." What I realised was that in being frustrated, angry, and concerned for my friend, I was alive, and therefore in some way dangerous for Andros. He had also reacted to me and probably felt more alive than usual. It seemed that we had moved beyond our usual stilted pattern of relating. The use of my countertransference associations and reactions to Andros formed a significant aspect our work together.

Therapeutic action

The nature of the therapeutic interaction between client and therapist is both conscious and unconscious and bidirectional in nature. Client and therapist cannot avoid having an impact on each other, and if the treatment is effective we cannot be sure whether that is as a result of the deliberate actions of the therapist or of unconscious processes. Ehrenberg (2010) suggests that we distinguish between a theory of technique or method (which has to do with what we do intentionally) and a theory of therapeutic action (which has to do with what is healing in the therapeutic encounter whether intentional or unconscious). I believe there is a danger that when we focus upon a theory of methods or techniques, we may lose sight of the intersubjective process that occurs between therapist and client that contributes to therapeutic action.

Therapeutic stance

The therapeutic relationship entails a certain degree of mutuality, while being asymmetrical. Within this process the therapist is identified by her stance and the structure of the relationship. My therapeutic stance involves curiosity about the nature of the transference-countertransference configuration that I am engaged in and the ego state relational units involved. Without ignoring back-there, out-there, my focus is on in-here, the here-and-now of the therapeutic dyad. I also attempt to occupy a resting place of optimal neutrality (R. Little, 2013). This entails allowing myself to be impacted and stirred by the client, engaging in the push-pull of the relationship. My stance and goal is to work through the old, while co-creating the new, with myself as an integral part of that process. This involves being engaged, and participating whilst at the same time observing and reflecting.

I see myself as drawing the fire, offering myself as a target, looking to see where the fire comes from, and offering the client the opportunity to show himself, drawing the projections my way, understanding that I am reacting to the client, both consciously and unconsciously and perhaps participating in a reciprocal manner. I see the structural change that emerges out of this process as the integration of split-off or dissociated states and the reorganisation of intrapsychic structure, the internal world. The therapeutic focus is on the deconfusion and reorganisation of Child–Parent ego state relational units, thus supporting psychic evolution.

Three aspects of my current focus that I would see as consistent with Berne's (1961) writings, are: analysis of ego states, as relational units (structural analysis), analysis of transactions, primarily as they occur between therapist and client, and analysis of games, and enactments, which I believe are inevitable.

Methods and techniques

There are a number of methods/techniques which I use to enable therapeutic action. These include: maintenance of the treatment frame; management of optimal neutrality (R. Little, 2013) and the therapeutically required relationship (R. Little, 2011b); integration of countertransference reactions; transference-countertransference analysis, including both negative and positive transferences; empathic listening; exploratory inquiry and clarification; interpretation and clarification of unconscious determinants.

Therapeutic frame

When the therapist manages to provide a consistent, reliable, holding, and containing environment, this offers the client an opportunity to relax his defences, transforming his experience. The therapeutic relationship provides the background against which dissociated experience can be associated to and integrated. The frame not only supports the work but can be the catalyst for it, offering protection and also a creative tension (Davies, 1994). I see myself as both, a "magnet" that draws out the unconsciously internalised relational units, and the "architect" and builder of the "transitional arena" in which the struggle takes place, and where relational experiences become free to emerge and reconfigure (ibid., p. 157).

It is the therapist's reliable, consistent frame with its safe, predictable, physical, and psychological structure that creates the transitional arena which supports the emergence of the transference-countertransference process. As well as enabling the expression of the positive transference, with its love and idealisation, this also supports the emergence of the negative transference, with its feelings of anger, hostility, and disappointment towards the therapist. Maintaining our therapeutic frame enables us to detect any erosion and slippage resulting from unconscious processes. I see maintaining the treatment frame as an essential ingredient in transference-countertransference focused TA psychotherapy. However, holding the frame can be experienced initially by clients as cruel, as well as liberating and containing.

Andros (a further session): emerging vulnerability, a reaction to disruption in sessions

In the third year of therapy Andros had begun tentatively to express something of his emotions to me, and on one occasion described feeling very low. He told me he had contacted an old friend with whom he'd tried to be more himself. Initially his friend listened to him but had then become frustrated and short-tempered with him (a familiar experience for him).

In our sessions Andros would keep his feelings to himself and would describe his interactions in a detached manner. This time, instead of pretending, he let me know how lonely and depressed he felt. I reacted by feeling sad. When I reflected upon this, and his depressed and lonely feelings, I realised that they had emerged during the summer break when he was on his own, whilst others were with family and friends.

Holiday breaks and even weekends can evoke feelings around separation and loss that are rooted in a client's attachment patterns. How these interruptions are managed will probably be significant. On resuming therapy there may be a retaliation, where the client does to the therapist what he feels the therapist has done to him.

Andros started the following session saying he had been thinking about our last session. He also said he was still feeling depressed, particularly the previous night. He realised as he spoke that he had felt low before our previous session. He mentioned having contacted his friend again, but this time pretending he was OK. He needed to see someone otherwise he felt he would go mad—possibly a reference to needing to feel contained by seeing me. After he had left his friend he realised that his needs had not been met because he had kept them hidden. Perhaps this was also an expression of how it was to leave me having kept his feelings hidden.

He began to look distressed, became tearful, and grabbed a tissue. This was the first time he had reached for a tissue since beginning therapy. We began to talk of his feelings. I was sad and tearful as he spoke of his loneliness. After some time I said, "I was thinking about how this had all kicked off after my holiday. I wonder if there is a connection." I continued with, "Maybe what we are missing is to do with the impact on you of me being absent over the summer. Perhaps you felt disappointed and deserted, leaving you feeling hurt and angry. Perhaps this is a part of the jigsaw puzzle that we haven't talked about." Initially there was some anxious denial from Andros, and then he acknowledged that it was probably true.

As we explored his feelings and fantasies about my holiday and absence he acknowledged that on returning to therapy after the break he was ready to tell me he was going to end therapy. This is a common response from him after holiday breaks. I said, "So you wanted to punish me and let me know how it feels to be discarded at such a critical time in our work."

Holding the frame and boundaries serves several functions. As well as being containing, the frame enables the therapist to observe unconscious acting out against the boundaries that the frame offers. For example, if I move out of my frame this is an indicator that something is being acted out. The boundaries and frame also give the client something of me to react against.

Empathic transactions

One of the initial tasks is to form an alliance with the client. This process may be impeded by the transference (Mills, 2005, p. 30). To enable the therapist to do the necessary work, a relationship of mutual trust needs to develop. We establish an alliance through empathy (Erskine, Moursund, & Trautmann, 1999), which involves appreciating and understanding the other's inner world and experiences. It needs to include not only the subjective experience, but also those aspects that have been dissociated, repressed, and are unconscious.

I make use of empathic transactions (B. D. Clark, 1991) in the deconfusion process, offering my client my understanding of his experience, through which the client feels understood. I do believe empathy needs to pay attention not only to the client's immediate subjective experience, but also to his dissociated and split-off unconscious self. I agree with Cornell and Bonds-White (2001) when they state that empathy and attunement are necessary conditions but are not in themselves sufficient for enduring change (p. 80). We obviously need to do more than offer an attuned empathic response.

Particularly in the initial phases of therapy the therapist needs to be attuned to the "lived subjective experience" (Mills, 2005, p. 133). The therapist's attempts to understand the client's inner world will promote the therapeutic alliance and support attachment. Gradually empathic attunement will allow the exploration of the dissociated and repressed aspects of the client, with the goal of integrating defensive relational schemas and ego state relational units. Empathic transactions will address selfobject needs (Wolf, 1988) that support the development of the "self", described by Erskine (1993) as relational needs that have been thwarted or underdeveloped.

On occasions the therapist may make statements to the client that appear empathic, and may originate from an empathic understanding of the client. However, this may be a defensive transaction used by the therapist to close down the gap between them, thus collapsing into a merged/fused state, eliminating difference, separateness (J. Benjamin, 2004, p. 12), and possible aggression in the therapist *or* the client. This represents a countertransference enactment on the part of the therapist.

Integration of countertransference

Empathy, as an aspect of countertransference, can be established through projective and introjective identification (Ogden, 1982). Following on from various psychodynamic theoreticians, I have come to see and use countertransference within a two-person psychology (Maroda, 2004; Stark, 1999). As well as my countertransference reaction consisting of thoughts, feelings, behaviours, and associations in response to the client, I think of it as communication from the client (Ogden, 1982). Combining both the client's feelings and behaviour with my countertransference begins to give me a guide to the internal world of the client and how he may be experiencing me.

In addition to inevitable self-disclosure when working face to face, the integration of countertransference processes leads to questions about the explicit disclosure of any countertransference reactions. Whether or not to reveal such reactions (amounting to therapist self-disclosure) is something I have suggested elsewhere needs to be undertaken judiciously (R. Little, 2011a). I agree with Aron (1996) that whether or not we disclose, our position needs to be open to reflection and comment by both client and therapist, a position aligned to the relational principle of engagement (Fowlie & Sills, 2011). Self-disclosure of the countertransference (Maroda, 2004) increases the opportunity that dynamic conflict will be resolved within the therapeutic dyad, enhancing the here-and-now relationship. This is consistent with my approach.

Interpretations

Among Berne's (1964) list of basic techniques and therapeutic operations (pp. 233–258) is "psychodynamic interpretation" (p. 241). This was one of the methods by which he deconfused the Child ego state, addressing its pathology. He defined interpretation as "a therapeutic operation" (p. 365) and wrote that the "Child presents its past experiences in coded form to the therapist, and the therapist's task is to decode and detoxify them, rectifying distortions, and help the patient regroup the experiences" (pp. 242–243). I would suggest that deconfusion, rather than addressing the Child ego state alone, addresses both the Child and Parent ego states as a unit.

Lew Aron (1996) stressed the positive use of interpretation, describing it as the therapist's "creative expression of his or her conception of some aspect" (p. 94) of the client. I view interpretations as attempts to make meaning and to symbolise the current experience of the transference-countertransference matrix (R. Little, 2013). Interpretations by the therapist are offered as an experience and understanding of the way the therapist and client are relating, addressing how they are interacting with each other, the roles in which they are cast, and the feelings, fantasies, and associations they have about each other, and any underlying motivations. The task in offering an interpretation is to describe and clarify what the client and therapist are experiencing in the present moment, facilitating an intersubjective process which is likely to be emotionally charged. Along with corrective experiences I see interpretations as an aspect of a two-person psychology (Stark, 1999). The overall goal is to facilitate integration and differentiation. Aron (1996) described an interpretation as connecting the therapist and client, "linking them in a meeting of minds" (p. 121).

Optimal neutrality

In taking a position of optimal neutrality (R. Little, 2013) I attempt to find a balance, over time, between engagement and observation, that is, involving the experiencing and observing egos, as well as holding a stance between being perceived as the new *and* the old object (Greenberg, 1986).

A balance also needs to be struck between participation and non-intrusiveness (Aron, 1996, p. 106). This involves accepting all parts of the client *and* therapist. This enables the client to work through the old object relationship (repeated), find the new object (needed), and reclaim the self. I see it as essential to work through the old and co-create the new.

"Optimal" refers to what is most favourable to a given client and therapist relationship. "Neutrality" refers to non-alignment with any *one* aspect over another. I do not see it as a rigid position but one that takes into account the push-pull of the therapeutic dyad.

Optimal neutrality represents that which is appropriate for the therapist to provide. This is in contrast to what was needed from the primary caregivers earlier in the person's life but was missing, insufficient, or part of a traumatic experience. What was missing and/or never sufficiently provided will need to be understood and grieved for.

I believe we need to face the more primitive processes (R. Little, 2005), including the darker sides and more conflicted aspects of ourselves, if we are to help the client fully integrate dissociated relational units. From this perspective the therapeutic goal is to help the client, where appropriate, to alter his internal world and intrapsychic structure.

Two transference-countertransference domains

The therapist listens to and reflects on the manner of their relating, gradually examining the nature of the self-other schemas that are active within the relationship. Initially, as a result of the therapist's stance, the vulnerable part of the client, which has been wounded in some way, is reawakened. The therapist's presence, attunement, and empathic understanding (Erskine, Moursund, & Trautmann, 1999) will be likely to stir relational, selfobject, and ego development needs previously sequestered. Alongside this reawakening of the possible satisfaction of the need, will be the fears of frustration and re-traumatisation (Novellino, 1985). The impasse that emerges out of this process occurs not only within the personality of the client but also within the therapeutic dyad, with the joint involvement of the therapist. Interpersonally, the impasse becomes manifest as two types of transference-countertransference matrices: the repeated relationship and the needed relationship (R. Little, 2011b). A distinction between these was made by Mitchell (1988) when he described the relational-conflict (the repeated relationship) and developmental arrest model (the needed relationship). In the Transactional Analysis literature, Novellino (1985) referred to the positive and negative poles of the transference. I began exploring the notion of two aspects of the transference clinically in 2001 (R. Little, 2001).

The repeated relationship (R. Little, 2011b), is potentially traumatising, non-gratifying, attacking, and/or rejecting possibly evoking defensive behaviours. Stephen Stern (1994) described it as "being organized in terms of familiar pathogenic relationship patterns" (p. 318). This relationship involves the bad object, whom the individual "hates and fears … experienced as malevolent" (Rycroft, 1968, p. 100). It is the source of conflict, with its expectation of selfobject failure (Stolorow, Brandchaft, & Atwood, 1987). This is the repetitive dimension of the transference and gives rise to the anti-relational Child–Parent unit that is focused on preventing the individual from forming an attachment with the therapist. Jealousy of the emerging therapeutic relationship may be the motivating force. The emerging therapeutic relationship may also include the exciting but disappointing object (Fairbairn, 1952; R. Little, 2001).

The needed relationship consists of the other as a "self-facilitating object" (S. Stern, 1994, p. 317), including a desire for an object who can attend to the vulnerable self with its unfulfilled need for growth and development. This addresses a selfobject function that was "missing or insufficient during formative years" (Stolorow, et al., 1995, p. 102) and represents the sought-after good object described as the one "who is experienced as benevolent" (Rycroft, 1968, p. 100). This relationship may contain the unmet needs for attachment and an empathic, attuned secure base (Bowlby, 1979, p. 103) and gives rise to the relationship-seeking unit.

The old and the new

For effective therapy, the client needs to experience the therapist both as someone new and someone from the past (Cooper & Levit, 1998). We need to balance staying with the old while understanding the "therapeutically required relationship" (R. Little, 2011b, p. 34) so that the new may emerge (R. Little, 2006). Therapy is the search for a transformational experience (Bollas, 1987) that will allow the client to understand the repeated relationship as well as to experience the therapeutically required relationship (R. Little, 2011b).

Angus: "Am I boring you?"

Angus, an intelligent young man, who had been attending weekly sessions for several months, came into my consulting room telling me how anxious and annoyed he felt about being late today. Angus always arrived punctually, but on this occasion was eight minutes late. Whilst I had been waiting I thought how unusual this was. I wondered what might have happened and started to feel anxious for his well-being.

I thought, "He's not usually late, what's happened?" As he continued to tell me of his anxiety I felt the pull to reassure him and say, "These things happen. It's OK." My reaction and the pull to reassure him felt like it would close down on something and so I kept my thoughts and feelings to myself. I used my reactions to his lateness to begin to explore what he might expect. I said, "I wonder whether you expected me to be anxious about you because you were late." He agreed, saying, "That is what I imagined you would think. Particularly as I am usually on time." After some hesitation he continued, "Anyway, if you are concerned because I am late, it shows you care about me and what happens to me." He appeared to be seeking a caring reaction in me.

Although on the surface it seemed to make sense, my feelings were at odds with his fantasy and statement. He went on to discuss his struggle at college where he was doing some research. As he spoke I found myself drifting off, not feeling engaged. I allowed my mind to wander, and then I remembered the previous session. At the end of that session he had become irritated with me because he wanted to shift his appointment and I didn't have any alternative times, which meant he would either have to cancel our session or change his arrangements. He didn't want to change his arrangements in case he upset his friends. He said he likes to stick to things rather than change them. (Despite wanting to change our appointment!)

Angus seemed to notice my withdrawal. He said in an anxious tone, "Am I boring you?" He then began to apologise. I said "I was wondering about what is going on between us today. It feels important." I continued, "I wonder if when you arrived here today you were anxious about who you might meet. Scared I might be cross with you. I think you might be frightened of me right now." He said "Why do you say that?" "I found myself thinking about our last session and how we ended. It felt to me like we were wrestling with something." Noticing a change of expression, I asked him, "How do you feel right now?" He said, "Anxious about my studies and whether my tutor will like my essay. I don't think she approves of my point of view." He continued without hesitating, "I am also confused by what you are saying. Why would I think you're cross with me?" As I listened to his response I wondered if the story about his tutor was an association to what was happening between us. Was it a coded story about how he felt with me?

His anxiety at the beginning of the session may have been an attempt to engage me in being concerned for him because he was scared I would be cross as he had been irritated with me in the last session. If he could arouse my concern for him, then perhaps I would be less likely to be angry with him, a defensive procedure to protect himself from me. This would fit with my reaction to him which was incongruent with what he was expressing, and is consistent with his expectations of the repeated relationship.

Angus appreciates our work and is beginning to feel understood. At the same time he fears my criticism. There is an emerging impasse between the feared/repeated relationship and the needed/longed for relationship (R. Little, 2011b); the old punishing and unfulfilling other that he needs to defend himself from and the new that is beginning to tolerate his feelings.

I went on to say, "I wondered if you were anxious about who you might meet when you arrived today, because in our last session you were irritated with me for not changing my schedule to accommodate you. I wonder if in a part of your mind, you thought that, if you could arouse anxiety in me, I would become someone concerned about you rather than someone who might be angry with you for being cross with me." I was aware of the historical antecedents but I didn't make a there-and-then comment or interpretation, I wanted to stay in the present moment, therefore wrestling with both the new and the old.

He had unmasked his feelings in the previous session, expressing his anger. This represents the needed relationship, one that can tolerate aggression. However, he then expected a retaliation from me, an indication of the repeated relationship.

He responded with silence. We both sat quietly for a few moments. Then he said, "Well, my father would always shout at me if he didn't like something." A technical option here is to pursue the memory of father (the repeated/old relationship), but I believed that would be defensive and dilute the present moment and the feelings we were experiencing with each other (the therapeutically required relationship). So again I stayed with the "now". "So right now, you're frightened and you are expecting me to dismiss you." "Yes, I suppose so." Again we sat in silence for short while. Then he said, "I am waiting for the pain I feel inside when I am shouted at and the way it shakes me up." It was as if he was experiencing a tension between the historical expectation and the emerging new. I felt a pull at this point to sympathise with his fear of pain and I also felt a need to stay with his fear of me. This might indicate an impasse between staying with the uncomfortable feelings with his fear of me on the one hand and closing down the gap between us by empathising on the other. I said, "You are managing to let me know how you feel as you sit with me. Although you are afraid of me, another part of you wants to be here." Then he replied with, "This is the only place I get to talk about anything." I felt seduced by this last comment, but it was probably true.

The longed-for secondary selfobject

As the client and therapist work through feelings and needs in the here-and-now, emotional memories may be stirred up and connections with earlier traumatic experiences made. The therapist may then become the "longed-for secondary selfobject" (Stolorow, 1994, pp. 43–55) and a witness to the expression of previously repressed and dissociated feelings. Thus, the therapist offers a relationship that hears and witnesses these feelings, maybe for the first time in the client's life. The therapist is a new object who responds to the client at an appropriate level thus providing the needed relationship.

Early trauma can occur in two phases (Stolorow, 1994). The first phase is the original trauma, abuse for example. The second phase is the rejection or neglect of the child's need to have the original trauma responded to in a caring, soothing, and understanding manner, therefore making some sense of it. As therapists we cannot change what happened, but we can fulfil the secondary requirement of hearing and integrating the original trauma (Erskine, 1993, p. 185).

When the client speaks of a particular historical abuse or trauma and begins to feel the emotions that accompany the experience, we become engaged in the process of helping the client contain, in a new way, a previously dissociated affect. Davies (1997) suggests that the secure attachment and the trust of the therapist are the antidote to the previous defence of dissociation. The client begins to reconnect to the traumatic memories and unformulated experience *with* its associated feelings.

When this occurs, I experience the client as more real and less defended. Sometimes, it can be difficult to stay with the intense emotions that are emerging. The therapeutic task is to enable the client to find himself mirrored in the therapist's response. This may include finding someone who is horrified, shocked, and reacting to the experience as he describes it.

Gertrude: an embodied countertransference

As Gertrude begins to relax her defences, and connect to the feelings associated to the memories of her mother's violence to her, I am aware of feeling quite shocked emotionally, although I had heard her describe some aspects of these stories before. Dissociating from her affect and maintaining an unemotional appearance had been her previous defensive position. She was beginning to associate to the underlying affect.

Gertrude started this particular session by saying, "I don't want to remain cold and hard. I want to connect with my feelings. I know what my mother did was cruel and nasty and she was a shit to me. But I haven't been able to feel much about it before." I was aware of feeling mild excitement while listening to her. We had been working towards this position for some time. She continued, as if in some sort of hurry, by saying, "I have been remembering again her forcing me to eat cat food." As she said this her colour changed just slightly. I began to feel a repulsion, more intensely than I had done before. I felt my throat tighten as she spoke. We were sitting facing each other, but at this point she wasn't quite looking at me. "She would grab my hair and pull my head back, forcing my mouth open." In response, I could feel my throat tighten further. I also felt horror and revulsion at the thought of what she was describing, and what would happen next if I had been her. As she spoke I was aware in one part of my mind that she did not seem upset. I was the one who seemed to be feeling the emotions. She then turned to me and seemed to take in my reaction, a non-verbal disclosure of my countertransference.

The way Davies describes these moments is that we have "engaged in helping the patient to contain traumatic levels of disorganizing affect" (1997, p. 244). What she further suggests is that the client can watch the therapist feel *for* him, and begin to know something of what he felt. Then they can begin to explore together what the client felt but had previously dissociated. The feelings that I felt in response to Gertrude would have been difficult to hide from her and at that time I would not have wanted to. This process could be described as concordant identification, in the sense that it was her "self" I was identifying with. She was finding in me feelings that she had dissociated from. We had spoken of the memories in a more cognitive manner, but on this occasion she was connecting with the emotional memories. This process seems akin to projective identification as it occurs between mother and infant

(Ogden, 1982, 1992), consistent with the child beginning to internalise a containing object/other.

Gertrude described feeling sad, she looked and sounded sad, but quickly moved away from the emotions and started speaking of her younger brother. I felt a kind of judder in response to her moving on. I responded by saying, "You seemed to have moved away from your sadness just now." She came to a stop, and began to cry, becoming very flushed. She often tells me she has trouble caring for herself. She seemed to be feeling sad for herself and what she had been through. I was feeling sad with her, but also incredibly angry that she had gone through such brutal inhumane experiences.

Davies (1997) suggests that the client has a need to find in the therapist a responsiveness to his affect, a wish to see in the expressions of the therapist a mirror of his states. It is as if the therapist holds the affective experience for the client, which in turns enables the client to begin to integrate previously unintegrated experiences. In these moments, Davies suggests there is a collapsing of past and present.

Initially the client may find a mirror of his feelings in the therapist, as an infant finds his feelings being mirrored by his caregivers. The client is having an impact on the therapist that helps him begin to associate and reintegrate his own emotions.

The therapeutic encounter: becoming the new bad object

I believe that the therapeutic encounter is shaped consciously and unconsciously by both myself and the client. In this process we will at times project onto each other aspects of our own ego state relational units, and sooner or later we may become entangled in enactments of early, unformulated experience with significant others. These experiences can help both client and therapist to begin to understand the client's current interpersonal and intrapsychic difficulties (Davies, 1994). Therefore games (Berne, 1964) and enactments emerge out of the co-created analytic third (Ogden, 1994) which is the result of mutual projective and introjective processes.

I see games and enactments as inevitable aspects of the work and if counterbalanced by interpretation and working through, the result is a co-creation of a progressively new interpersonal experience.

The therapist and client will eventually engage with the bad object of the repeated relationship. This consists of the client experiencing me as someone he fears and likewise, I could also encounter the bad object in myself. If I remain involved but maintain a reflective mind, then I am an aspect of the bad experience, whilst offering a response which goes counter to the client's expectations in the moment.

In essence, the therapist is offering the client a different subject to relate to and therefore becomes a "new" bad object (Cooper, 2010). Even if the client interprets my behaviour in a manner that is consistent with his expectations, if I manage to think about my countertransference reactions and, for example, offer an interpretation, in that moment I, as Hoffman (1983) described, cast "doubt on the transference-based expectations" (p. 415).

Even though I am offering an interpretation and/or self-disclosing, I find myself wondering if I can ever be anything other than a "new" bad object in the transference-countertransference relationship.

However, when I have been deeply involved in an enactment I may only begin to understand what has transpired afterwards, or during supervision. In letting myself become the "bad object" of the repeated relationship I believe I am supporting the expression of the client's more aggressive, hateful, and malignant thoughts (Davies, 2004), an essential aspect of the therapeutic endeavour of integration. What is less easy, is when I emerge in therapy as my "bad self". Then I may unconsciously wish to get rid of the client, to rid myself of the "bad" feelings that have been evoked.

Apparently I had "allowed" Barbara's friend to come and see me as a client. In doing so I had destroyed her sanctuary. I was flummoxed: I had no idea what, or who she was talking about. "But what of me? This is my space," she exclaimed. I was being attacked, yet again. She began to bombard me with accusations.

I felt useless. I feared that this could go on for weeks, or months. I felt hopeless. She was threatening me again and had threatened me with ethics charges before. I felt frightened. She knew how to bring charges against me, having worked in a lawyer's office. I wanted to be free of the torment of these feelings and phantasies. I wanted to wipe her out, obliterate her from my life. I felt the rage run through my body like an electric current. This must have affected how I was with her. This was not how I liked to think of myself. Who is this that has emerged in me?

What gets stirred up in games is our "bad" self-other relational unit: a repeated transference. It is one thing when the unit is stirred and we remain reflective; it is another, when involved in an enactment we lose our reflective capacity. What we need to do is to understand and work with these engagements. In this way and over time the therapist becomes the new bad object and the new emerges out of the old.

Conclusion

If we as therapists tend to focus on the repetitive element of the therapy process (R. Little, 2001), in the form of games (Berne, 1964, 1966), we may overlook how new capacities for relating are emerging out of the old. On the other hand, those who work within the relational model may be too quick to offer a new relationship, thereby defensively welcoming aspects of the new and, in doing so seek relief from the old, repetitive, problematic relationship with its games. I believe we need to find a balance between these ways of working (R. Little, 2001, p. 41).

To understand the nature of the therapeutic relationship and the transference-countertransference matrix we need a map of the terrain; one that identifies the nature of what is happening and is visible on the surface: the geography or behavioural aspects. We also need a map to help understand something of the history and structure and what is below the surface: the geology or intrapsychic processes. Finally, we need an understanding of the way the surface structure and natural features interact with the human element: the topography or interpersonal elements. Our scripts unconsciously supply us with a map with its predetermined routes and description of the terrain. This may blind us to the various other routes with their particular vistas. Therapy could be described as an excursion into the interior, exploring the interpersonal landscape and the intrapsychic structures that underpin the terrain and co-creating a new edition of the map.

As the client and therapist gradually realise that the map is not necessarily the terrain, they then begin to move into uncharted territory, with the landscape spread out before them: not knowing what lies ahead, who or what they might encounter, what feelings might be stirred, what longings and desires may emerge. At the same time they may encounter resistance both internally and externally to the journey.

CHAPTER THREE

The heart of redecision therapy: resolving injunctive messages

John R. McNeel

In the beginning

In the autumn of 1969 I came walking through the student lounge of the Louisville Presbyterian Theological Seminary and was startled to see an odd looking older man sitting there. He had long unkempt hair, a shaggy grey beard, and deep cigarette stains on his front teeth. As he sat there smoking I couldn't help but notice his shoes were untied and he looked like he had slept in his clothes, with his shirt tail out. He was hunched forward over his cigarette with his shoulders up around his ears. He reminded me of a vulture. Having taken note of this odd apparition I went on to my breakfast.

An hour later I was startled when this apparent homeless person walked into class with my professor Dr. David Steere. David was teaching us how to conduct group therapy using Transactional Analysis as the primary treatment strategy. The week before he had cautioned us not to miss class on this day because it was going to be taught by a visitor: "Dr. Robert Goulding and I consider him to be the greatest therapist alive today."

As I was recovering from my shock Bob began to talk. He described his approach to doing therapy. He called it redecision therapy. He described the power of injunctions and how to change them. Within minutes I said to myself, "This is the smartest person I have ever heard and he can help me." I was entranced. In an interview with him later that week, Bob invited me to come to California the following year to train with him and Mary at their Western Institute for Group and Family Therapy. I accepted without hesitation and found myself on the West Coast the following autumn. I thought I would be there for a few months, two semesters at most.

In my wildest imaginings I did not anticipate I would be invited to become a faculty member of the institute or be encouraged by Bob to return to school to get a PhD in psychology, but that is exactly what took place. For my dissertation I researched one of Bob and Mary's weekend workshops, which they called "marathons". They were my teachers, my mentors, my friends, and my drinking companions. We had enormous fun. Bob inscribed a book to me with the words, "John, you are like a member of the family." I got married forty years ago on the front lawn of the institute with Bob and Mary looking on with tears in their eyes. I conducted Bob's memorial service. My memories are legion.

A disappointment and a disagreement

By the time Bob and Mary published their signature book, *Changing Lives through Redecision Therapy* (1979), I had been deeply immersed in the processes of redecision therapy for a decade. I had learned it, I had researched it, I practised it, and I was teaching it across the United States and internationally as well as at the institute. Bob and Mary were very excited about their book. It had been highly anticipated by all of us on the faculty. None of us had seen it. It came out amid great expectations. Lots of friends and colleagues gave them copious praise and congratulations. I did too. I was happy it was out. I thought it had a lot of good material.

In their typical fashion they recognised everyone who had ever helped them develop and formulate their material throughout the International Transactional Analysis Association. They made sure that each of us on the faculty had a piece of transcript from our own work so we could be featured. They were remarkably generous and loyal to their friends. For that I felt admiration and gratitude. And, I felt disappointed.

By the time the book was published I had been using their methodologies and theory in clinical settings for a long time. In conversations with other colleagues with similar training I realised we were having the same experience. We were executing the redecision methodology meticulously but we were not seeing the lasting behavioural changes we expected. Even though we subscribed to the brief therapy model we were finding it necessary to see our patients for a longer period of time than had been prescribed. We all had Mary's voice in our heads as she had stated on numerous occasions, "Any therapist who sees a patient for more than a year is ripping that person off!" She was unequivocal.

As time passed and my own experience accumulated, I had the growing suspicion that the discovery of identifiable injunctions was more important than even the theory and methodology of redecision therapy itself. Given the freedom to greatly expand on each of the injunctions by the latitude that only the length of a book can provide, I expected a much greater dissertation on this vital theory. I was disappointed when I found that the twelve identified injunctions were discussed in only four pages (pp. 34–38), with only a brief description of each. I believed there was much more there than they had written.

There was a wonderful celebration in 1985 at Pacific Grove, CA to mark the twentieth anniversary of the creation of redecision therapy. Ellyn Bader, Carol Solomon, Ellen Pulleyblank, and I presented a panel discussion on "Sins we have committed while doing redecision therapy". This playful title actually hid a much more serious agenda as we had all found ourselves performing outside the playbook. First off, we were all routinely seeing people for more than a year. It may sound odd at this point in time, but we were all profoundly relieved to find this out. We were all wondering what we were doing wrong that this was happening.

Turns out we had all reached a point of disagreement with Bob and Mary. We were not seeing evidence that people could effectively reprogramme their long-established neural pathways by a single therapeutic action, no matter how poignant or powerful. These focused moments could definitely be helpful, but only as building blocks in a longer process of helping people arrive at lasting change. There was a need for extensive reprogramming if a person was to mend the psychological damage from the injunctions. It was not enough to proclaim freedom from them or a determination not to be influenced by them. They were more powerful and pervasive than that. You might say they are a worthy enemy.

The historical perspective

If any of the preceding is heard as me being hard on my beloved teachers, it is important to put their work into the context of their time and what was happening in the world of psychotherapy. It was a time of remarkable ferment. Eric Berne and Fritz Perls were among those turning that world upside down and they were only two of the actors on a much bigger stage. They were very influential to Bob and Mary. It was a time of rebellion against long drawn-out and staid psychotherapy with its focus on pathology, which had dominated the profession since its earliest days. Bob and Mary were in open revolt against what they called the psychotherapies of "making progress". They disdained a system which to them conferred all power to the therapist and none to the patient. It is no accident that the title of their first book, a collection of their earlier writings was entitled, *The Power Is In the Patient* (1978).

In the introduction to *Changing Lives through Redecision Therapy*, Bob wrote:

> Our approach is creative, as we constantly look for new methods. We do not blame the patient when there are failures or make lists of "untreatable patients" to present to the Annual Meeting of the American Psychiatric Association. Rather, we search … to find a method, a way of creating an environment that will facilitate change. (1979, p. 4)

Earlier in that same introduction he wrote, "Eric Berne, the genius who fathered Transactional Analysis … wrote and talked about curing people, rather than 'making progress'" (p. 4). This summed up their approach to psychotherapy. They wanted to find a shorter, more effective and potent form of therapy, especially one in which the patient felt challenged to be the agent of power in his change. Their work was an artefact of their times.

Virginia Satir wrote the foreword for *Changing Lives* (ibid., pp. vii–ix). She reminds the reader that the theory contained in this book was shaped by the existential crisis created by World War II. She spoke of the material being "occasioned by the survival necessity during" the war. Everything was "… essential to stopping this scourge. In the armed forces, this meant that when service personnel were psychologically injured, they needed to be restored as soon as possible. … There had

THE HEART OF REDECISION THERAPY

to be a more immediate and successful approach (to psychotherapy)" (ibid., p. vi).

From this milieu, Bob and Mary created their system, partly in revolt and partly inspired by a new confidence in the capacity of people to change and take charge of their lives. Satir noted that out of the cauldron of the war, "[I]t was soon discovered that people had far more potential for recreating themselves than had ever before been thought. New possibilities began to loom" (ibid., p. vii). Bob and Mary seized upon this confidence and capacity and created their original model.

Their model and expectations

Bob and Mary took the concept of personal responsibility back to a very early age. They identified the original twelve injunctions, but emphasised their belief that the injunction had to be "accepted" by the child to have any power and that even small children possessed the agency and autonomy to reject an injunction that was being given. "No injunction is 'inserted in the child like an electrode,' as Berne believed" (ibid., p. 4). Given that belief they created a system where the original "acceptances" by the child could be effectively overturned in a relatively short period of time.

> Our objective is to establish an environment for change. We create an intensive, rather than extensive, environment, encouraging the patient to change himself in a short period of time—a weekend, a week, two weeks, or a month—and then go out and practice his changes without further therapy. (ibid., p. 7)

This was their ideal. It was their goal to help individuals return experientially to those early scenes in their childhoods and, with the group's and therapist's help, overturn those earlier acceptances which they called "early decisions". Hence they named their process "redecision therapy". The goal was to create a safe environment so that the process could be carried out.

Their process consisted of three steps: contract work, impasse clarification, and redecision work. They liked specificity in their work and would help the participant enter into a clearly understood contract regarding the goal of the immediate therapy. Impasse clarification was an educational process where the past, including injunctions was connected to the current difficulty in life. The redecision work involved helping the person access an early scene from childhood and bring it into the present. In this present moment the person was invited to make a new decision to counter the earlier collaborative decision from their childhood. This process frequently involved the Gestalt technique of two-chair work. When a redecision was successfully accomplished the group was encouraged to act as supportive witnesses.

The expectation from this process was a demonstrable change in the person's behaviour and a perceptible ability to act in a more autonomous manner. Eric Berne (1964, p. 178; 1966, p. 310) cited autonomy as the goal of successful therapy and called it "the recovery of three capacities: awareness, spontaneity and intimacy" (1964, p. 178). Bob and Mary emphasised the concept of responsibility as a means to move individuals from feeling like victims to a place of personal empowerment. "We ask the client to claim his own autonomy whenever he gives it up" (Goulding & Goulding, 1979, p. 4).

Bob and Mary saw the injunctions as having limited power. I would often hear comments in referring to an individual's work such as: "He finished with that injunction today," "She completed her issues with her father," "She finished her grieving for her mom," or "He resolved his 'don't exist.'" In their theoretical system the person had engaged with the injunction in an autonomous way and he could separate himself from it given the right opportunity. They disliked any language that alluded to powerlessness and they were loath to consider that injunctions might have had a shaping influence over time that was inevitable.

They would agree that injunctions created adaptive behaviour, and they would argue that this behaviour could be changed rapidly and conclusively. Without saying so specifically, they posited that long-established neural pathways, vast behavioural patterns, and habits could be modified easily. They thought the main ingredient necessary for change was taking responsibility for having been licit in the decision process and then changing that decision. They challenged people to speak in a manner in which they took total charge of themselves.

Anyone who spent time with them at the institute will remember Bob's "try bell", which was a dinner bell he kept beside his chair. He rang it vigorously any time someone in the workshop used the word, "try". In the interest of taking responsibility and empowerment, he insisted that people use the words, "can't" or "won't" in place of "try".

As the late faculty member, James E. Heenan noted in his observation of their work, "It is not only great therapy, it is great theater." That was certainly true.

In my doctoral dissertation (McNeel, 1975) I carried out research on one of their weekend workshops. This included extensive pretesting and interviews with each of the eighteen participants as well as post-testing and post-interviews. The marathon was observed by six of my colleagues who independently rated each piece of work. They judged if the work had been contract work, impasse clarification, or redecision work. The workshop consisted of both lay and professional participants. As a group, three months after the event they had a deeply positive memory of the event and of the group leaders. They had been influenced, encouraged, and educated. It is not known if they felt the same way ten years later, but the short-term impact was very favourable. One participant wrote enthusiastically three years after the event that her new decisions were still vivid and useful (McNeel, 1984, p. 4).

From "injunctions" to "injunctive messages"

We all have treasured experiences. Certainly one of mine is the years I spent as a faculty member of the Western Institute for Group and Family Therapy. That experience profoundly changed my life. Of course if Bob could hear me say that he would shout, not merely say, "John, you changed your life! We didn't!" No, actually I participated and those two boundlessly generous geniuses and my colleagues did change my life. They loved me, guided me, adopted me, and gave me endless opportunities.

Another treasured experience from my past is a training group I conducted monthly in southern California for over a dozen years, beginning in the late 1980s.

By that point in my career I had come to the conclusion that the realm of injunctions had not been fully appreciated or explored. This group of very dedicated and intelligent clinicians humoured me as we engaged in a multi-year exploration and investigation of them. It would take a separate paper to describe the hours spent in proposing, arguing, discovering, and arriving at some very new conclusions; the greatest being just how important the theory of injunctions is and the amount of impact they have upon people.

As we did our investigation we continued using the word, "injunction" in talking about these early messages. As we became convinced of the powerful and enduring impact of the injunctions, the word did not seem to suffice in describing their full nature. There were two problems. Bob and Mary emphasised the person's decision in response to the injunction, even including the option of not listening or responding to it at all. This did not appear to be an option. To us, that was like saying someone could grow up in a Spanish-speaking household but choose not to learn or respond to the language that surrounded them on a daily basis. This led to our second objection. The word is often used as a legal term and it does carry a negative connotation in that it is often an order to desist from or suspend a certain activity. The problem is that in the legal world, injunctions can be reversed or removed, which means they disappear, perhaps forever. "Psychological injunctions" cannot be removed nor do they disappear.

For these reasons, we began to use the phrase, "injunctive messages", because it more accurately describes the limiting and prohibitive power of injunctions, while also clearly conveying that, like any message, it might be disregarded but it does not entirely disappear. We do not remove injunctive messages from our developmental make-up so much as we become more and more adroit at recognising their presence. Then we can become skilled in choosing healthier responses to them. One does not "finish" with an injunction "once and for all", but learns to disbelieve injunctions when they reappear and spend less and less time in their thrall. This is a learning and maturation process as opposed to the result of one propitious action at a powerful moment in time.

New discoveries

In brief, we expanded on many concepts and created new ones (McNeel, 2000, 2002a, 2002b). We found that there were actually two responses to each injunctive message: a despairing decision and a defiant decision. There is a coping behaviour that arises out of the defiant decision. The coping behaviour is a defining characteristic for each message. The recognition of that behaviour is the main method of diagnosis, not just intuition or biographical report. The redecision is a process of integrating a new belief that over time replaces the despairing decision. This in turn obviates the need for the defiant decision. There is a necessity to engage in resolving activities. These are drills that allow a person to practise new thoughts and behaviour in order to establish new habits.

And, finally it is vital to alter the internal parental voice. Consciously or unconsciously, the familiar parental voice in a person's head is to some degree in league with the injunctive message. It is vital to the change process to replace this voice with one that supports the person's autonomy from the influence of the message.

The charts at the end of this chapter contain twenty-three injunctive messages. The process of growing the list from the "canon" of twelve injunctions (Goulding & Goulding, 1976, 1989; Stewart & Joines, 1987a, 1987b) to the number of twenty-five injunctive messages is described in detail by McNeel (2010).

Two decisions

Except for the injunction, *don't exist*, the Gouldings (1978, p. 217) did not propose any specific possible decisions for any of the others. They did propose seven possible decisions for this one and they are discussed elsewhere in this book (Chapter Eight). We operated from the basis that injunctive messages were real phenomena and certain ones were possibly embedded in the environment while a person was growing up. Obviously not all injunctive messages are in every home. Lots of people are given permission and adequate modelling for surviving, thriving, and attaching. It is the injunctive messages that are ubiquitous which exert the most negative influence. And like a language, the person has no choice but to respond in some manner.

To these preponderant messages, we found that there are two decisions, not one. The first is the despairing decision. It is what the young child's brain presumes when no one touches her, ignores her, or shows her no warmth or reassurance. The despairing decision has great power because it seems true. Like its name it creates despair, but the despair feels congruent to the message being received. After all, for a small child the environment is experienced as being part of herself.

Because there is a powerful instinctive drive lodged in every brain to survive both physically and emotionally, the growing child will fasten on whatever forms of empowerment she comes across. These form the basis of the defiant decisions. In general these decisions all share a quality of "I'll show you" about them, even though the quality of defiance is more readily apparent in some more than the others. The important issue with these decisions is they are the person's best attempt at finding a solution for the despair that accompanies the earlier decision.

The powerful thing about the defiant decisions is that they appear to work, at least to some degree. They do relieve, at least temporarily the feeling of despair. It is problematic in that what worked in an earlier context today expresses itself in a self-limiting or self-destructive behaviour that the person feels compelled to do. An example of this is someone who is financially secure, but still works compulsively sixty hours a week. It is important to note that the creation of the defiant decision was the person's best attempt at healthy adaptation to an impossible situation.

The coping behaviors

All of our work and investigation rested on two assumptions, the first being that the Gouldings had discovered real phenomena. We concluded that there really are identifiable injunctive messages, that they are most often discreet, that they have the possibility to profoundly affect someone's life, and they can be resolved. A second conclusion was that each injunctive message has a distinct signature. We called this signature the coping behaviour and it is the main device for diagnosing specific injunctive messages.

Just as a physician will ask questions of a patient to obtain relevant data, she will know which signs are indicators for certain diseases or other medical conditions. She would never ask someone, "Do you think you have pneumonia or multiple sclerosis?" In the same way we do not ask someone, "When you look at the list of messages, which ones do you think you might have?" Obviously a person might be able to make a correct guess, but without conviction. Often the injunctive message that has most affected his life might very well be hidden from view. His habitual responses to it might be so integrated with his sense of self that they appear to be ego syntonic. It takes an outside observer knowing what to look for to properly diagnose injunctive messages. As one wit noted, "It is hard to see the picture when you are standing in the frame."

Redecision as a process

The most distinct departure from what the Gouldings taught concerns the methodology for helping people accomplish the redecisions that are in pursuit of lasting and sustainable change. Even though the literature lacks a concise definition of the Gouldings' concept of redecision, Bob came close when he spoke at the first Milton Erikson Conference:

> Now I want to talk about redecision therapy. Redecision therapy is not simply making a decision to be different. It is the process in which we facilitate the client getting into his or her Child ego state. From that state, he relives an old scene and changes his or her part in it. (1985, p. 303)

For us this statement spoke to an unsubstantiated optimism. As much as we wanted to subscribe to the notion that one act of empowerment could result in knowing how to behave and feel differently in a variety of settings and stimuli, it did not appear realistic. This becomes more evident given the severity of the person's psychiatric diagnosis and developmental history.

The argument is not whether there is a process of redecision. There is. But it has a more incremental nature over time, notwithstanding the occasional dramatic moment of insight or catharsis. We do not eliminate the original injunctive message so much as we learn how to respond to it in a different manner. It is possible to replace the despairing decisions with something more satisfying and functional than the defiant decisions. The adequate replacement is a new belief that by its nature counters the power of the injunctive message. These new beliefs do not occur in a flash, but can be obtained over time. However, these new beliefs must be spelled out because they are as specific as the two decisions and coping behaviours are to each message. We began to call the redecision process "one of new belief acquisition".

The resolving activity

It is not enough to subscribe to a new belief in the expectation that a change in behaviour will naturally follow. It is necessary to consciously engage in new behaviours. These behaviours are not intuitive to someone under the sway of a particular injunctive message. The goal of these assigned activities is to empower the individual and his ability to make autonomous choices. These additional choices bolster confidence that change is possible. The drills seek to help people attain this by consciously practising the new behaviours that lead to exactly what Berne was describing.

The new parental stance

In its complete form, we call this, "the new parental stance that heals". For many people the parental voices they have in their heads hark back to their childhood and are not kind or wise. If an injunctive message exists, you will find an earlier parental voice that is somehow in collusion with that message. People need to have voices inside them that contain compassion, wisdom, and love. In this section we created voices that are counter to the original injunctive message. These new voices are strong, clear, wise, and protective. It is good for people to memorise them.

The five categories of injunctive messages

As already mentioned, we discovered many new injunctive messages in our process over the years. When there were twelve identified injunctions, they appeared to stand separately. However, when the number of injunctive messages swelled to twenty-three (as of this article) it became apparent that there were logical categories into which they fell. Through our process we identified five. The five categories are logical and intuitive: survival, attachment, identity, competence, and (sense of) security. The first five injunctions that the Gouldings identified were: don't be (exist), don't be close, don't be you, don't be grown up, and don't be a child. It is interesting to note that these first five injunctions almost perfectly parallel the five categories of injunctive messages presented here.

The survival injunctive messages

Don't exist
Don't be well (don't take care of yourself)
Don't trust
Don't be sane
Don't touch.

The attachment injunctive messages

Don't be close
Don't feel attachment
Don't belong
Don't be a child.

The identity injunctive messages

Don't be you
Don't be separate
Don't be visible
Don't be important
Don't (be engaged in your own life).

The competence injunctive messages

Don't make it
Don't grow up
Don't think
Don't feel successful.

The (sense of) security injunctive messages

Don't enjoy
Don't be grateful
Don't feel
Don't relax
Don't be happy.

Themes of resolution by category

The Gouldings were adamant that injunctions could be resolved individually if the work was done correctly. "Correctly" meant that the crucial work is done while the person is in the Child ego state, rather than in the Adult ego state:

> But if the Child makes the redecision, with the approval of the Adult, then the Child looks for ways to changing his stroking pattern, his time structuring, with considerable enthusiasm. (1972, p. 110)

They said that there would be no experience of despair if one made a redecision in this manner. They said this in direct rebuttal to Eric Berne and his contention that one might feel despair after making a significant change:

> Eric used to talk of the despair people felt when they made a decision, or dropped their script, or stopped playing some major game.

> Some of this was probably self-fulfilling prophecy if you know that
> if you change something you are going to despair for a while, then
> you will probably despair … then of course the Child may despair.
> (1978, pp. 222–223)

I believe that the experience of despair is inevitable in the process of redecision work because the early despairing decision is there from early development. It is both consciously and intuitively believed by the person. In reading transcriptions of the Gouldings' work, it is not unfair to say that they would often help people energise or reenergise their defiant decisions. For some people it may have been the first experience of feeling the power that does stem from the defiant decision. After all, feeling a sense of power trumps feeling powerless and hopeless. A person "looks better" when being defiant versus despairing. However, there is a significant problem connected to the despairing and defiant decisions in that they both maintain an interactive relationship with the injunctive messages.

If redecision therapy is to have lasting effect, it needs to be part of a larger process in which the patient knows about both his despairing and defiant decisions. Through understanding his despairing decisions he may gain empathy for himself that was absent in his early environment. In understanding his defiant decisions, he may learn to feel an admiration for his early fortitude, courage, and resiliency. In the moment of origin these decisions may have been survival genius. However, acting from the defiant decisions in real time often leads to exhaustion and crushed expectations. The behaviours that flow from these decisions are defeating to the goals of self-care, intimacy, satisfaction, love of self, and feeling secure.

This paper ends with a brief description of the impact of each category of injunctive message. There is a description of what individuals need to learn and do in order to have a healthy response to the messages. The process in each category represents the acquisition of new data, insight, and empathy. The most important and optimistic point is that the original despairing responses to all injunctive messages can be effectively altered without resorting to any of the defiant decision strategies.

The injunctive messages that impact survival

The messages in this category do not necessarily lead to an overt wish to die. However, together they do present a world that is absent of warmth, love, trust, and consistent dependability. There are often powerful models from the parental figures of how to be seriously self-destructive. This results in defiant responses that have a serious "I'll show you" and a "me against the world" quality to them. People with these messages often misinterpret the world as being more threatening than it actually is. This leads them to feel in a state of constant struggle with concomitant stress behaviours leading to physical and emotional exhaustion. This can place a person's long-term physical survival at risk. These behaviours erode the vibrancy of the personality as well.

Because the impact of these messages has been to create a belief that the world is a cold place where self-sufficiency is the greatest good, it is necessary to discover that unconditional love does exist. The resolving of these most dreaded messages is centred on this discovery and on allowing other people to bestow their affection. The affection needs to be warm, verbal, physical, and emotional. A second necessary discovery is that there are trustworthy people in the world. These people have never known how deeply reassuring it is to trust others. The most important decontamination is learning that affection cannot be earned whereas recognition and approval can be. From these discoveries the individual is able to learn to feel empathy and that is the great healer in this category.

The injunctive messages that impact attachment

These messages create a world of immense loneliness, where closeness and attachment are inhibited. This is a world where there is no permission to be childlike and dependent. One does not have a strong sense of belonging and it is difficult to know how to satisfy emotional longing. In response, people typically seek to control relationships and try to harden themselves to any potential disappointment by professing not to care. There is pride in being tough enough to handle isolation. There is an unexpressed rage in giving abundantly to others what the person actually craves but never seems to receive. From the safety of detachment the person is often trying to "get" and "possess" the benefits of relationship.

Resolving these messages is paradoxical because it means learning to give the love that has always been longed for and denied. It is not possible to satisfy the longings of the heart from a distance or from a safe non-vulnerable position. As with the survival messages, there is a need to recognise the presence and the unconditional nature of affection. Here the central issue is in giving affection, generously and abundantly. It is important to say the words, "I love you" often. In this way the world is transformed into a much warmer place. Resolution also means learning how to protect others from controlling and manipulative behaviours. Finally, it means learning how to request emotional satisfaction from others.

The injunctive messages that impact identity

The original emphasis was with gender identity, but the scope of these messages is much larger. The sum of them all communicates that there is something wrong with the person. This fills the person with a deep sense of shame for somehow having been "born wrong". The defiant decisions inspire a need to be superior in some grandiose manner, or despairingly hide oneself from the world. In either case, the effort is devoted to creating a persona and projecting it to the world. By hiding behind a false front the person hopes to satisfy the voices that say, "You shouldn't be you".

Resolving these messages has its heart in claiming the imperfection that exists in all our lives. There are no perfect people. Nor are there people who never feel anxious or vulnerable. Personhood is defined by the individual in congruence with an awareness of one's innate gifts and shortcomings. As these messages are resolved, curiosity to know oneself replaces the desire to be someone else or to envy others. There is great relief in sharing all aspects of life including one's own vulnerabilities.

The injunctive messages that impact competence

The sum of these messages leaves a person adrift in a world where there seems to be no viable way of knowing how to gain the feeling of adequacy. It isn't measured by achievement because the devil of expectation always diminishes it, no matter how great the accomplishment. The recourse is to be in competition with the world, always trying to prove that one is better than everyone else. There is a pressure to excel regardless of one's limitations. For many, it is inconceivable to learn from the modelling of others or to recognise their wisdom. Contempt for others is often seen as a facet of feeling competent.

As these messages are resolved the concept of feeling competent in the world takes on a vastly different meaning. Competition is left to pleasurable activities, not the boardroom of life. Life becomes full of admirable people who can be mentors and teachers. The idea of dominating others in order to feel competent becomes foreign. Feeling successful in life is based on confidence that one is making a mark in life and being a beneficial influence on others. The pressure drops away to know absolute truth and ambiguity becomes a sign of a mind at work, rather than a sign of ignorance or confusion. There is comfort in the new belief: "There is no such thing as failure, only learning".

The injunctive messages that impact (a sense of) security

Unfortunately many people grow up in spiritually stunted environments where unattended suffering is often present. Material security may be present but not what is needed for emotional security. Joy and gratitude are rarely expressed. Emotional experience is often painful. In these settings, happiness is rarely recognised and there are few moments to savour. In response they create an unobtainable vision of what a happy and secure life looks like. Goals for the future take on the metric of measurability when "enough" will be gained. Understandably, people feel in a hurry to achieve this better world. This focus on the future creates urgency about time, which removes people from engaging in the present moment.

It may sound strange to say, but one must understand suffering to have a happy life. There are many strategies that people employ to avoid suffering, from constant vigilance to numbing out with addiction. None work. Life has a mysterious and spiritual component that will not be satisfied by any metric. A greater wisdom about life informs us that joy does exist, that gratefulness is the secret to being content, that if we feel alive we will feel our emotions, and that happiness is largely unconnected with our circumstances. Because suffering does exist, it will visit our lives. People often feel defeated by this, thinking they have failed. Or, they take away a greater confidence in facing the future. It is this confidence which powers a true feeling of security. Secure people are optimistic and happy, but they have no illusions that being "bulletproof" is an attainable or even a desirable goal in life.

Making use of the charts

These five charts are designed to be of use to the clinician. Of course, they can also be a great aid to the client. They are an honest estimate of the logical flow from each injunctive message. The coping behaviours are at the heart of the diagnostic process. They are shown in bold type on the charts. They provide the key for the clinician to accurately diagnose each injunctive message and be able to relay that information to the patient. The coping behaviour can be recognised through attending to voice tone, body language, facial expression, biography, and presenting problem. From the coping behaviour, the clinician can go in either direction using the material in the other columns by asking curious speculative questions. This will aid in the process of ruling in or ruling out a particular injunctive message.

The clinician can also use the last two columns that are under the heading, "self diagnosis". These statements were created so that an individual could have a means to ask reflective questions in the quest to identify relevant injunctive messages. If someone is deeply in the thrall of one of these messages, he will find the material in "the healing response" to be foreign to his thoughts and to his experience.

Taken together, the material contained in "the new parental stance that heals" column and in "the healing response" column can create a bridge to insight. This is revelatory. It is not uncommon for people to report that they have had very few warm or supportive thoughts such as these.

In a similar manner, if one is to read down "the despairing decisions" column and "the bitter response column", it becomes clear how bleak life can feel for some people. Reading down the "defiant decisions" column gives a good picture of the many forms of "I'll show you" that exist.

Clinical acumen and intuition are the informing factors in determining how best and when to share these charts with patients.

The material in the charts is continually being updated. This version is not gospel. When it becomes apparent that a more potent formula is available, the wording is changed. Since this chart was last published (McNeel, 2010) the message, "don't touch" has been moved from the security category to survival. "Don't share", "don't want", and "don't invest" have been removed entirely, their effects having been covered adequately by other messages. "Don't be important" has been moved from the survival category to identity. And there is a newly identified injunctive message, "don't be happy", which is included in the security category. "Don't be thankful" and "don't feel attached" have become "don't be grateful" and "don't feel attachment" respectively. Close reading of the material will reveal extensive wording changes since 2010.

Table one

The Survival Injunctive Messages

The Injunctive Message *A believable falsehood*	The Despairing Decision *What the person fears to be true*	The Defiant Decision *The person's best attempt at health & resiliency*	The Coping Behavior *Which stems from the defiant decision*	The Redecision *A new belief based on better data*	The Resolving Activity *A process to create new habits*	The New Parental Stance that Heals *Spoken with wisdom & compassion*	Self Diagnosis	
							The Bitter Response *Reinforces a pessimistic view of life*	The Healing Response *Reinforces an optimistic view of life*
DON'T EXIST	I'm a mistake & I shouldn't be here	I will stay here & justify my existence	**Driven to seek approval & recognition**	Unconditional love exists	Consciously appreciate your courage	Your life has meaning	It's a fact that my life is a heavy burden	My life is precious
DON'T BE WELL *Don't take care of yourself*	I'm not worthy of attention	I will prove myself a strong person	**A pattern of exhaustion**	Boundaries are essential for wellness	Contemplate: What matters & how much is enough?	You are worthy	I'm tired & exhausted, but no one cares	I am well loved & well cared for
DON'T TRUST	I'm defenseless in the world	I will only count on me	**Super controlling**	There are people worthy of trust	Discern the character of others	You are smart enough to tell good people from bad ones	I often feel I am used & betrayed	I count on the good people in my life
DON'T BE SANE	The world is crazy & there is no protection	I will be super normal (& *disdainful of others*)	**Hatred of self or others, vengeful**	There is a way out of misery	Getting the reassurance, "you are not alone"	The harm that was done to you was real but not personal	I would be defenseless in life without my hostility	I feel love for me and forgiveness for any who harmed me in the past
DON'T TOUCH	I'm unwanted	I will be self sufficient	**Projecting an attitude of "nothing hurts me"**	I actually like & need affection	Allow people to give nurture: physically, verbally & emotionally	There is great goodness in expressed warmth	I feel proud of the harshness I endured during my childhood	I feel love & empathy for my young self

Figure 1.

Table two

The Attachment Injunctive Messages

The Injunctive Message *A believeable falsehood*	The Despairing Decision *What the person fears to be true*	The Defiant Decision *The person's best attempt at health & resiliency*	The Coping Behavior *Which stems from the defiant decision*	The Redecision *A new belief based on better data*	The Resolving Activity *A process to create new habits*	The Parental Stance that Heals *Spoken with wisdom & compassion*	Self Diagnosis	
							The Bitter Response *Reinforces a pessimistic view of life*	The Healing Response *Invigorates an optimistic view of life*
DON'T BE CLOSE	I feel abandoned	I demand perfect love	Looking for a love that doesn't exist	I can survive living with an open heart	Use the words, "I love you"	Be generous with your love	In relationships I am watchful & try to leave before others leave me	There are people in my life to whom I am loyal & loving
DON'T FEEL ATTACHMENT	I'm alone	I won't be denied: I will get what or whom I feel entitled to	Control others by being possessive, manipulative, & judgmental	There are people who have genuine affection for me	Know what brings pain to those who love you & refrain from those behaviors	Treasure the people who give you their hearts	In relationships I withhold compassion and understanding	I am protective of the people who have affection for me (especially from myself)
DON'T BELONG	I'm outside looking in	I won't seem to care	A pattern of isolating & being remote	My longings can guide me to good people	Show active caring to others	There are people who are ready to care about you	No one is loyal to me	I celebrate the people in my life
DON'T BE A CHILD	There is no room for my emotional needs	I will be strong & endure the neglect	Constantly attending to others hoping the gift will be returned	I am a person with needs, not a machine	Remember this, "you can ask for anything"	You can confide your needs	I give up easily & adapt to the needs of others	I love & treasure the people I depend on

Figure 2.

Table three

The Identity Injunctive Messages

The Injunctive Message *A believeable falsehood*	The Despairing Decision *What the person fears to be true*	The Defiant Decision *The person's best attempt at health & resiliency*	The Coping Behavior *Which stems from the defiant decision*	The Redecision *A new belief based on better data*	The Resolving Activity *A process to create new habits*	The Parental Stance that Heals *Spoken with wisdom & compassion*	Self Diagnosis	
							The Bitter Response *Reinforces a pessimistic view of life*	The Healing Response *Reinforces an optimistic view of life*
DON'T BE YOU	I'm unacceptable	I will be perfect	**Playing a role in someone else's play**	I claim my imperfect life	Consciously love both your gifts & flaws	You are beautiful & I love you	I fear being belittled	I am curious to know my innate wants, desires & talents
DON'T BE SEPARATE	I can't be me	I will be me in spite of you	**Leading a double life so as to avoid conflict**	I am the only person with the right to define my personhood	Use conflict as an opportunity to define personhood	Be yourself: other people are more resilient than they appear	I'm stuck in a role I didn't choose and don't want	I am me and no one else
DON'T BE VISIBLE	I feel ashamed	I will hide behind my public self	**Appearing confident & having no problems**	I don't have to be ashamed of being vulnerable	Revealing your true self to safe people	What you keep hidden deprives you of being known	I show my public self, not the real me	Certain people know me & my vulnerable self
DON'T BE IMPORTANT	I am nothing	I'll be great, bigger than life	**Dominant, expansive, competitive, & grandiose**	Hard won pride brings me no lasting sense of importance	Think about the people you love rather than the conquests you seek	You are important because you exist	I exaggerate, therefore I exist	Those who will "love me for the rest of their lives" inform me as to my true identity
DON'T *Be Engaged in Your Own Life*	Whatever I do is wrong	I'll defend my inaction in life	**A well defended anxiety that is not amenable to facts**	It is not possible to remove risk from life	Seek daily to do things that had been postponed due to anxiety	Life is rich beyond your comfort zone	Fear & anxiety constrict my life	My life is a pretty interesting story

Figure 3.

Table four

The Competence Injunctive Messages

The Injunctive Message *A believable falsehood*	The Despairing Decision *What the person fears to be true*	The Defiant Decision *The person's best attempt at health & resiliency*	The Coping Behavior *Which stems from the defiant decision*	The Redecision *A new belief based on better data*	The Resolving Activity *A process to create new habits*	The Parental Stance that Heals *Spoken with wisdom & compassion*	Self Diagnosis	
							The Bitter Response *Reinforces a pessimistic view of life*	The Healing Response *Reinforces an optimistic view of life*
DON'T MAKE IT	I am never good enough	I will prove I'm better than everyone	**Striving always to excel while preoccupied with failure**	I have it in me to make a mark on the world	Recall & own your many accomplishments	You stand alone and I am proud of you	Secretly, I feel my life to be one of failure	It's remarkable how much impact I have in life
DON'T GROW UP	I feel lost & never know what to do	I will fend for myself in the world	**A "little person" striving to look grown up**	It's OK to need good models in life to show us the way	Seek to see the admirable qualities in others	It's good to find & accept influence	I might look great but fear being seen as inadequate	I seek to lead an admirable life
DON'T THINK	I feel inadequate	I will force others to think as I do	**Defensive of rigid beliefs & prejudices**	I have the courage to learn & face ambiguity	Practice seeing two sides to every argument	"Truth" is a moving target & life is too complex to get it totally right	My beliefs are basically unassailable	As I learn I feel an evolution & a deeper satisfaction
DON'T FEEL SUCCESSFUL	I feel I am always to blame	I will fix everyone & everything	**Habitual use of blame toward self or others for anything wrong**	The pain of the world (my parents) is not my fault	Consciously enjoy being beneficial to others	The person you seek to be makes you successful	I easily feel remorse when I think about my life	I love the effort I put into living a sincere life

Figure 4.

Table five   The (sense of) Security Injunctive Messages

							Self Diagnosis	
The Injunctive Message *A believeable falsehood*	**The Despairing Decision** *What the person fears to be true*	**The Defiant Decision** *The person's best attempt at health & resiliency*	**The Coping Behavior** *Which stems from the defiant decision*	**The Redecision** *A new belief based on better data*	**The Resolving Activity** *A process to create new habits*	**The Parental Stance that Heals** *Spoken with wisdom & compassion*	**The Bitter Response** *Reinforces a pessimistic view of life*	**The Healing Response** *Reinforces an optimistic view of life*
DON'T ENJOY	Life is empty	I will construct a joyful world	**Time urgency driven by "event greed"**	Joy does exist but is not under my control	Consciously saying "no" to "ego" events	Recognise & savour moments of joy	I "comfort" myself by being busy, irritated & in a hurry	I am never more than a memory away from reliving moments of joy
DON'T BE GRATEFUL	There is never enough	I won't be denied	**A life of insatiability**	Abundance exists & is not a function of getting more	Practice having thoughts of gratitude	Thankfulness is the source of contentment	I equate gratitude with complacency & setting for less	I value the gift of my life & all that is in it
DON'T FEEL	Feeling is painful	I will do whatever is necessary to deaden my feelings	**Response to feelings is mechanical, even "nice" but lacks empathy**	My emotional world can be rich if I learn empathy	Identify emotions and feel them	To be alive is to feel	I have no time for feelings & other trivialities	Feeling alive does not frighten me
DON'T RELAX (and feel safe)	Life is suffering	Staying alert will keep me safe	**Constant vigilance**	I've coped in the past and can again	Using memory to create a sense of confidence about capability	Remember: You are strong & capable of handling life	If I worry, maybe nothing bad will ever happen to me or mine	I'm confident I will have the resilience to handle what comes up in life
DON'T BE HAPPY	Life is sad	I will "get" happiness	**Constantly pursuing an external source of happiness**	Happiness is possible now and vital to my health	Practice smiling frequently esp. when reminiscing	Your sense of happiness exists separately from your circumstances	There is not much in life to smile about	Laughing & smiling are important aspects of my life

Figure 5.

In conclusion

In the appendix of my doctoral dissertation (McNeel, 1975, pp. 138–380) I included a verbatim transcript of the workshop. This is the only extant record of a Goulding workshop in existence. As such, it is an important document in the history of redecision therapy.

My brilliant, but psychologically unsophisticated mother read the entire transcript. In her succinct manner (she was a trained proofreader for the family weekly newspaper from the age of nine) she said, "They (the Gouldings) don't like parents very much." She made a subtle but excellent point. It was subtle because the workshop was oriented in a very positive direction and was overtly warm and enthusiastic, with a great deal of humour. The point was excellent because there was an "us against them" attitude towards original parental figures. There was the sense that accomplishing a redecision was an act of victory against them, as if they had been enemies.

In fact most parents did the best they could with what they had. In my clinical experience, very few parents wished to harm their children, even if what they were doing was in fact very harmful. Parents are more often vehicles through which injunctive messages are communicated, having received them in their own childhoods. Ultimately the issue is not with the parents. It is with the messages.

These messages don't go away. It is possible to recognise them and respond to them in an entirely different manner. In learning to do so people do work through issues with their parental figures in the service of gaining a greater wisdom and empathy for themselves. In this way one is not saddled with a lifetime of struggle against an enemy, but is presented with tools for resolving impasses that have become internal.

This work is never completely done. Over time individuals do gain autonomy by being able to respond with new choices to these confounding messages that had implied they were not to survive, be attached, feel confident in their identity, be able to claim their competence, or feel deeply secure in life. The acquisition of these new beliefs and the new choices in behaviour that stem from them are worthy goals.

Recognition

It is my custom to dedicate any writing I do in the area of redecision therapy to my late beloved friend, Dr. James Edward Heenan, 1925–1998, "a redecision therapist of penetrating perspicacity, the kindest humor and infinite sweetness" (McNeel, 1999, p. 115).

CHAPTER FOUR

Opening to the vitality of unconscious experience

William F. Cornell

My view is that the analyst's technique is his attitude actualized, and that what matters most is the passionate curiosity tamed in the service of the patient's self inquiry, the analyst knowing a bit about how analytic work unfolds, not about how the patient should live his life.

—W. S. *Poland*, personal communication, January 4, 2015

I trained simultaneously during the 1970s in Transactional Analysis and Radix, neo-Reichian body education, becoming a trainer in each modality. On the surface these two methodologies were rather strange bedfellows, in that TA was profoundly cognitive and rational, with a strict rule against touching clients, while Radix was, to an equal and opposite extent, profoundly emotional, with touch and bodily expression at the core of the neo-Reichian techniques (Kelley, 1988, 2004). However, what these two modalities held in common was a positioning of the therapist on the *outside* of the therapeutic process as the one who assessed the client's difficulties from a specific theoretical frame of reference and then *acted upon* the client's way of being so as to promote change. It was the task of the TA therapist to identify games and scripts so as "cure" the client. It was the task of the Radix practitioner to confront the interpersonal and bodily character defences so as to promote emotional catharsis and ultimately establish "orgastic potency". This active, knowing positioning of the therapist had great appeal to me as a young, rather frightened, and overly responsible psychotherapist. It served me well, but I gradually began to see that it did not always serve my clients so well. I took my questions and clinical concerns to my TA and Radix supervisors. The supervisory responses were uncannily similar: the problems were rooted in the depths of my clients' resistances and character defences. I was doing fine; I was simply to do more of the same—longer, harder. I did as I was told, and some of my clients got worse. I decided to look elsewhere for consultation. I knew the fundamental difficulties were in my working style, not in the resistances of my clients. I sought supervision outside Transactional Analysis and the Reichian worlds, and I began to read, searching for an understanding of the problems I was finding in my clinical work.

I began supervision with a Kleinian therapist, whose style was unlike anything I had ever known. I hated the process, and I hated her, but I knew she was up to something important. We worked from session transcripts. She said nothing about my clients—no diagnoses, no interpretations. She made no technical suggestions, nor did she challenge what I was doing. She essentially asked one question in seemingly endless variations, "What was going on inside of you that you chose to speak right then? Why did you feel the need to do something just then?" Gradually, reluctantly, I began to see how often my interventions—be they verbal, bodily, supportive, or confrontational—were precipitated by my own anxiety and my need to *do something*. I also began to recognise that my affinity for these active methodologies was an enactment of my script. In my family of origin, I was the doer, the caretaker, and the problem solver, so here I was again playing out these roles in my professional work, whether or not they suited the needs of my clients.

I then sought supervision from a Jungian analyst, in spite of my stereotypical view that Jungians were all overly intellectual and spent their time diagnosing archetypes and drawing mandalas with their clients. This man proved to be a gift to my professional development. He gave me my first lessons in listening rather than doing. He taught me to manage my anxiety and to soften my style. Most important, he listened for the more growth-oriented impulses of my clients, helping me to shift out of my habitual game/character/defence listening mode.

During this period of time, I suspended most of my Reichian style therapy and invited several of my body therapy clients to meet and read with me to see if we could figure out what was wrong with the way we had been working. It was our reading of the Vietnam-related literature on PTSD that gave us our first insights into the impact of trauma and to distinguish dissociative defences from those of the more classical repressive sort that both Berne and Reich emphasised. The result was an evolution in my understanding of working with body process, which I've written extensively about over the years (Cornell, 2008b, 2011, 2015; Cornell & Landaiche, 2007; Cornell & Olio, 1992, 1993).

Without my busy, allegedly empathic, "useful", "good parent" therapist-self in high gear, I often fell into a muted, rather empty silence. I needed not only to learn how to listen differently, I needed to learn how to speak differently. I returned to the psychoanalytic literature, now exploring contemporary analysts. The discovery of the work of D. W. Winnicott (1965, 1971), Christopher Bollas (1987, 1989, 1999), James McLaughlin (2005), and Warren Poland (1996, 2013) was like a revelation to me. Here were accounts of the force and vitality of unconscious experience that stood in stark contrast to the classical psychoanalytic theories of the unconscious that Berne had rejected in his development of TA. Here were analysts who each in their own way described how to listen, to spend long periods in attentive quiet, and to tolerate uncertainty. It was a fundamental task in classical psychoanalysis to render the unconscious conscious. For Bollas the thrill of psychoanalytic explorations was that of enriching conscious experience with the depth, mystery, and vitality of unconscious experience.

My immersion in their writings and my good fortune to work closely with both McLaughlin and Bollas provided the basis for much of the work I will describe in this chapter. Jim McLaughlin and I were never in supervision or therapy together; our working relationship was around his writing and mine. As he became familiar with my writing, he made a pointed and unforgettable interpretation, "It seems to me that the closer something is to your heart, the quieter you become. It is as though you imagine that silence can best protect what you cherish." In supervision with Christopher Bollas during this same period of time, he made the comment that I seemed to be afraid of the unconscious— of my own as well as that of my client. These were transformative interpretations.

My discovery a few years later of the writings of Muriel Dimen (2003, 2005) and Ruth Stein (1998a, 1998b) radically transformed my understanding of the meanings and functions of sexuality, returning attention to sexuality to my clinical work. My reading and meeting with these analysts made fundamental changes in my understanding of my work through the 1990s and the first decade of this century. The impact of these analytic perspectives on my work will be the focus of this chapter.

This chapter is based in my evolution as a psychotherapist. However, the force and vitality of unconscious realms are present whenever we work as professionals involved in facilitating psychological change, regardless of our particular field of application.

A brief pause with Eric Berne

Reading Winnicott and Bollas opened new ways of reading and understanding Berne, which led to a series of papers exploring both the richness and the limits of Berne's writing (Cornell, 2000, 2005; Cornell & Landaiche, 2006, 2008; Cornell, 2015b). In rereading Berne with a fresh perspective, I began to see a depth and an often conflicted wisdom in his work that had not been apparent to me in my initial study of his books or in the rendering of Berne that had been in my TA training.

I found in rereading Berne a concept that proved to be a key in my unravelling the clinical dilemmas I was trying to find my way through. In his theory of games, Berne (1964, p. 64) made distinctions between what he called "first, second, and third degree" games, which I have further extended to the understanding and differentiations of script. By "first degree", Berne was describing levels of intrapsychic and interpersonal defences that were reasonably available to conscious awareness and change through cognitive interventions and understandings. Berne saw games at the first degree level as serving a "social" function, which is to say, to make relationships more predictable.

Second degree games and scripts serve defensive purposes that operate outside conscious awareness and control. At the second degree, Berne saw a split between the conscious level of communication and another, which is more psychologically significant, that represents more unconscious motivations. Second degree games are understood as serving a more fundamental psychological function—that is, maintaining script—rather than a social function. Defences operating at this level are not so readily amenable to change through cognitive interventions.

Berne (1966) developed his model of group treatment primarily as a means of helping clients identify and alter their second degree games.

Berne characterised third degree games and scripts as held and lived at the "tissue" level, by which he meant at the level of the body rather than the mind. Berne saw defences at this third level as being extremely resistant to change and ultimately destructive. As I read Winnicott and Bollas, I came to see Berne's pessimism for successful treatment of third degree (and sometimes second degree) defences was a direct consequence of his turning away from maintaining a place for working with unconscious experience and motivation in Transactional Analysis.

My emphasis here is on the use of Berne's differentiation of the degrees of games as an indication of intrapsychic organisation. Stuthridge and Sills (this volume) offer a further elaboration of Berne's model, emphasising the interpersonal implications and impacts of the degree of the game. It is important to recognise that while Berne framed his differentiations of the degrees of games in terms of levels of defence, these variations of psychic organisation are not in and of themselves defensive or pathological. The fact, for example, that aspects of one's experience are organised and experienced primarily at non-verbal body ("tissue") level does not make them pathological.

When writing about script theory, Berne (1963) introduced the concepts of protocol and palimpsest:

> A protocol or palimpsest is of such a crude nature that it is quite unsuitable as a program for grown-up relationships. It becomes largely forgotten (unconscious) and is replaced by a more civilized version, the script proper … . (p. 167)

In this way he described a level of unconscious, somatic organisation without the attribution of defence and pathology he attributed to third degree games (Cornell & Landaiche, 2006).

In the fifty years since Berne's death, the study of attachment patterns, implicit memory processes, the sub-symbolic mode of organisation, transference/countertransference, and neuropsychological research have radically shifted our understanding of these somatic, and often unconscious, realms of experiences. Protocol and palimpsest are not inherently pathological, but are grounded in what we might call "the good, the bad, and the ugly" of our earliest experiential that live on within us in what we would now call implicit, procedural memory. At the third degree level, *living the experiences* with our clients precedes and informs whatever comes to be analysed and spoken.

Berne's differentiations helped me see that I needed to develop a much more varied approach to psychotherapy. I could see that while my more active, interpretive interventions, be they the more cognitive style of TA or the more somatic interventions of the neo-Reichian modes, were often sufficient for clients whose defences were organised primarily at the first and second degree levels. But for other clients and the deeper, more troubled phases of treatment, there needed to be fundamental changes in my customary ways of working. I did not need to trash everything that I had been doing, but it was abundantly clear that I needed to expand my ways of working.

Two-person, separate

It was a painful period of learning in which I gradually shed my manic, overly active, relentlessly useful style of psychotherapy. In my personal psychoanalysis I was able to painfully face the defensive functions of my manic need for action and efficacy. Here was the mother's presence in the unconscious motivations for my manic overdoing. My father's absence underlay my dread of silence and separateness, which I felt to be the equivalent of neglect and isolation.

My consultants gently, but persistently, pointed out how often my apparent "empathy" for my clients served the needs of my self-image more than the needs of my clients. Bollas repeatedly spoke to how an overinvestment in "empathy" foreclosed the experience of the client, taking away his right to self-exploration. McLaughlin argued, "Here I emphasize the working of two separate minds so that I can make clear that the central focus on the patient's reality view does not mean seeking unbroken agreement and oneness in the dyad" (2005, p. 207). Poland's writing over the years has emphasised the fundamental separateness of the subjectivities of the therapist and client, exerting a quiet but persistent influence on my working style. Recently he expressed the essence of what a therapist needs to convey to a patient in this way:

> Whatever the analyst then says, from the most trivial clarification
> to the most profound interpretation, whatever the content of the

words, a crucial message buried deep in the structure of the very making of the statement is one that states, "*No*, I am *not* you, nor am I one of your ghosts, but as separate people we can speak of what is involved. No, I am not part of your dream, but as a person who cares for what you are doing but who is separate, I can help you find the words to say it. (2012, p. 947)

The willingness of the therapist to respect that essential separateness gives the client the space and freedom of self-discovery and self-definition. I came to see how a therapist's self-disclosure or the valorisation of mutuality further risks an impingement on the client's psychic realities and struggles.

Gradually I learned to be *informed* by my countertransferences, and for the most part to keep them to myself, so as to allow my clients to inhabit their own intrapsychic wishes and struggles:

> Psychoanalysis takes place between two people yet feels as if it lives within the deepest recesses of my private life.
> ... For every encounter with a patient sends me deeply into myself, to an area of essential aloneness processed by voiceless laws of dense mental complexity.
> ... the analyst and his patient are in a curiously autobiographical state, moving between two histories, one privileged (the patient) and the other recessed (the analyst), in the interests of creating generative absence, so that the patient may create himself out of [these] two materials ... . (Bollas, 1999, p. 11)

Bollas's position often seemed frightening and alien to me as a therapist who habitually used his work with clients to escape himself. His sense of a "generative absence" was a startling and liberating contrast to the meanings of absence that I had internalised with my father.

Deeply depressed during her graduate school years, Catherine was desperate to have a place where she could figure out her life and her sense of self. She had lived her life being seen only through the demanding and judgemental eyes of those around her. It was with Catherine that I learned with particular poignancy the importance of keeping our histories separate and of tolerating my countertransference.

We had been working for four years when her mother was diagnosed with a recurrence of an earlier cancer that had metastasised to her bones and brain. During that same period of time, my sister was terminally ill with massively metastasised cancers. My sister died while Catherine's mother was still undergoing treatment. Many times, as I listened to her, I thought of my sister, who was the same age as Catherine's mother, and of my niece's and my nephews' anguish. At times I found it nearly unbearable to listen to her as I anticipated what lay ahead for her and her mother. I said nothing to her of my sister's plight or the impact that listening to her had upon me. I could not, in the sessions themselves, sort out which of my reactions had to do with Catherine and what were mine—they were too immediate and intense. Her father was as emotionally self-absorbed and oblivious to his children as was my sister's husband, so my countertransference was intense and risked being intrusive. I kept it to myself and worked it through with myself, so as to remain open to her experience.

Catherine's parents were each in their own way so profoundly self-involved that there was no room for her struggles or needs as she faced her mother's illness. She needed a space with me that was entirely hers. Her relationship with her mother had been turbulent and deeply conflictual but also loving and intimate. She felt an intense need to avoid conflict as her mother grew more ill. Catherine often said, "if my mother dies", which I never corrected. However, when I spoke of her mother's illness, I always said, "when your mother dies". She asked me one day why I said "when". I told her that her mother's cancer was terminal, and that her mother undoubtedly knew that. When Catherine, her father, or other family said "if", they were lying. "It is a lie intended to comfort," I said, "but it is a lie nonetheless. Perhaps it is a lie that comforts your father and family, but it signals to your mother that there are things that cannot be spoken, cannot be faced together, and that she may be facing her death alone. I'm not willing to participate in the lie with you. You may make a different choice with your family." In time, Catherine learned to speak freely to her mother, and her mother was able to respond in kind, and, fortunately, they did not lose their capacity to argue with each other. Catherine found her way to accompany her dying mom. They could speak the truth to one another.

As her mother approached death, Catherine was often told that she was too emotional and that her feelings would upset her mother. As her mother became less and less able to communicate verbally, Catherine wanted desperately to hear from her mother her beliefs and feelings about dying. Catherine wanted to say goodbye, to tell her mom how much she would miss her, and how angry she was at the cancer. But Catherine was rendered mute by her family, who insisted that her mother needed to be "protected" from the fact that she was dying. I was silently furious with her family and frightened that she would lose this precious opportunity with her mother. I felt certain that her mother knew she was dying and did not need to be "protected" from that reality. I had to make a decision about how and if to speak to what I was thinking and feeling. I was not at all certain what to say, if to say anything at all.

Self-disclosure is not a casual decision, and I didn't want to speak just to alleviate my own distress (Aron, 1996; Cornell, 2014; Jacobs, 2013; Maroda, 1999; McLaughlin, 2005). I did not want to be another person telling Catherine what to think and feel, intruding my feelings upon her. I finally decided to speak to her directly about my own experience with my sister and her family. "You may remember last summer when I took some time off from work. My sister died last summer of cancers very much like your mom's. I took time off to be with her and her children. I learned some painful but important things with my sister in her illness and dying that I would like to share with you, if you think that would be helpful. It is different from what you are hearing from your family." She agreed, and I talked with her about how important it was for my sister and her children to stop pretending there would be a miraculous recovery, to give up hope together, and to speak openly about her impending death. These conversations gave my sister some final peace and intimacy before dying.

The conversations with Catherine about my sister and her family, typically very brief, continued after her mother died. My focus was on my sister, her children, and their needs, not my own experience. Catherine never asked me what it was like for me—she knew that was not the point. The stories from my sister's dying gave Catherine the courage and freedom to go against the pressures of her family and speak with her mother as she needed to. Her mother welcomed the opportunity.

Catherine is now a mother herself with a baby girl. Our sessions have been a place in which she can grieve for her mother's absence during this very precious period of life. Her mother is never mentioned in her family.

The therapist as an unconscious object
in the evolving psyche of the client

I have been reading Winnicott for more than two decades. His way of writing, as well as his way of working as an analyst, was highly idiosyncratic. His ways of writing and working have required years of study to understand. His way of thinking about the psychotherapeutic process has deeply informed and transformed my understanding of psychotherapy. At the heart of Winnicott's understanding of human development, be it within the parent/child or analyst/patient dyad, is the necessity of aggression, ruthlessness, and object usage (1965, 1971). Winnicott (1984), through his work with children and adolescents as well as his adult patients, came to understand that the expression of aggression and destruction was an effort to force the external environment to respond to internal needs. Winnicott saw aggression as a manifestation of hope that the object (other) will survive one's projections and demands, thereby facilitating the differentiation of self and other.

In ego development and the elaboration of the "true self" of a child or a patient (Winnicott, 1965), the unconscious intention in the use of the object is not the destruction of the object but the discovery of the self. My long-standing wish to be a *useful* therapist foreclosed the possibility of my clients to *use* me in their own ways in the discovery and elaboration of themselves. They did not have the freedom or space to find themselves, because I was always there first. My reading of Winnicott and consultations with Bollas began to show me ways to get out of the way of my clients to open a different kind of therapeutic space, so as to be available to be *used by* my clients rather than be *useful to* them. Bollas, deeply influenced by Winnicott, described the core of Winnicott's attitude towards life and psychoanalysis in language I found deeply compelling:

> The issue Winnicott addresses can only be understood if we grasp that he does not assume we all "live" a life. We may construct a semblance of such and certainly the false self attests to this. But to live a life, to come alive, a person must be able to use objects in a way that assumes such objects survive hate and do not require undue reparative work. (1989, p. 26)

I learned the true meaning of object usage through my work with Alessia. She first burst into my office like a storm cloud, a dark and broiling presence that filled the room. She commanded attention, and she immediately had mine. A graduate student in her late twenties, she seemed simultaneously a lost girl and a powerful, self-possessed woman. She was married but was fed up with her husband and contemplating leaving him. "Oh," I thought to myself in that initial session, "a simple job—helping her to make a decision about her marriage." That was not to be the case at all.

Alessia's parents were both prominent medical professionals who had related to their daughter as the identified patient, since probably from about the time she had learned to walk. Barely into elementary school, she had been sent off for psychotherapy. I was, perhaps, her eighth or ninth psychotherapist (she'd lost precise count). As she described the range of diagnoses she'd been given over the course of her relatively young life, I had the fantasy that the DSM would require continual revision so as to afford her parents new opportunities to assign diagnoses.

While her parents were relentlessly concerned with the psychopathology of their daughter, they paid little attention to her actual life. As a young teenager, Alessia had fashioned a secret life, completely outside the awareness of her very busy and preoccupied parents. Her secret life was full of sexual exploration and encounters. In her sexuality, she felt herself most fully alive. By her college years, she had married. Her marriage was a poly-amorous arrangement, accompanied by multiple lovers of both genders. What more, I wondered as I heard her stories, could a young person ask for? I found myself envious. During those formative years of my life, while my sexual fantasies had been closer to the life Alessia was actually living, I had limited myself to the safety of a single, heterosexual relationship. Alessia, on the other hand, seemed to devour lovers and other intense experiences as food and fodder for her life.

For the first five years of our work any comment, observation, reflection, or interpretation I offered was dismissed out of hand. Most of the time, I was left with the sense that what I said was simply unheard as irrelevant, but there were times when Alessia's response to my interventions was to make it abundantly clear that what I said was quite dumb and unwarranted. I couldn't have explained why at the time, but I did have the very clear sense that the only thing that would have been even dumber than what I'd already been saying would have been something like, "Have you noticed that you reject everything I say?

I wonder if we could talk about that." Or worse yet, "I think you are putting your father's face on me."

My countertransference was intensely mixed up. I always looked forward to seeing her, being rather thrilled by her passionate and aggressive nature. At the same time, I felt reduced to an audience watching some kind of one-woman theatrical performance. My negative countertransference found relief through diagnoses that could situate the problem squarely within her way of being. I could fall back on my Reichian characterology and declare her (to myself silently) as a hysteric, perhaps even a psychopath. From my TA frame of reference I could fill a short lexicon of games: "If it weren't for you"; "Now I've got you, you son of a bitch"; "Corner"; "Uproar"; "Ain't it awful"; the list could go on. It was interesting, and not accidental, that she never asked me for anything, except for a diagnosis, which she asked for repeatedly! Here I had the tact to quietly reply each time something like, "You've had a lifetime of diagnoses. I can't possibly see the use of another. I want to get to know you, not diagnose you." But anything else I offered would be immediately rejected. Had I been working with her a few years earlier, I would most likely have destroyed the therapy through some form of confrontation rather than tolerate and learn through my countertransference.

Alessia never stopped talking. We had no "contract" in the TA sense of an explicit purpose or goal for our work. She came to sessions; she spoke; I listened. That seemed to be the deal. As the months passed, I felt like a therapist without a job, certainly not the job I typically cast for myself. Although I felt like I had no personal importance to her whatsoever, the sessions were clearly important. She was never late. She never missed a session. When she travelled (which she did for her work rather often), she always arranged a phone session. Strangely, I did not feel irritated by her. Quite the contrary, I felt a growing paternal countertransference of admiration and protectiveness towards her. I didn't know what was going on, but I "knew"—in the Bollas sense of the unthought known (or perhaps "unthinkable known" was closer to the truth)—that something important was going on.

Although she never said so, I was reasonably sure that my admiration of her registered somewhere inside her. It was, perhaps, most important that I never called into question her sexual activities, which by conventional standards would only be seen as perverse. It was clear to me that her sex life was an essential platform for her well-being.

At the same time, I feared that it left her open to being exploited. She would often express surprise and/or outrage when some sexual partnership collapsed or exploded. I had the distinct impression that she was also hurt, but I kept my observations to myself. I grew more comfortable with the erotic aspects of my countertransference. I could sit with Alessia and feel my growing affections for her, relishing her passionate sexuality.

Fortunately for both of us, by the time Alessia came to see me I was working with McLaughlin and Bollas, each of whom, in their own way, was teaching me how to live in and with my countertransference, rather than acting it out through confrontation, interpretation, or "sharing" it in self-disclosure. Bollas writes of the necessity of "countertransference receptivity", which he describes as "a capacity to receive life and bear a not knowing about what is taking place even though a profound mulling over and playing is the medium of such reception" (1999, p. 44). What became clearer to me was that my willingness, indeed the necessity, to keep a distance was serving an essential function. I began to get the sense of my paternal presence being that of a father who cared but could stay out of the way.

Her automatic dismissals of my comments in the early months of the therapy were deeply instructive. Seen through the lens of Berne's degrees of games, it was clear that we would not be working at the level of cognitive insight and/or transferential projections and relations. Our work together was not to be at first or second degree levels. We were not together to *solve* a problem. We were together to *live* the problem together. Our work was at the third degree level. Years passed. If I was travelling, a request for phone contact was never made. She never asked where I was going. She had never asked a single question about my life or work. After about five years she asked at the end of a session, "So what do you think?" I was startled. Why now, I wondered. I no longer recall what she'd been talking about or how I answered her question. I do recall her response, "Well, I don't know how the hell you came up with *that*." Oh well. Maybe there would be another time when she would ask again.

As is so often the case for me when I'm working with a client during periods of not-knowing and uncertainty, various bits and pieces of things I've read come to mind as objects to be used. Thrashing my way through difficult authors is one of my favourite and most productive forms of object usage. The first bit that began to press itself into my consciousness was Berne's (1972) accounting of script forming a wall around the child's "secret garden" to protect one's most precious wishes and fantasies from the intrusion and harm of others. I thought about how Alessia had managed to keep so much of her life secret from her parents. I found new meaning in Alessia's honesty with me; she did not seem to need to keep any secrets from me. Some sort of understanding was taking shape as another association to hiding and privacy came to my mind, this one from Jim McLaughlin:

> It is this private self that provides inner stability and nourishment. Yet it is also a hiding place for those most unwanted and troublesome aspects of what we fear and wish we were not. It is this aggregate that we zealously protect, keep mostly hidden, and cling to as our essence. It is what we bring to the other when we engage in the analytic dyad. (1995, pp. 434–435)

I found new understanding and regard for the careful, attentive distance I was maintaining. I continued to "consult" with various authors as I sat in session.

Winnicott also "visited" me during several sessions. Something from him nudged the edge of my consciousness, but I couldn't quite catch hold of it. At the time Alessia had started working with me, she had pretty much cut off all contact with her parents, especially her father who she found to be boorish and "way too full of himself". Over the course of our work, she was feeling more settled in herself, so she felt confident enough to begin re-establishing more contact with her parents. Her father rapidly returned to his intrusive and opinionated self. She was telling me, angrily, of her most recent phone conversation with her father that ended with her shouting at him, "It's none of your damned business." As I listened to this latest encounter with her father, Winnicott returned to the room.

Now I knew what "Winnicott" had been trying to tell me, and that evening I found the piece I needed to read. Winnicott was writing about the early roots of the capacity for aggression, in which he is describing the young child's "motility" through which "the environment is constantly discovered and rediscovered" (1950, p. 211). Motility is the word he used to characterise the infant's and young child's sensorimotor explorations of the world around her. He describes three patterns of the environmental (usually parental) response to the child's bodily explorations: 1) freedom to explore and experience, 2) the environment *"impinges"* thereby restricting the child's freedom to form her own experience, and 3) a persistent and extreme pattern of impingement. The result of such "persistent and extreme" impingements is that:

> There is not even a resting place for individual experience … . The "individual" then develops as an extension of the shell rather than of the core … . What is left of the core is hidden away and is difficult to find even in the most far-reaching analysis. The individual then *exists by not being found.* (p. 212, emphasis in the original)

I developed a keener and keener sense of Alessia's vulnerabilities— which I *sensed* but never *spoke about.* I also felt a growing recognition of my identification with her manic energy. As I allowed her energy and that of my own to register more and more intensely in my body, I began to find a way forward, a way of creating a slightly different space with her. I knew I had to find a way to speak past her relentless energy and activity.

From the accumulation of now more than five years of working together, I knew I could not speak to her directly. I could not say something like, "You got mad at your father, but it must have also been quite painful." I had to speak in the third person, "Fathers can be so infuriating." "Yeah, tell me something I don't already know." "And they can be so disappointing." This time her reply was in a soft voice, "Yeah, they sure can." A new space opened between us. I could find ways to begin to speak to (or for) her vulnerability, sadness, uncertainty—qualities I knew from my own experience can be so deeply hidden under manic defences. I learned to speak to her (and for her) in the third person: "Sex would be so much easier if there didn't have to be someone else there." To this she replied, "Yeah, well *that* can certainly be arranged. Half the people on the planet have their best sex by themselves. The porn industry makes billions. But it is kind of empty that way." There were, of course, many variations in my third person reflections: "Partners can be so clueless"; "People often don't recognise that starting a business is like having a child—it's very precious"; "Sometimes the words that come out of someone's mouth are not what they are actually feeling"; "Anger is so often only part of the picture"; "It's hard enough to bear disappointment—it's nearly impossible to speak it"; "It's a mystery how people ever come to understand one another". Gradually she began to speak from and for these places within herself. She began to ask me, "So what do you think?" and mean the question. Our sessions became increasingly and more reliably conversational.

Winnicott makes an important distinction towards the end of his discussion of object usage: "I wish to conclude with a note on using. By 'use' I do not mean 'exploitation'" (1971, p. 94). On the contrary, he argues, "It is the greatest compliment we may receive if we are both found and used" (1989, p. 233). He placed great emphasis on a child's or patient's *right* to *find* the object reliable. The therapist does not simply *provide* a supportive atmosphere that the grateful patient can lap up. The therapeutic environment needs to be *used*, tested, and sometimes attacked, so as to be found to be reliable. It is a process that is simultaneously impersonal and intimate. Winnicott goes on to suggest, "Alongside this we see many treatments which are an infinite extension of non-use, kept going indefinitely by the fear of confrontation with the trouble itself—which is an inability to use and be used" (ibid., p. 235). For years Alessia had held me as an object to be used for her own intrapsychic development, an object that was present and interested but unintrusive, undemanding. I had been found to be reliable, and now we could move gradually to confront "the trouble itself".

Sexuality and Eros in psychotherapy

Sexual and erotic desires, while so often mired and distorted by the shadows of the past, have—at their best—the relentless evocation of the future:

> Sexual desire, therefore, educates us throughout our lives. It often reflects our longing for something that we do not currently have. Since almost all of our lives are periodically unsatisfying, our new sexual desires inform us about our felt deficiencies in ourselves and our relationships and how they might be improved.
>
> (Levine, 2003, p. 284)

Sexuality can be a wonderful contributor to our erotic capacities, but sex can also be deadening, numbing, distracting. There are very few clients with whom discussions of sexuality do not become a part of our work together.

Alessia's sexuality was always very apparent, but its multiplicity of meanings—and, perhaps, of "trouble itself"—remained to be explored. Her day-to-day life was filled with overt sexual activity. Here, together, we had slowly, quietly fashioned a different kind of erotic space, a space for the erotics of thought. I can imagine that this may strike some readers as a rather bizarre pairing—Eros and thinking—especially from a writer often known for his body-centred approach to psychotherapy. The force of the erotic is about coming more fully into life, the establishment of the capacity for deeper and more robust vitality with which to meet life, be it body-to-body or mind-to-mind. Thinking together can be a wonderfully erotic experience.

Ours was a vitally necessary psychic space allowing each of us a very particular kind of solitude. The underlying Eros of our working couple became more apparent. In a brilliant essay on the erotics of transference, Jessica Benjamin observes:

> In the solitude provided by the other the subject has a space to become absorbed with internal rhythms rather than reacting to the outside. ... This experience in the transference has its countertransference correlate, in which the analyst imagines her- or himself sharing with the patient a similar state of intense absorption and receptivity, immersed in a flow of material without the need to actively interpret or inject her- or himself. (1995, p. 141)

It is perhaps most fully and persistently in our sexual relations that we encounter "object usage", both as the user and the used. Sex carries the same paradox that Winnicott attributes to the use of the object—it is at one and the same time the possibility of being profoundly impersonal and gratifyingly intimate. Human sexuality simultaneously forces us towards the other and into ourselves.

Contemporary models of psychotherapy and psychoanalysis have seemed either to ignore or domesticate sexuality (Cornell, 2003, 2015a; Green, 1996). As Muriel Dimen has rather cuttingly noted, "Sexuality has become a relation, not a force" (2003, p. 157). Over the past couple of decades, contemporary analysts such as J. Benjamin (1995), Davies (1994, 1998), Dimen (2003, 2005, 2011), Slavin (2003, 2007), and Stein (1998a, 1998b, 2008) have been articulating anew the *force* of sexuality and erotic life. Stein, for example, argued that it is in the very nature of "the excess of sexuality that shatters psychic structures ... so as to enable new ones to evolve" (2008, p. 43). It was only through the more contemporary psychoanalytic literature I found meaningful and provocative clinical discussions of sexuality that informed my clinical practice (Cornell, 2003, 2009a, 2009b, 2015).

With many of my clients, our work involved fostering a capacity for more aggression and object usage in their sexual relations. But for Alessia, her sexuality needed to become not only a force, but also a relation. Sexuality had long provided an essential function—and I stress *function*, in contrast to defence—of knowing through sensation and action that she could manage and contain the intensities and potential intrusiveness of others' sexual desires and practices. The vigour of her sexual relations needed to expand to make room for her longing and vulnerability.

My speaking in the third person about loss, sadness, vulnerability, uncertainty, and disappointment could resonate within her without defining her personal experience. The space created by the third person allowed me to speak and allowed Alessia the freedom to consider, consciously and unconsciously, the relevance for her of what I was saying. She began to look for different emotional qualities and capacities in her partners and friends. Her sex life has remained as robust as ever.

I have never engaged in transference interpretations or reflections with Alessia. The nature of our relationship has been lived and *experienced* rather than discussed and analysed. I have no doubt that my quietly, respectfully attentive ways of being with her created at an unconscious level a sense of new possibilities for relatedness. She began to look for more consistent and attentive relationships in her life. She seems to have managed to coach her mother to be a better listening and receptive parent. Her father remains problematic.

What I hope I have illustrated with this accounting of our work together is that it was not the content of Alessia's talking that informed me, it was *how* she spoke and related to me. This is the core of unconscious experience organised at the third degree (or protocol): it is in one's very way of being. Many clients, of course, can and do make use of much more frequent verbal (and somatic) observations and interventions. This was not the case for Alessia. The relentless intrusions of her parents were like the air she breathed—for a very long time. Our sessions needed to provide a very different atmosphere—for a very long time—and I needed to bring my attention and care to her in a very different way from what she had always experienced. I was to be shaped by her, rather than the other way around. The consistency and reliability of my non-intrusive interest gradually allowed her the freedom to relate to me and to herself differently.

In closing

I have been in practice for over forty years now. Through all those years I have had the very good fortune to learn from a remarkable, challenging, and inspiring group of consultants and mentors. Ours is a profession rich with the opportunity, the necessity really, to constantly think anew.

I was first drawn to Transactional Analysis by Berne's deep regard for his patients. My academic training had been in phenomenology, a foundation that has afforded the best possible base for the psychotherapeutic endeavour. I saw in Berne the beginnings of an integration of the phenomenological perspective with psychoanalysis. At the time of my initial training what was most important to me was the TA gave me a structure for thinking and some idea what to actually *do* with the people when they were in my office. That was such a rich gift to a nervous, novice therapist.

Phenomenology and transactional analysis have been my ground. For the past twenty years my readings of and studies with contemporary psychoanalysts have carried me "under" that ground into the rich domains of unconscious experience and communication. In recent years my learning has been particularly enriched by studies with Maurice Apprey (2006), a classically trained psychoanalyst who is also deeply versed in phenomenology and is bringing these two disciplines into an exquisite dialogue. With Apprey I have found a deepening integration of these two modes of psychological investigation that I first saw as a possibility reading Berne.

As I look ahead, I also continue to learn how to create space for the emergence of the unconscious domains in my work with groups. I've long been much more at ease in dyads, and as a group leader have found much security in the typical structure of a TA treatment or training group. But in recent years I have grown more tolerant, sometimes even eager, for the discomfort, unpredictability, and depth offered through the models of analytic and process-oriented groups (Landaiche, 2012, 2013; Nitsun, 1996; Van Beekum, 2012). Herein is the leading edge of my ongoing learning.

CHAPTER FIVE

From impenetrability to transparency: the "I" of the beholder

Elana Leigh

G rappling with the evolution of theory and the process of integrating it into our practice is a complex and demanding but essential responsibility. The task is not an easy one in an environment of polarities, which can leave us feeling like we are wedged between one place and another in our search for a truly authentic therapeutic identity. Bromberg captures this experience when he says, "It is only because the line between 'personal' and 'professional' is permeable rather than hard edged that it is possible for the therapeutic relationship to exist" (1996, p. 13).

In this chapter I will explore how the relational turn in contemporary thinking has affected me as a transactional analyst. By highlighting our psychoanalytic history and Freud's theory on mourning and melancholia I will emphasise the importance of integrating the old into new theories rather than disavowing the place of the old. I will argue that addressing the evolutionary development of theories and practice facilitates integration and this involves necessarily revisiting the past in order to integrate disavowed parts of the self. This facilitates the creation of a consistent and continuous personal narrative, and it is this that creates the authentic "I" in our therapeutic identity and relationship with our clients.

Psychoanalyst Stephen Mitchell (1988), often credited as the father of relational psychoanalysis, invites us to find and create our own relational methodology and this has provided permission for me to integrate my humanistic Transactional Analysis history with my current relational psychoanalytic perspectives. This invitation opened a decade of exploring what this integration meant for me. This paper outlines my personal evolutionary process as a psychotherapist from impenetrability to transparency, which to some extent was my version of Freud's struggle with the dilemma of the psychotherapist's subjectivity in the therapeutic relationship.

Ever since Freud one of the ongoing debates within the field of psychotherapy has centred on subjectivity versus objectivity of the psychotherapist. Freud had a deep aversion for the analyst's subjectivity being used in the treatment and in fact warned Jung about this when he suggested that the psychoanalyst should be opaque to his patients and, like a mirror, should show them nothing but what is shown to him or her (1912e).

This underpinned his lifelong struggle with the locus of therapeutic action, as he was concerned that the use of the analyst's self would interfere with the scientific nature of psychoanalysis, and lead to its expulsion from the sciences. In his desire for psychoanalysis to be taken seriously as a science, he seemingly had to minimise the importance of the therapist's subjectivity.

Freud's dilemma highlights the dynamic that in the process of creating something new we are often simultaneously separating from someone or something. As we enter this process of separation we simultaneously enter the paradoxical struggle to be recognised by those we are departing from. This complex bilateral dynamic can create a narcissistic injury for both parties: the one being left feels betrayed and the one departing may experience a sense of grandiosity covering more complex feelings of shame, guilt, and fear. When the rupture is too great for the relationship to be renegotiated there is no alternative but to find one's own way alone. I believe this speaks to the many splits that have occurred since Freud. These unprocessed dynamics have been carried collectively and perhaps have contributed to the fragmentation and inability to walk the talk of difference in the psychotherapy field.

The desire and the consequences of separation

Freud wanted to separate and create a new science of the mind and yet he spent much energy consciously or unconsciously attempting to get recognition and acceptance from the scientists. The same has been true for the humanistic tradition where there was an attempt to break from the medical model and again it did not take long before the attention shifted from the excitement of creating a revolution to the desire to get recognition from the psychoanalytic family from whom the humanists had separated.

Right from the outset the issue of inclusion/exclusion and recognition and acceptance played a central role in how psychotherapists positioned themselves and how theories have been informed. Although psychoanalysis has devolved into a range of different approaches and sensibilities, in classical psychoanalysis the rigid, opaque boundaries that were expected from the analysts ruled out any dangerous subjectivity that could interfere with the scientific evidence of the model, which Freud was avidly protecting.

In my view it was Freud's ambivalence about the analyst's subjectivity that informed his rather rigid theories and practice. This phenomenon of creating an opposite behaviour in order to protect that which is feared is common and included in Freud's theory on defence mechanisms as reaction formation. This has been described as "… converting a socially unacceptable impulse into the opposite. The conscious is opposite to the unconscious" (Baumeister, Dale, & Sommer, 1998, p. 1085). I am hypothesising that the rigid, opaque boundaries that were expected from the analysts not only protected psychoanalysis from falling foul of the sciences, but was also a form of reaction formation, protecting Freud from his own narcissism.

The natural attraction to subjectivity

Freud's deep compassion shaped a quality of responsiveness to his patients that firmly located him as a significant subject in relation to his patients, in a manner that contradicted the tight analytical frame that we have come to know. This contradiction illuminated his ambivalence and conflict about this central discussion and this has continued to keep clinicians and theoreticians questioning.

He believed that the analyst did contribute strongly to the analytic process, not by bringing subjectivity into the dyad but by giving "equal notice" to the analyst's and the analysand's material in an effort to be in a state of evenly suspended attention (1912e). This allowed for a shared process of association, which informed interpretation.

He also believed that in order for an interpretation to be used the repressed material needed to be close to the surface, and the patient needed to feel firmly attached to the analyst. The secure therapeutic relationship together with the accessibility of the material created a safe container for the delivery of the interpretation, thus protecting the patient and the analysis. It was therefore quite clear that Freud *was* working closely with the meaning and the significance of the therapeutic relationship, and that the analyst should remain both objective and open to the process. These features, he believed, led to psychic continuity, which was the road to mental well-being.

The early signs of binary thinking

At that time the emphasis was on the patient's intrapsychic structure and psychotherapists were operating from a one-person psychology (Stark, 1999). This meant they were *administering* treatment as opposed to being a mutual partner. The centrality of the patient's intrapsychic structure did not, however, detract from Freud's grappling with the analyst's internal world and its place in the analysis, and wondering what to make of it.

Indeed, I believe that the struggle with the boundary between analyst and analysand, therapist and client, subjectivity and objectivity, is part of the human struggle of negotiating the boundary between self and other and is often key to most conditions that enter consulting rooms.

It was a natural progression for followers of Freud to actively begin to play with the role of the analyst and to keep the debate of subjectivity versus objectivity alive. The need to be engaged with our patients seems to be a natural phenomenon and yet its very essence is what is questioned and feared.

We thus see the field move from drive theory to ego theory to object relational theory and finally to contemporary relational theory. Each paradigm shift was informed by a new and different position regarding the question of subjectivity versus objectivity. The different theoretical frames influenced the role of the analyst as well as the theoretical positions on what constituted cure.

The introduction of the analysis of the interpersonal relationship was thought to be revolutionary as it dramatically changed the methodology of psychotherapy. The emphasis of the work was no longer only on the intrapsychic structure of the patient but now the nature of the interpersonal dynamics was equally in focus.

According to Stark (1999) the original classical psychoanalytic models were interpretive and operated from a one-person psychology where the analyst stood *outside* the dyad to focus on the internal dynamics of the patient. The field then moved to corrective provision models, which paid attention to the developmental deficits in the patient, in the belief that they could provide that which was missing from childhood. These approaches were seen as one-and-a-half person psychology as the analysts stood *alongside* the patients, attending to the developmental deficit, but still essentially standing outside the relationship and doing psychotherapy as opposed to being in it.

Stark referred to the contemporary relational model, which developed into the authentic model as the psychotherapist privileges both her own and the patient's subjectivity. Mitchell's (1988) relational matrix focuses on three "poles"—self, other, and the interaction between the two, requiring the psychotherapist to step into the therapeutic dyad and be fully immersed in what Stark called an authentic relationship.

This question of how the psychotherapist uses herself in the service of the psychotherapy continued to be central. What an interesting conundrum: on one side models of abstinence precipitate problems associated with the psychotherapist's absence and at the other extreme the over-intrusive therapist occupies perhaps too much space creating a different but equally damaging effect.

The relational turn and its impact on the author's evolution

I now turn my attention away from the positioning of the therapist within the classical psychoanalytic tradition and towards the evolution of this central value within contemporary relational theory.

In the mid-1980s the contemporary relational turn led by Stephen Mitchell was seen to have been revolutionary. I believe, however, that this turn was in fact a natural evolution. The inclusion and emphasis on the interpersonal nature of the psychotherapy dyad was by then present in the field. Self-psychology and Sullivan's interpersonal psychoanalysis, for example, were already experimenting with ways to work with the subjectivity of the therapist and the patient and the interpersonal relationship. Within the humanistic tradition this had been happening since the 1950s. Much of the time, however, the therapist was still standing slightly outside the therapeutic relationship and had not actively entered into the dyad as a partner; the genuine "I" of the psychotherapist had not yet arrived within the clinical encounter.

The active introduction of the psychotherapist's self, encouraged by the relational turn, immediately caused the fear and excitement of the old debate between subjectivity and objectivity to resurface. How is it possible to be both unequal in terms of power and yet be genuinely mutual? This paradox underpinned many discussions, which did then and still do create confusion and dissension.

Reflecting on the above questions I turn to my own history. I trained as a transactional analyst in the 1980s and I found myself caught in an ongoing dilemma, between a revolutionary humanistic approach and the classical psychoanalytic model. Berne's unconscious drive to be separate and different had infiltrated the very fibre of our Transactional Analysis community. There was a philosophy, theory, and methodology that we adhered to. Its brilliance lay in its difference from the medical model, in that it provided an interactive way of working with both the intrapsychic as well as the interpersonal dynamics of the patient and the therapeutic dyad. Within the integrative Transactional Analysis psychotherapy community, however, there came a moment when working in the prescribed one-and-a-half person, reparative, corrective provision style was questioned. I, too, began to notice the repetitive requirement for "more of me" and began to question what was missing; I was giving and supplying but for some not repairing.

Doubts about the reparative model

It became clear to me that even though my desire and intention was to provide "a better childhood" for my clients, this was both unrealistic and created complexities in the power dynamics. I was troubled with the thought that perhaps working within a reparative model led to a dependency within the therapeutic relationship that created a vulnerability to abuse from both parties. Within this model at that time the practitioner had not fully stepped into the therapeutic relationship. This in itself meant that the psychotherapist was still "doing" psychotherapy and that the use of the countertransference was informing the psychotherapist about the client's pathology. The power imbalance was still present. This imbalance was manifest in the language both within and outside the consulting room. The "I" of the psychotherapist had not fully arrived.

Case vignette

> In the late 1980s when working weekly with a client for four years I became aware of the following pattern. She would arrive at a session distressed about something in her life where she felt helpless and despairing. I would explore her despair and mostly relate this to her history where she felt unsupported by her family and left alone. I often used two-chair work (Erskine & Moursund, 1988; Goulding & Goulding, 1979) to highlight the intrapsychic impasse she was experiencing in her Child ego state. This would often lead to her spending a period of time being regressed and crying with me holding her.
>
> In my mind she was able to cognitively understand where the impasse lay, affectively able to express unexpressed emotions, and this all provided in my mind a reparative experience. Towards the end of the session she often stated that she felt clearer, stronger and able to re-enter her world as an adult and not function as if she was still the young girl who felt so helpless and alone.
>
> She left satisfied and I experienced a feeling of competence—all was well.

The problem that emerged about the scenario outlined above was that it became a repetitive pattern, which ultimately led me to question what I was doing.

I instinctively knew that all was in fact not well and I confronted both my own and the modality's limitations: something more was required and I at that stage was unclear what this was.

On reflection what was required was for me to bring this very dilemma into the psychotherapy relationship where we could explore together both the failures of the past as well as in the present with us. This requirement speaks to what I believe is a central difference between a one-person psychology where the problem mainly lies in the client and a two-person psychology where the therapist and client hold the problem together.

Grappling with the relational in Transactional Analysis

The relational turn in the 1990s was a natural progression for some transactional analysts (particularly the integrative transactional analysts). The language, philosophy, and interactive approach felt familiar. It began to provide a platform to grapple with some of my concerns and questions emanating from the reparative models of practice.

This coincided with transactional analysts having a need to reclaim some of their psychoanalytic roots (Moiso, 1985). This meant that for many of us we began to refrain from touch, regressive, and most experiential techniques and moved into working within the therapeutic relationship using the transference and countertransference to inform us moment to moment. If we could have observed the transactional analyst working we would have perhaps seen that we looked very different to the revolutionary humanists we once were.

At that point I was thinking as a transactional analyst, using the foundation canon of TA theory, but at the same time, having begun to immerse myself in the work of Mitchell, I was in an evolutionary process of learning how to truly bring the "I" of myself more fully into the therapeutic dyad. When thinking about Mitchell's three poles I had only superficially begun to introduce the self-pole as I had not discovered how to fully bring myself into the therapeutic relationship. This therefore affected the whole relational matrix that I was operating from at that time.

For me there was a significant synchronicity in the work of the neurobiologists who were writing about the necessity for right brain-to-right-brain communication in the development of a sense of self with others. Siegel's (1999) writing about the interpersonally developed brain and mind depict the contemporary relational psychoanalysts writing about working from a two-person psychological perspective. This new learning began to clarify that whilst in the 1980s I actively used and valued my right brain it was in isolation from the "other's" right brain (one-person psychological perspective). My new insight and knowing from the contemporary writers was about right-brain-to-right-brain communication and the inevitability of this shared two-person dynamic.

The result of my awareness was that while this new home base initially felt comfortable and familiar for me it soon became clear that for me to work authentically from a two-person perspective a paradigm shift was required inside myself.

Searching for a coherent relational frame

This next chapter in the story gave rise to many questions and confusion about my professional identity. There was no one relational infrastructure housing a formal training and theory, for which I was searching. I couldn't identify a solid container in which to settle. I had not found the next island to land on. I felt like I was in no man's land. I was preoccupied with questions such as: What is relational theory? Whose relational theory? What did it mean to work from a two-person psychology? Where was relational methodology? Could the new contemporary theories and practice accommodate the old Transactional Analysis methods?

Multiple relational theories emerged each having their roots in different historical theories and methods. Despite their differences, concepts such as transparency, self-disclosure, and therapeutic spontaneity unified these theories, all of which are practised within a frame whose central tenet is the focus on the interplay between the self, other, and interaction poles described by Mitchell.

For a long while these concepts remained somewhat arbitrary theoretical constructs due to the fact that there was no defined methodology linked to a coherent theory. As a result, multiple individual interpretations of these constructs in the form of case studies peppered our discourse, with the onus on the individual to integrate these concepts into his own thinking and practice—a far cry from following a prescribed theory and methodology.

This shift towards a more individually determined process of integration provoked further questions about what it means to work from a two-person psychology; if I am fully present moment by moment, engaged in a two-person dynamic, with what emerges from within the client, myself, and the interaction, does this exclude my previous theoretical knowledge which I learnt predominantly from within a one-person psychology? Are the two psychologies incompatible or not? Is it possible for old and new to stand together? If so, how, and if not, why not? Does being a relational two-person psychotherapist require me to only focus on the interactional, interpersonal poles of the therapeutic dyad or can I also include the focus on the intrapsychic elements of both the client and the therapist?

Case vignette

When working recently with someone with a borderline structure he became angry with me. It was clear to me that he was angry because I had recently taken leave. I felt anxious and slightly defensive as I felt responsible for creating this disruption in him, me, and us. I noticed how I wished to use his borderline structure as a way of interpreting his anger particularly after a break. I also noted how my own anxiety was interfering with our contact. I responded, "I felt anxious to meet with you after our break, and think it is hard for us to manage the comings and goings especially after a break." He quietly responded, "I agree and it really helps when you share your part in this as opposed to blaming me for my strong feelings."

Traditionally, I would have felt all the feelings I experienced in this situation, but because of my own vulnerability, I may have defended myself by perhaps bringing in an interpretation. In this way I would have kept myself outside the relational moment and maintained a one-up position. In so doing, I would have evaded the relational truth that we were both experiencing anxiety. Conversely, responding as I did this time, I was transparent to myself in my acknowledgement of my own defensiveness and anxiety. Although I did think of his borderline structure, this time I did not use it to further persecute him but to share how coming and going is complex and that we are there to make sense of this together since what we share is a co-constructed dynamic.

While philosophically I hold the belief that the relationship is shared and that in this instance, we were both contributing towards the felt anxiety, I nevertheless still experienced discomfort within myself about my intervention. In bringing the "I" of myself so intimately into the therapeutic space it provoked in this instance my narcissistic injury which is to doubt my own intention: was I in this moment authentically sharing my client's anxiety or was I using my new found relational sensibility to soothe him and protect us both? Surely on the other hand, it's easier and safer to keep myself out of the therapeutic matrix?

My ambivalence inherent in this personal account talks to the heart of the debate concerning subjectivity and objectivity and to the question about whether to self-disclose or not. It also talks to my own struggle when transitioning between an old and new frame. The combination of the internalised collective fear of transparent subjectivity and the absence of a coherent theory and methodology within the relational paradigm fuelled my discomfort. The metaphorical parent, symbolised in a unifying theory and methodology, was missing.

I long for the certainty and security that this metaphorical parent can offer. I long to know with certainty what belongs to me, and what does not. I long to know that bringing my personal thoughts and feelings into the therapeutic relationship will not be narcissistic and therefore damaging. At the same time I know that I cannot have this certainty to protect myself from myself.

Case vignette

A long-term client came to a session feeling frustrated and stuck in both his life as well as in his therapy. He felt disillusioned that after all these years of therapy he still experienced feeling stuck. This he stated was limiting his life choices.

At this moment I began thinking about the Parent ego state and how historically I worked from the premise that sometimes when a client was experiencing feeling stuck it could be a symptom of some unresolved material within the Parent ego state. I thought with fondness about the Parent interview (McNeel, 1976) and wondered whether I would dare to step out of my existing relational therapeutic frame and introduce this "old" technique.

My internal thoughts were the following: I feel helpless and slightly incompetent. Historically in this moment I would have introduced the technique of the parent interview as I think the aetiology of this impasse resides with his father. I feel ambivalent to introduce this as perhaps I am avoiding working with my own discomfort of his disappointment in his therapy and in me. Is my desire to introduce the technique an enactment? And equally if I refrain from doing this is it another form of an enactment? I too feel stuck between my old and new paradigms. I smile, and experience understanding our joint stuck feelings with more depth.

I said the following: "My thoughts about feeling stuck are that this can happen when we are caught between desiring something new and that something new is in conflict with something old. For me right now

I would like to introduce you to a technique, which works with feeling stuck. This is new for us here, but old for me in terms of my history as a psychotherapist and this creates ambivalence in me. My hunch is that for you your frustration is about desiring to do new things in your life that are in conflict with your father and your history. What do you think about these thoughts and my suggestion?"

He smiled and said, "Well, at least you too have internal conflicts and ambivalences and I do feel caught between something new and old but I don't understand it. It feels like the real knowing is hidden and that is what is so painful and frustrating. I would really like to try this technique and feel moved at how much thought you are giving me and our process."

I both introduced and reintroduced us to the parent interview technique. I placed two chairs in front of us and invited him to stay with his frustrated stuck feeling and slowly move into the chair, symbolising his father. (I chose to interview his "father" as we had recently been working with issues relating to him.) I invited him to evoke his "father" as fully as possible. He closed his eyes as he moved into the chair where he was to be his "father".

He slowly opened his eyes and we entered into a moving conversation where I felt curious about who this man was, particularly in relation to the current stuck feelings of his son—my client. There was a pivotal moment where he (father) became moved while talking about scarcity in his childhood and at that moment I felt equally moved and we sat quietly together acknowledging how hard life can sometimes be.

In this moment I experienced closure and chose to conclude the conversation with father and move back to my client. I thanked him for his willingness to trust and be with me and we said goodbye. I invited my client to move back to his own chair. As he moved and sat down he wept for both his father's life and his.

I sat quietly waiting for him to feel ready to re-engage with me. As he slowly looked up at me he said, "How does this work? I have never felt these feelings with or for my father and it makes such sense to me how hard it has been for me to move forward in my life since it provokes feelings of abandoning him. I am now thinking that perhaps I am ready to live my own life and perhaps I can do this because I can also hold feelings of love and understanding for my father. I can have what he never did have and not take anything away from him." This was a significant turning point in his therapy and his life.

I sat quietly with him as I marvelled at what had just occurred and in that moment I too realised that I did not have to lose aspects of my own psychotherapy professional history when stepping into a new paradigm.

The difference in the way I worked with this client in 2013 as compared to in the 1980s and 90s was that I was not following a prescriptive technique but rather using a technique where I was fully present to myself, the client, the father, and to our relationship. I used both my and the client's subjectivity to inform me, which is different to historically using technical indicators (change in ego state).

The agency in this exploration lay with both my client and myself—we were co-explorers and the outcome was astonishing. He has subsequently made new decisions in his life and no longer feels stuck.

This does not feel magical but liberating for me to experience and know that old and new can, in such moments, sit together. The "I" of myself is the integrator of my past and present and it is this "I" that allows this process to be an authentic therapeutic experience.

The relational turn emphasises the requirement for the psychotherapist to take up a position as an authentic mutual participant and in doing so confronts us psychotherapists with issues of narcissism in a new way. Our narcissism has nowhere to hide and, in its exposure, is demanding examination in a manner that Freud and others were not ready, willing, or able to do.

I think we experience responses to narcissism at a body level and at the primitive primary aspects of self, the very places where the original narcissistic injury occurred. We instinctively know when someone is genuinely with us as opposed to when we are being used as an object for another's needs. It is this faculty that makes children great detectors of incongruity and narcissism. Adults have forsaken this natural ability by over-accommodating for the purpose of seeking or maintaining attachment. When in the presence of our own known or unknown narcissism of needing to be seen and known we perhaps simultaneously feel shame and disgust for these needs. The overcompensation and displacement of this shame is what unconsciously traps us into our discomfort with narcissism. I think that this is perhaps the shadow of the relational paradigm.

Knowing this intellectually, however, did not provide me (or us) with tools to engage in the practice of including the therapist as an authentic, mutual participant. Indeed as stated previously no relational theory and methodology existed in which to seek refuge, thus creating a struggle for me in both the area of knowledge and the fear of my narcissistic exposure.

We psychotherapists have learnt to protect and defend ourselves from the discomfort and shame of self-exposure and through the process of reaction formation, have attempted to deny ourselves and overvalue theories and techniques.

This shame, I suggest, arises out of vulnerability in the domain of self and therefore mistrust in our own reality. Is this not what underlies most narcissistic injuries? We have learnt not to be self-centred, self-orientated, but to be "other" focused, leaving us with a need to be seen and recognised. When this need to be recognised is not healthily met it runs the risk of being professionally enacted with our clients, fellow professionals, or both. Freud's theory of reaction formation has yet again proved to be a brilliant temporary solution to protecting our narcissistic injuries.

The melancholic effect of change

Freud in his seminal paper on "Mourning and Melancholia" (1917e) spoke deeply to my struggle at the time of the relational turn. Freud explains how, when in a state of melancholia, we are either caught in an unrelenting experience of depression or in a manic defence. These two reactions are the ego's attempt at protecting itself from the emptiness.

In retrospect I wonder whether, in my process of evolving and transitioning from one modality to another, I may have entered a state of melancholia, having lost the object of my desire (Transactional Analysis as I knew it) which, whilst I was attached to it, I also knew that it provided me with a sense of omnipotence and grandiosity. This sheltered me from potential shame of not knowing and thereby allowed me to hold onto my illusions of being able to heal and cure. The more authentic experience, but the experience harder to tolerate, was the mourning of the loss of one paradigm and facing the void.

Freud's concern of subjectivity, I suggest, kept him safe from his own potential melancholic state and gave rise to a collection of beliefs about transparency that we came to think of as a doctrine. The same may be true for us at the time of the relational turn. Could we, too, be defending against the depression associated with the mourning of the loss of certainty and knowing in our original chosen modalities, by jumping to a defensive new position and then believing that we have found a revolutionary relational way of working?

In the 1980s and 90s, I carried the map of my own psychotherapy, working primarily within a reparative model of Transactional Analysis. I experienced both the agony and the bliss of this model that, at the time, I could not challenge. What was missing, in hindsight, was the capacity to tolerate two minds in the consulting room. However, this was the spirit of the time; injuries, mistakes, healing, and growth occurred.

As a psychotherapist, I did not work interpersonally with my countertransference reactions. Disruptions were not worked with as part of the psychotherapy as our model had not evolved enough to know about disruption and repair as part of the therapeutic healing process. The self of the psychotherapist needed to firstly enter the therapeutic space before this healing could occur. Before even that could happen, we needed to collectively be willing and able to work with our introjected omnipotence inherited from Berne. I believe that Berne too may have been in a reactive defensive place in himself after his rejection and departure from the psychoanalysts.

Mills in his recent book *Conundrums* (2012) raises important questions and critiques of contemporary psychoanalysis that resonate strongly with me. He asks, "Does the analyst's subjectivity foreclose the question of objectivity? And does a two-person model of intersubjectivity minimize or cancel the force and value of intrapsychic reality and lived individual experience?" (pp. 22–23). Mills's questions talk to my discomfort and uncertainty and to my belief that it is the false binary of either/or that traps us. The solution to any binary I suggest is inner knowing and outer knowledge. This releases us to be free to choose, to know, and to hold the difference between both positions.

Integration—the gift of the contemporary relational turn

I am now able to read Mitchell's words without experiencing the original loss and confusion they evoked in me all those years ago. Mitchell, in his own evolution was offering a proposition to the broader psychoanalytic community that cut straight to the heart of the repetitive splitting that had occurred throughout time. He subtly implored us to reflect on our personal need and desire to have one coherent relational theory. Perhaps he believed that in gratifying this need, we satisfy the illusion of grandiosity and omnipotence that never stands the test of time. Is it not fascinating to notice how grandiosity in all forms is vulnerable to being challenged and popped and yet the same is not true for humility? Again, a reminder of Freud's hypothesis that grandiosity protects the experience of defeat and yet, it is our capacity to tolerate defeat which is the royal road to humility.

Mitchell contended that everything occurs within the matrix of the therapeutic relationship (1988). "The relational conflict matrix emphasises the conflict both internally and in between. This requires those of us in the field to have an interest in all that has come before and all that is contemporary. How we hold this together depends on our individual frame of integration" (Mitchell in Aaron & Harris, 2005, p. xvii). Mitchell in no way intended that there should be one relational theory. He was proposing instead that within the relational frame, a thinker could integrate a variety of relational concepts drawn from different traditions and reorganise them in a new coherent individual theory. This to my mind is the true definition of integration: the bringing together of ideas through an internalised process, the central integrator being the individual who combines knowledge, values, philosophies, and a sense of self.

Mitchell requested for us as professionals, scholars, and practitioners to stay close to our own history and professional training and from that position to integrate contemporary concepts and philosophies. The onus is on each individual therapist and through our own integration process we thus authentically bring ourselves into the therapeutic dyad.

There is a difference between following a theory or method as a protective veil and having one's own assimilated and integrated thoughts and knowledge. This I believe is what Berne meant when he spoke about moving away from models that adhere to the belief of "doctor knows best". Perhaps it is natural in the evolutionary learning cycle to take on a belief that speaks to you, copy it, deconstruct it, and finally integrate the original belief and make it your own. When we skip over steps in this process of learning we disavow old in order to make the new more relevant. When all these steps take place we hold the old and the new together. This was my "ah ha" or eureka moment. I finally realised that as long as I followed a methodology from an introjected position I was not fully present in the therapeutic relationship. I had grasped that the onus is on me, as on each individual therapist, and that through our own integration process we finally authentically bring ourselves in the therapeutic dyad.

The debate on the subjectivity and objectivity of the psychotherapist continues in contemporary relational psychotherapy but with language that differs from the past. Transparency, therapeutic freedom, and self-disclosure are examples of contemporary language used to discuss the plight of the psychotherapist's role in an interpersonal paradigm. In my journey of integration and my search for my own relational methodology I have arrived at my own meaning of relational concepts such as transparency, self-disclosure, and therapeutic spontaneity. I additionally think that within relational psychotherapy the skill set has moved from being external to the psychotherapist to more internal (Leigh, 2011). Historically the methodology was externalised through the use of techniques to facilitate the therapeutic process and in contemporary times this has shifted to a more internal reflective process held inside the psychotherapist.

When experiencing a strong countertransference feeling of anger, for example, I would have, historically, held the belief that this was being projected into me so that I was able to deepen my understanding of the client's experience. I might have externalised this in the form of an intervention such as "I am wondering if you are feeling angry right now?" This intervention assumed that my clinical hypothesis was correct and it overlooked and foreclosed on the client's experience, my genuine curiosity, and my capacity to, in D. B. Stern's words, "court surprise" (2013, p. 253). Today I would take time to reflect on my anger, stay curious, and bring in my reflection of my anger in order to wonder with my client about what this might be informing us both about each other and our dynamic.

To be genuine to this process I need to be willing to face the possibility that this may require some disclosure of myself in the service of the client, the therapeutic process, and myself. In this instance I am as vulnerable as my client and a mutual participant in the dyad. The techniques and skills I employed here are to notice my internal response; I pause, reflect, inspect, and am transparent to myself. From this reflective open and curious position I open up the possibilities of a mutual understanding of what is happening. This process is different from an historic, grandiose, but possibly safer position of assuming I know and thus I am equipped to interpret the client's inner world.

Case vignette

A client entered the session crying and sobbing, unable to talk. I sat with her observing her body and her pain. I soon began to feel tension in my own body. I sat with my own tension and began what Symington (1986) would have called my own reverie or free floating attention. In this free associative state I imagined my client lying on the couch where she would be able to allow her body to guide her painful process. I imagined her curling up and sobbing like a baby and me sitting quietly next to her holding the space.

This thought grew and I felt the restriction of the chair that my client was sitting on, as if for this little baby holding herself upright was almost impossible. Perhaps the cries were coming from a baby who physiologically could not yet sit?

I noted that the more this thought was present the more restricted I became. I was conflicted with what I naturally wanted to do, as I believed that in this contemporary paradigm, this is not the way to work. As I heard and observed my thoughts I was no longer with both the baby and the client in the room. I was lost in my own struggle and the baby was yet again missed.

I said, "I feel your tears are about never trusting or knowing that anyone was and is with you in your pain."

Her cries increased and I moved to bring a folded mattress into the centre of the room.

I said, "Your body looks like it needs to lie down and do whatever it needs to do. The mattress is here and so am I. I know this perhaps feels new for us both but then so do your tears. Feel free to stay where you are or move to the mattress."

She responded with a scream of fear saying, "I am so scared I will fall apart."

I responded with "I can see your fear and also know how much we have spoken about how this fear stops you feeling free to live your life as you wish to live it."

She moved slowly to the mattress and cried while her body shook and moved. I was sitting besides her, holding the space, not touching her but reflecting from time to time what I experienced and observed.

After twenty minutes she became calm and looked at me. We gazed at each other and I began to enquire how she was feeling. She talked about her shame and her sense of exposure and together we reflected on how hard it is to touch those parts of ourselves that feel unacceptable and yet when they stay locked up inside we never quite know whether we have the resilience to survive them.

She and I survived our own separate fears: mine to follow what felt was the right intervention even if it meant crossing an internal conflict about right and wrong, and hers to allow herself to express her feelings in a manner that was exposing and a risk to the part of her that believed she would fall apart. We experienced our joint resilience and something new emerged.

What differentiates this work from that of the 1980s was that throughout this process I was cognisant of the fact that this was my client's process as opposed to me providing her with a reparative parenting experience. I was not attempting to be a better mother to her than her own mother but responding and trusting both her and my competence to allow something new to occur. My multiple psychotherapy trainings, our strong alliance, and my inner personal psychotherapy map held me competently through this process.

Knowing the difference between providing from a one-person psychology and mutually negotiating from a two-person psychology felt central to my own sense of congruence and authenticity. I was not mixing paradigms but was integrating old and new ways with contemporary relational sensibility.

The therapeutic process resides inside me as opposed to being prescribed. I have come to know that I am a collection of my past and present training, knowledge, values, and philosophies. Both my integration of one- and two-person psychotherapies and my personal evolution are what create the "I" that sits moment by moment with my clients. "In most moments we depend on our own analyses, training, and clinical experience, which are in our bones. In the end our participation is educated and at the same time we are doing our best to find a response that is adequate to our clinical and human purposes. We are feeling our way and courting surprise" (D. B. Stern, 2013, pp. 251–252).

Stern speaks not only to that which resides in our bones, but also of the importance of mind and heart being equally present in our presence as psychotherapists. I am coming to know the difference between moments when I hide behind my theories as opposed to using them in ways that keeps my clients and me mutually and authentically engaged in the intimacy of the relationship. We stand naked together.

Conclusion

As a transactional analyst my therapeutic freedom today lies in my responsibility to reclaim my revolutionary humanistic self in the presence of my contemporary relational sensibility. Who I was and who I am coexist, and in this knowledge I have come to know that old and new methodologies too can stand together. The integrator of them is "I".

As psychotherapists our struggles and joys are many. We have grappled and always should continue to grapple with the questions of how to be in this complex paradoxical conundrum of being both human and a psychotherapist. In having the courage to stay with our many losses, through our humility we find ways to hold difference and complexity, past and present, heart and mind. If having the desire to heal and make a difference is part of our collective narcissism, let's claim it, employ a watchful eye ensuring this is never at the expense of another, and in this way continually honour the challenging, healthy tension between "I" and beholder.

I am indebted to those learned, curious individuals who have generously shared their thoughts and who have had the courage to push the boundaries of our profession.

CHAPTER SIX

Changing transgenerational scripts

Gloria Noriega Gayol

"How can I change my transgenerational script?" is the question clients often ask once they become aware that they have been repeating in their own lives patterns that are similar to those lived out by a parent or grandparent. To facilitate such changes, I have developed a methodology that combines individual psychotherapy with an intensive weekend workshop in which I integrate psycho-education and therapeutic interventions using Transactional Analysis theory and techniques in conjunction with psychoanalytic concepts, systematic therapy, and psychodrama.

The workshop facilitates a direct, immediate existential experience of what I refer to as *unknown knowledge* (Noriega, 2010) about oneself and one's family. It motivates clients to change their life scripts, thereby interrupting the chain that has been unconsciously repeated in their family for two or more generations. The objective is to empower clients to recognise and be able to change dysfunctional scripts while still allowing them to retain for themselves and their descendants any healthy legacy left to them by their ancestors.

The intergenerational approach in Transactional Analysis

As Eric Berne said in his last book, "The most intricate part of script analysis in clinical practice is tracing back the influences of the grandparents" (1972, p. 318). I think he would have continued developing this concept had he not passed away unexpectedly in 1970 at the age of sixty. When I began researching and developing a working method (Noriega, 2004, 2009, 2010; Noriega, Ramos, Medina-Mora, & Villa, 2008), there was little in the Transactional Analysis literature on this topic, most of it over a decade old.

English (1969, 1998) described the *episcript* as a hot-potato game, which involves passing on the end of a tragic script. Dashiell (1978) created a process for applying *redecision therapy* (Goulding & Goulding, 1979) to incorporated psychic presences from ancestors that are found in the Parent ego state of someone in a subsequent generation. J. James (1984) explained the importance of the grandparents' relationship when choosing a partner. Massey (1985, 1989; Massey, Corney, & Just, 1988) integrated script theory, family systems, the use of genograms, and the script matrix, and Campos (1986) highlighted the importance of empowering children to prevent script formation. From a cultural perspective, Said and Noriega (1983) described some Mexican cultural scripts for men and women, and Tholenaar de Borbon (1983) described the cultural script in the Dominican Republic and its repetition in new generations.

Nowadays, interest in this topic has been rekindled, and more contributions have been published in the *Transactional Analysis Journal*. For example, Jenkins and Teachworth (2010) used redecision therapy in the treatment of adult children who repeat their parents' partner scripts. Salters (2013) described a method that integrates Transactional Analysis with sandplay and family constellations in work with children and adults. McQuillin and Welford (2013) compared the humanist philosophy of Transactional Analysis with proposed systemic values in family constellations. Recently, Welford (2014) explained the importance of grief work for the family system, and Novak (2014) described a psychotherapy method for working with clients who feel hated by their abusive parents.

Transgenerational psychotherapy

Transgenerational scripts are introjected into the personality through Parent ego states, which means someone may be unconsciously thinking, feeling, and acting in a way that is similar to one or more of his ancestors. This causes the person to project in current relationships an enactment of an unresolved issue from the ancestral figure with whom he is identified.

Usually the need for transgenerational script work becomes clear after several psychotherapy sessions, although occasionally it can be the initial motive for a consultation. When doing Transactional Analysis psychotherapy, it may be important, if not essential, to carry out some preparatory steps prior to working with Parent ego states, unless a particularly destructive introjection is involved that might put the client's safety at risk (Clarkson, 1992, p. 100). Therefore, when applying transgenerational treatment, I recommend simultaneously going through the steps described in the following paragraphs here so that the client can recognise his Child ego state needs and, at the same time, develop a robust Adult ego state that will allow the person to widen his consciousness to develop more of his own resources.

As experienced clinicians know, the first step in any therapy is to foster a therapeutic alliance that allows a relationship of trust to develop between the client and the therapist. I use integrative psychotherapy principles to establish such a relationship, which goes beyond empathy to facilitate clients' contact with their thoughts, emotions, and relational needs (Erskine, Moursund, & Trautmann, 1999). Later, a verbal contract is made. This is a bilateral agreement to focus, as the first treatment objective, on the initial motive for consultation while simultaneously determining session frequency and resolving any questions about how the therapy will be managed. Sessions generally occur weekly, and depending on clients' needs and interests, I may also invite them to participate in one or more workshops on transgenerational scripts.

The following steps are carried out during the weekly sessions and in some ways in the workshops. They do not need to be followed in a set sequence and should be adapted to suit the client's needs. They can also be used as a sound and safe foundation for ongoing, in-depth therapy beyond transgenerational psychotherapy.

Decontamination of the Adult ego state

If considered necessary, some or all eight of the therapeutic operations recommended by Berne (1966) are applied: interrogation, specification, confrontation, explanation, illustration, confirmation, interpretation, and crystallisation.

Deconfusion of the Child ego state

I use the model described by Hargaden and Sills (2001), which assumes that a lack of development of the client's early self emerges during the transference within a client-therapist relationship. This includes types of attachment, ruptures, and fragmentations during various phases of treatment and is why the transference relationship is used as the main vehicle for decontamination.

The intrapsychic relationship

Clients become aware of the internal dialogues between their Parent and Child ego states and recognise in them the *original introjected transaction*. This is the type of relationship they used to have with their parents in childhood and that they now project onto their relationships with other people. Two-chair work allows these internal dialogues to become explicit so that clients can stop persecuting themselves and learn to establish clear limits. This is necessary to stop them from abusing both themselves and others.

The development of an internal nurturing Parent

Self-reparenting techniques (M. James, 1981) are used to facilitate the creation of a new Parent ego state that is more suited to clients' needs and that can look after and protect them while they learn how to be in charge of themselves (Noriega, 1995).

Emotional development

I recognise and accept everything clients think and feel in such a way that they learn to understand the language of their feelings and emotions and, at the same time, how to express them (or not) in a safe and effective way. This fosters affective expression and open communication.

Redecision therapy

By using the seven components of redecision therapy (McNeel, 1977), clients learn to recognise their early decisions as adaptation methods or survival conclusions taken on in childhood to help them face adverse situations. At the same time, they discover other possible options that better serve them in their current lives so that they can ultimately leave behind their life scripts (Goulding & Goulding, 1979).

As preparation for transgenerational work, at some point during the therapy I suggest that clients write a biography of their family over the last three generations. This can be a useful and interesting, although sometimes difficult, exercise in family research and personal reflection. It allows them to discover the influence of their ancestors more broadly in their lives. It is not the same to know something about one's family secrets and sensitive situations as it is to take a step back and see it written down on paper. At the same time, the written account gives me a better understanding of the relationships between the client and his family members as well as the traumatic and painful issues that need to be resolved in that particular family.

Mechanisms of script transmission

The processes just described allow us to do important groundwork before delving into transgenerational script dynamics, which usually occur through unconscious communication (Novellino, 1990) by means of the following four mechanisms:

- *Ulterior transactions* (Berne, 1961, 1964) are the non-verbal communications transmitted by tone of voice, gestures, facial expressions, and body attitudes as well as some words that contain implicit hidden messages.
- *Psychological games* (Berne, 1964) contain an unconscious wish to understand or give meaning to unresolved issues from the past, even when the social transaction appears to be something different. They usually have a negative payoff, which reinforces the early decisions as the basis for the script system (Erskine & Moursund, 1988).
- *Transference psychodynamics* (Moiso, 1985) contain the emotional tone and relational patterns that characterised the client's early relationship with one or both parents. This triggers a countertransference reaction in the therapist based on the dyad from the symbiotic *original introjected transaction*. This dynamic has also been described as *symbiotic structures* (Joines, 1977) and *relational units* (Little, 2013).
- *Projective identification* seems to be the main way scripts are transmitted from parents to children. This defence mechanism was described

by Klein (1957). Laplanche and Pontalis (1968) defined it as "un mécanisme qui se traduit par des fantasmes, óu le subject introduit sa propre personne en totalité ou en partie à l'intérieur de l'object pour lui nuire, le posséder et le contróler" (a mechanism revealed in phantasies in which the subject inserts his self, in whole or in part, into the object in order to harm, possess, or control it) (p. 189). By this means, the person projects onto someone else his unpleasant and unacceptable feelings, thus provoking in the other an experience of those same feelings. As a result, the former can blame or devalue the latter.

These mechanisms work in a systemic way, that is, they do not occur independently because all four are related. In Transactional Analysis terms, ulterior transactions give rise to psychological games, these games manifest themselves in transference psychodynamics, and projective identification surrounds them all through emotional "contamination", which also reinforces the ulterior transactions. In the client-therapist relationship, these four mechanisms manifest themselves just as they do in their other relationships. That is why they can be used during the enactment for either diagnosis or treatment, with the aim of moving from unconscious to conscious communication.

Berne (1961) described the *finer structures of the personality* as subdivisions of the ego states. Using case studies, he illustrated how the Parent ego state contains the introjected personalities of parents, grandparents, and great-grandparents. As a result, individuals may be enacting the kinds of relationships that their parental figures used to have. My interpretation is that this is the way clients unconsciously use the therapeutic relationship to communicate an ancestor's unresolved emotional or relational conflict. They are seeking the therapist's help to free themselves from the generational chain that has been damaging their current relationships.

Mucci (2013) referred to this phenomenon when explaining her work with traumatised patients, particularly citing Kogan (p. 175) in defining "enactment" as the compulsion of Holocaust survivors' offspring to recreate their parents' experiences in their own lives through concrete acts. However, not all the experiences from our ancestors are introjected as defensive ego states dissociated from consciousness. Little (2013) explained the nature of the relationship by making a distinction between tolerable and intolerable experiences that have been internalised as relational schemas. Those that consist of the tolerable, good-enough experiences in "nonconscious" implicit memory are non-structuring internalisations and an aspect of the integrating Adult ego state. These represent autonomous functioning in the here-and-now and an open system with the ability to assimilate and accommodate (p. 107).

The term *nonconscious* was used by Summers (2011) to describe tolerable, non-defensive experiences that do not reside in ego state relational units but nevertheless influence our behaviour.

Therefore, although we internalise both tolerable and intolerable experiences, it is the latter that we introject and that stay in the dyad of our Child-Parent ego states as a symbiotic *introjected transaction*.

Therapeutic mourning

Working with grief and its various stages is relevant in transgenerational psychotherapy because clients need to leave behind their fantasies of revenge or superiority and abandon their judgemental attitudes (e.g., excluding a family member for bad behaviour). The exclusion of an ancestor damages the family system because everyone has a right to belong to the family, and excluding someone leaves issues unresolved in the family history. Such issues may then be taken up by a young member of the family, generally someone who arrived later. Thus an episcript is created, like a hot-potato game that will continue passing through subsequent generations (English, 1969, 1998). As Mucci (2013) wrote, "Trauma itself is defined by the destruction of that bond, and recovery has to come from that place of reconstruction of the internal link between self and other" (p. 196).

Forgiveness and liberation from script

For clients, forgiveness represents relinquishing the illusion that other people change. It will also help them to heal if they can forgive themselves for any error they may have committed and recognise that their true power lies in repairing the relationship they have with themselves and, as far as possible, the damage they have caused to other people.

It is important to note that forgiveness is not the same as forgetting and should not be forced or imposed on the individual by religious beliefs. Forgiveness arises naturally once individuals are able to broaden their consciousness and understand the motives that caused their ancestors to commit the mistakes that have damaged their descendants.

> Forgiveness happens spontaneously, and it alters the relationship between the victim and the wrongdoer. But if, in a sense, forgiveness when achieved "just happens," in order for forgiveness to come about, all the previous steps mentioned in the clinical work with those traumatized … must be accomplished. Working through mourning, anger, and the internal representation of the perpetrator are the fundamental steps. (V. Jankélévitch as cited in Mucci, 2013, p. 207)

Physis and spiritual development

Physis was defined by Berne (1957) as "the force of nature, which eternally strives to make things grow and to make growing things more perfect" (p. 89). Clarkson (1992) wrote that "Physis is Berne's unique addition to the other two great unconscious forces (Eros and Thanatos) in human life, and he sees all three as the background of psychological life" (p. 11). Physis is the source of resilience, which allows us to overcome adversity. It is the strength of the human spirit, which goes beyond religious beliefs. Berne (1972) illustrated this force by using a vertical arrow rising from the Child ego state up through the Adult and the Parent ego states, thus representing physis as a force for the liberation from script.

In their contribution to Transactional Analysis from a spiritual perspective, M. James and J. James (1991) described the "inner core" as a strength similar to physis, one that houses the spiritual self and that can be expressed by the ego states and the body through seven urges: to live, to be free, to understand, to enjoy, to create, to connect, and to transcend. Trautmann (2003) recognised the spiritual dimension of each person as an important part of the therapeutic process for finding words to express this dimension; in exploring the meaning of this experience with possible historical, introjected, and/or traumatic origins; and as valuable in the search for deeper meaning and mindfulness. Frankl (1962), a Viennese psychiatrist who survived Nazi concentration camps, coined the phrase "the defiant power of the human spirit" to describe the tenacious determination that we can call on in dealing with life's challenges.

CHANGING TRANSGENERATIONAL SCRIPTS   127

I recommend to my clients the practice of mindfulness through Vipassana meditation (Goldstein & Kornfield, 1987), which is based on the principles and techniques of the Theravada Buddhist tradition. These are simple, but it is only possible to obtain the benefits through daily practice. This method facilitates the development of the Adult ego state because it teaches how to maintain contact with the body and sensations in the here-and-now. It also fosters significant changes in brain function in those who practise it (Siegel, 2007). Hatha yoga is also recommended as a method of meditation through body movement.

Thus, the strength of physis drives us to overcome adversity. However, lack of awareness about transgenerational scripts can produce an impasse between this strength and family script injunctions that represent the entangled knots on our genealogy tree. These injunctions may include Don't Exist, Don't Be You, Don't Be Close, Don't Think, Don't Feel, Don't Grow, Don't Be a Child, Don't Do, Don't Belong, Don't Be Well and Sane, Don't Be Important, and Don't Be Successful (Goulding & Goulding, 1979).

In transgenerational script workshops, after identifying their injunctions, clients may then look for options for change through corresponding permissions for breaking free of transgenerational scripts. The following are examples of permissions created by clients for themselves: I'm willing to live unconditionally, I can remodel and reconstruct my life, I can be myself and accept the sex I am, I can be close and trust the people with whom I choose to share love and intimacy, I can grow and accept myself as a mature person, I can enjoy my life and find a balance between work and fun, I may think clearly and make my own decisions, I can feel and share my feelings, I can make things happen, I can be healthy and well, I can belong to my family as well as to groups and relationships, I can be successful, I am important, I can surpass my ancestors, and I can change.

Transgenerational scripts workshop

The objective of the workshop is for participants to discover painful topics or traumatic situations in their families of origin that are repeating themselves in current relationships. Having done so allows them to then make necessary changes to improve their quality of life and contribute to a healing of their family system. Workshop participants are usually my clients and sometimes other people who are interested in the subject. With the latter, I do a preliminary interview because the workshop is not recommended for psychotic individuals or those suffering from an acute personality disorder. In addition, participation requires a confidentiality agreement.

For clients in individual psychotherapy, the group work can provide an opportunity to identify themselves with other participants because their experiences can have an effect on others. This dynamic facilitates recognising unresolved issues that clients may not yet have taken into consideration and stimulates them to express their emotions and repressed feelings. At the same time, support and feedback from other group members may motivate them to establish intimate relationships of acceptance and respect for other people.

The workshop is usually run over four to five days including a weekend, although the dates and times vary. I usually begin by asking group members to introduce themselves in a way that includes their family genealogy. Participants take two minutes to close their eyes and visualise their genealogical trees, after which they stand and proudly introduce themselves by saying their first name, the names of their parents, and the names of their maternal and paternal grandparents. I start by introducing myself in the following way: "My name is Gloria, I´m the daughter of Roberto and Isabel, granddaughter of Iñigo and Maria on my father's side and Roberto and Virginia on my mother's side." This exercise is usually exciting because, from the beginning, it allows us to sensitise ourselves to working with the psychic presence of our ancestors.

Participants then answer a brief questionnaire that allows them to recognise issues that have been repeated in their families over several generations. After that, I teach the following concepts interspersed with group dynamics and therapy work with clients who request it:

- How transgenerational scripts are encoded in ego states
- The introjected Parent–Child transaction
- The difference between individual, family, and cultural scripts
- That people belong to genealogical trees
- Script injunctions (Goulding & Goulding, 1979) as the knots that block the healthy energy flow in the genealogical tree
- Different ways that scripts are passed from grandparents to succeeding generations (Berne, 1972)
- What kind of life did your grandparents live? (J. James, 1984)

- Family secrets, an *unknown knowledge* (Noriega, 2010)
- Enactment of the family script through the mechanisms of script transmission (Noriega, 2004, 2009, 2010)
- The episcript (English,1969, 1998)
- The script system (Erskine & Moursund, 1998; Erskine& Zalcman, 1979)
- Therapeutic mourning (F. Clark, 2001; Erskine, 2014a)
- The dynamics of forgiveness
- The ethical concepts of justice and fairness in the family system (Boszormenyi-Nagy & Spark, 1973)
- Resilience and the force of physis (Siebert, 2007)
- Permissions for breaking free of the transgenerational chain (Allen & Allen, 1972)
- The integrating Adult ego state (Tudor, 2003)
- Recognition of the constructive legacy of our ancestors
- The Transactional Analysis practice of mindfulness (Verney, 2009; Žvelc, Černetič, & Košak, 2011).

In the workshop, participants also learn that personal growth is not linear but works like a spiral. That is why they may experience partial, not total, regressions that can be used to broaden the development of their consciousness and their Adult ego state.

Following here is a case study that includes a brief segment of an intervention carried out in a transgenerational script workshop after two months of weekly psychotherapy. The intervention described was useful to both the client and other members of the group and demonstrates the power that can be released by integrating individual and group therapies.

Paula's case

Paula arrived at her first interview with severe physical and emotional trauma following an episode of domestic violence in which her husband brutally beat her before throwing her out of the house. Paula's husband constantly insulted her by boasting about his multiple acts of infidelity. The violence occurred when she told him she wanted a divorce. He then verbally abused her by insulting, taunting, and humiliating her. Paula responded by crying, which made him even more enraged. He did not stop beating her until she fell down unconscious.

However, despite the gravity of the situation, Paula felt guilty because she thought she had caused the problem. She did not understand that psychological and verbal violence are also forms of abuse. She was confused and would say she no longer wanted a divorce and that she had asked her husband for forgiveness. She now wanted me to help her understand her husband and herself (in that order) because she felt like she was going crazy. During that first session, she also told me her parents frequently argued and attacked each other about infidelity. We agreed to continue with weekly psychotherapy sessions and that she would eventually attend a transgenerational scripts workshop. As our first therapy contract, we settled on clarifying her thoughts and emotions so that she could make good decisions.

Paula was twenty-eight years old and worked as a door-to-door cosmetics salesperson. She had interrupted her university studies to marry and was the mother of a four-year-old child, the product of her marriage. She frequently mistreated her son by screaming and hitting him. She said she did not have any patience and easily became frustrated with him.

During subsequent sessions, I learned that Paula had a younger brother who had received a privileged education from her parents because he was male. Beginning when they were children, her brother insulted and hit Paula constantly, and now as a young man, he continued to do the same thing with his girlfriends. Paula had always felt inferior for being a female. Her parents had wanted her to be a boy because they considered men to be the strong ones in a family and that women were only to serve them.

Paula's parents were also victims of severe physical abuse by their parents, with marked discrimination against women. As an adult, her father became addicted to alcohol and her mother became acutely depressed, which caused her to spend a large part of her time in bed away from her two children. When he was drunk, Paula's father harmed his wife, and when Paula intervened, he would also beat her. As a first result of therapy, Paula stopped hitting her son when she realised she was doing the same thing to him that her father and brother had done to her. However, radical change did not occur until she could clearly see that acts of domestic violence had occurred in her family over three generations.

During the workshop, Paula was interested to learn that suffering abuse, whether as a direct victim or as a witness to it between other family members, tends to remain introjected in the ego states of children. It then appears later in their adult lives in different ways: they let themselves be abused, they abuse others, or they abuse themselves. On learning this, Paula asked to work on these forms of abuse by establishing the following contract: "To stop the abuse I continue to do to myself and in my relationships."

The following paragraphs offer excerpts of the intervention carried out with Paula as we worked in her Parent ego state with her father's and paternal grandfather's introjections (P = Paula, Th = therapist, J = José; Paula's father as portrayed by Paula).

P: I feel scared and ashamed about what I am going to say (she cries and hangs her head.) When I was a girl, my mother yelled at me when I made a mistake on my homework. I think she was easily frustrated because she was stressed by fights with my father. I am now doing the same thing with my son. I no longer hit him, but I do yell at him in a nasty way. I know this is not OK, but I cannot control it.

TH: What are you thinking?

P: That I am stupid because even though I know what I have to do, I end up doing the complete opposite. It's the same with my husband.

TH: What do you mean?

P: My husband is always humiliating me by saying he is with other women and that I'm not worth anything as a woman. When I told him I wanted a divorce, he got very angry and hit me. I don't think I should have said what I was thinking.

TH: Why do you think that?

P: Because my parents also argued and fought all the time. I would feel terrified when my father came home drunk and hit my mother, and although my husband doesn't drink as much, I think I am provoking him.

TH: You decided to get divorced and stop having a relationship like your parents. That isn't provocation; it's putting a stop to the violence in your marriage.

P: Yes, I know, but now I am confused because to prevent my husband from being angry, I changed my attitude, and now I behave in a submissive way, just like my mother did. That hasn't worked either because my husband continues to insult and humiliate me.

TH: It seems that, like your mother, you also chose a violent husband, and now your marriage is similar to that of your parents.

P: Yes, but he doesn't want therapy, and I feel confused. Before I even realise it, I am fighting with my husband again, and it's my son who suffers the consequences. Later I regret it and apologise to the kid. I feel like I am going crazy because instead of doing what I know is right, I end up doing the same stupid things as always. Please help me.

TH: Well, what would you think about doing a role play in which you pretend to be one of your parents and I interview you?

P: OK, I like the idea.

TH: Good. We're going to invite one of your parents to this workshop (pointing to a second chair). I'm going to interview this person and you will listen.

P: (Changes chairs) I am a little scared.

TH: I understand. This is something new for you. Everything will be fine. Close your eyes for a moment and take on the personality of one of your parents. You're going to act and talk like that person. When you open your eyes, tell me what your name is and who you are.

P: (Opening her eyes) My name is José, and I am Paula's father.

TH: Nice to meet you José, and welcome to the workshop. Now tell me, what is your daughter Paula like?

J: Paula is a very rebellious young girl, and I am concerned because she has been drinking too much lately and also has lots of problems with her husband. I know it's partly my fault because I also drink a lot, but she is a woman and is foolish like all women. She insisted on marrying a boy who wasn't right for her, and, of course, now they spend their time fighting.

TH: José, what was your relationship with your parents like?

J: My dad was a drunk who beat my mother all the time. I defended her and so he would also beat me. I decided to leave home at fourteen and not ever go back. My life has been difficult and lonely. I hate my parents because they hurt me a lot (cries).

TH: I see. It would seem that the abuse you suffered as a child has affected you.

J: Yes, because I have also been violent with my wife, but she exasperates me because she is as stupid as my mother. For example, she is always threatening to divorce me and then doesn't do anything, so we fight all the time.

TH: Would you have preferred to get divorced?

J: I think so because we don't get on well. Well, I would have liked to be different from my father and not be a drunk who abuses and despises his wife.

TH: Does your story echo what Paula is going through?

J: I think so because my little grandson is also suffering as a result of his parents' arguments. It would seem as if my family was plagued by my father's curse.

TH: What do you mean?

J: When I left home, my father cursed me for being an ungrateful son. He told me, "You will pay with your children for what you're doing to your mother and me" (crying with despair).

TH: (Pointing to a third chair) José, put your father in that chair and tell him what you are feeling now.

J: Dad, I have been lonely and am frightened because my family is doing the same as you did. Alcohol has been my sole consolation, and my daughter Paula is also drinking a lot. I think she feels desperate like me.

TH: José, would you like to return your father's macho beliefs to him?

J: Yes. Dad, I no longer have to obey your curse by treating my wife and daughter badly. Disrespect and violence toward women is not going to continue in my family. Enough is enough. My wife and daughter deserve respect, and so do I.

TH: Repeat louder "Enough is enough."

J: Enough is enough!!! (shouting).

TH: José, how do you feel now?

J: Much better, I feel liberated.

TH: Would you like to extend this new decision to the women beyond your family?

J: Yes, of course! Actually, women as well as men have a value as human beings and deserve respect.

TH: Very good. It has been a pleasure to meet you, and thank you for letting me be witness to your new decision to respect yourself and women (I shake his hand to signal farewell).

TH: (Gesturing to Paula to return to her first chair) You are Paula again. How do you feel?

P: As if someone had taken a huge weight off my shoulders. I never imagined that deep down my father could be so vulnerable.

TH: Did you realise anything else?

P: Yes, that I was drinking like my dad because I did not want to be submissive and depressed like my mother. However, I did not realise that at times I am also like my mother, like when I shout at my son. Or lately with my husband, asking forgiveness for something I haven't done.

TH: OK, and now that you have realised that, what can you tell me about your own mistreatment?

P: Actually, I now realise that even though my father controls himself more, I still treat myself as he used to when I was small. At times I have felt as if I can hear his shouts in my head.

TH: What do those shouts in your head say?

P: You're stupid! You have to understand men because women are there to serve men!

TH: You can reply to him if you want.

P: What you are saying no longer makes sense. I deserve respect. I like being a woman, and what's more, I am learning to be a good mother.

TH: Do you want to tell him anything else?

P: Yes, that I reassert my decision to stop drinking and to permanently end the mistreatment of my son and myself and to not let anyone else mistreat me.

Reflections on the transgenerational work with Paula

Paula is among many people who benefit from transgenerational psychotherapy because they come to recognise that they are repeating a life script that does not belong to them. The transgenerational scripts workshop allows specific issues to be addressed that have not been dealt with in individual therapy sessions. In Paula's case, she was able to work on the domestic violence that crossed four generations in her family: her grandfather, her father, Paula herself, and her son. The intervention as described in the session transcript occurred with Paula's Parent ego states and involved working through the introjections of her father and grandfather. This work also allowed her to recognise the origin of her ambivalent behaviour and to deconfuse her Child ego state by realising that she had made the early decision in her childhood to not be like her mother and instead was acting like her father. However, when she was terrified after episodes of violence with her husband, she ended up adopting a submissive attitude that was similar to the one her mother had taken.

The technique used in the intervention with Paula was the Parent interview (McNeel, 1976), which integrates Transactional Analysis with Gestalt therapy and consists of inviting the client to pretend to be one of her parents. The therapist then interviews that parent as if he or she were really present. This helps the client to understand her parental figure in greater depth and to awaken feelings of compassion that may then allow the client to forgive the parent.

I usually add one or more chairs to work on a transgenerational level so that clients can also establish a dialogue with their grandparents, as well as with other members of their family, if necessary. I also tend to add some psychodrama techniques such as the role play Paula did. With her I also used the parent resolution process in the parent's Child ego state (Dashiell, 1978), thereby giving therapy to Paula's father as if he were really present.

In Paula's case, enactment of a family drama over three generations could also be seen through the mechanisms of script transmission (Noriega, 2010). These included ulterior transactions through verbal and non-verbal messages of disqualification towards women in the family system, psychological games in which Paula was drawn into repeating a family drama with episodes of violence with her husband, transference psychodynamics that caused Paula to interact with her husband in a way that was similar to how her mother used to interact with Paula's father, and projective identification contaminated with domestic violence as expressed in letting herself be abused, abusing herself, and abusing others (her son).

The feeling of rejection that Paula had felt since birth because she is female marked her life with two injunctions: Don't Exist and Don't Be You. The first is a lethal message of self-destruction that surfaced when she was young as feelings of depression, two suicide attempts, and exposing herself to situations that put her life at risk. According to her family history, apparently both her parents and grandparents had also received the same injunction and suffered from depression. The second injunction surfaced in Paula's life through an early decision: "It is better to be like a man because women are worthless." This was also reinforced through her relationship with her husband because to justify his infidelity, he humiliated her as a woman.

Another injunction Paula accepted was Don't Think. This was expressed through her states of confusion and feeling that she was going crazy when, in reality, what she was doing was rejecting the consciousness of her Adult ego state, thereby confirming the family belief that all women are stupid. As a teenager Paula was diagnosed with attention deficit disorder with hyperactivity, and she had been on medication ever since. However, once she started to think clearly, her distractions and agitated state began to dissipate, and she is no longer taking any medication. Paula is now in the process of obtaining a divorce, has resumed her university studies, has a stable job, and has stopped mistreating her son. She is also not abusing alcohol any more.

Paula's treatment diagnosis was dysthymia, which manifested as a creeping depression that had begun in early childhood and never been treated, as well as an anxiety disorder as a result of her confusion with her emotions (American Psychiatric Association, 1994, pp. 352–357, 443). However, Paula is actually an intelligent, capable woman, and thanks, in part, to the transgenerational script work, she is now in control. It has been a year since she attended the transgenerational script workshop, and she has continued with her weekly psychotherapy. She does well in her studies and feels valued in her job. She thinks clearly and has realised that the compulsion to repeat the family drama was her way of unconsciously denouncing the family script and, at the same time, claiming her identity as a woman.

As seen in Paula's case, in the transgenerational script workshop, psycho-education facilitates the decontamination of the participants' Adult ego state and the deconfusion of the Child ego state. As clients expand their consciousness, the group dynamic and therapy interventions enable them to understand and express their emotions. Clearly this was the case for Paula.

Conclusion

Unconsciously, we may be repeating in our current relationships the unresolved conflicts of our ancestors, even if we never knew them. These may be linked to issues such as alienation, illegitimacy, addiction, violence, infidelity, depression, and so on. In many cases, people hold family secrets that have run underneath the daily lives of several generations.

Combining individual and workshop group therapy can be a powerful resource by which clients and group members can broaden their consciousness about important issues in their transgenerational life scripts. We in the current generation are the owners of the link that can be opened to change by repairing the transgenerational chain that may be stopping our own development and the emotional fluency for our descendants. As we become conscious of this hitherto unknown knowledge, we can allow ourselves to modify our destructive family scripts and, at the same time, preserve and reinforce the constructive legacy of our ancestors.

CHAPTER SEVEN

Inference, re-experiencing, and regression: psychotherapy of Child ego states

Richard G. Erskine & Amaia Mauriz-Etxabe

In his chapter on "Regression Analysis" Eric Berne (1961) stated that his therapeutic goal was to create "the optimal situation for the readjustment and reintegration of the total personality". He wrote about the importance of the "phenomenological" experience of the Child ego states becoming "vividly revived in the mind of the patient". Such vivid emotional experience is often accompanied by intense emotional expression, characteristic of a young child. He equated these vivid emotional experiences with "gut-memories" or "abreaction" (pp. 224–231).

Although Berne wrote about the significance of doing age regression therapy, he did not identify the knowledge, skills, or quality of relationship necessary in facilitating a therapeutically supportive age regression. Berne wrote about his experimentation with clients' "role-playing" of their childhood experiences. His descriptions of his clinical practice seem to place the therapeutic emphasis on an "inferential" understanding of the child's experience (1961). However, his chapter has remained an inspiration to us and has provided some of the theoretical basis for including various forms of Child ego state therapy and therapeutic age regression in our repertoire of psychotherapeutic skills (Erskine & Moursund, 1988; Moursund & Erskine, 2003).

Central in the practice of Transactional Analysis in contemporary psychotherapy is the resolution of clients' Child ego state conflicts and issues of life script (Berne, 1972; Erskine, 2010a; Hargarden & Sills, 2002; Sills & Hargaden, 2003). It is in early childhood that the fixated relational patterns that constitute the core of a life script are established through self-stabilising physiological survival reactions, implicit experiential conclusions, introjections, and explicit decisions (Erskine, 2010b). To achieve an in-depth psychotherapy we psychotherapists must help our clients to resolve the childhood conflicts, neglects, and traumas that have become fixated in their lives. This requires that we think about our clients from a developmental perspective with a sensitivity to the child's physical and relational needs, the possible relational conflicts and losses that the child may have lived, the quality of influence provided by caregivers, and how the child managed to stabilise, regulate, and enhance his or her self.

Many therapists have had clients who claim to have no memory of childhood experiences before the age of eight or ten, yet those same clients have intense longings or repulsions, patterns of avoidance or compulsion, and tumultuous relationships (Wallin, 2007). These emotional and relational patterns may be the expression of memory— memory that is nonconscious because these experiences have not been transposed to thought, concept, language, or narrative (Bucci, 2001; Kihlstrom, 1984; Lyons-Ruth, 2000; Schacter & Buckner, 1998). If significant experiences are not acknowledged within the family, when there is no meaningful conversation, it may be impossible to put needs, emotional sensations, or relational conflicts into social language or even to think about them (Cozolino, 2006). Likewise, when important interpersonal experiences never occurred, such as patience, gentleness, kindness, or respect, the client will have no memory of those events or that period of time; there will be a vacuum of experience (Erskine, 2008). The client may say "I don't know" when asked about important events within the family. Instead these implicit procedural memories are expressed through physiological and emotional reactions, re-enactments in client-therapist relationship, the transferences of everyday life (Freud, 1912b), or through a vague sense of emptiness.

Remembering, reliving, and re-experiencing

In psychotherapy many of the therapeutic transactions involve facilitating clients with *remembering* their life's experiences, making sense of those remembered experiences, and realising how early reactions and conclusions influence choices made in their current life. When clients tell the various stories of their life they are drawing on explicit memory and together with the psychotherapist they create a consistent and comprehensive narrative that gives meaning and significance to their life experiences (Berne, 1972).

Reliving is different from remembering. In reliving, the painful experiences and conflicts of the past are repeated, the old mechanisms of self-stabilisation and compensation are reinforced, the survival reactions and script conclusions are not only confirmed, they are often intensified—the person may become re-traumatised. Reinforcement of old self-protective and self-stabilising patterns often takes place when a person relives a frightening or painful experience while watching a film or is in the midst of a family dispute. Reliving may occur when a person tells an emotionally charged story and loses interpersonal contact while talking. In reaction to the absence of interpersonal contact he may then escalate the intensity of affect and bodily sensations, thereby reinforcing early physiological survival reactions or script conclusions. Reliving may also occur when the psychotherapist fails to assess the significance of what is being transferentially communicated and the client therefore relies on old script beliefs to manage the situation (Erskine, 1991; Novellino, 1985; also see Ray Little's chapter in this book). When reliving occurs via the transference it is the psychotherapist's task "to take on the transference relationship" (Trautmann, 1985), to actively engage in the client's transferential enactments in such a way that the contactfulness of therapeutic relationship provides a new experience, one that is clarifying and reparative.

Reliving is the phenomenological description of what Freud (1920g) called the repetition compulsion—a person's acting out what he cannot form as explicit memory and therefore cannot put into language. The psychological functions of such reliving are twofold. The first homeostatic function serves to maintain a sense of stability, continuity, and predictability; the second function involves an assertion of psychic energy that is invested in health and vitality, the hope for a reparative experience, and the satisfaction of relational needs. This is the urge to heal, repair, and grow, similar to what Berne called *physis* (Berne, 1972; Cornell, 2010). These diverse functions are in dynamic balance—the internal dilemma is to remain the same or to grow and change (Beisser, 1971).

Re-experiencing is almost reliving; the same affects, body reactions, and internal conflicts emerge; the archaic means of compensating and self-stabilisation are reactivated. But, before the point of reinforcement, the psychotherapist and client co-create a different outcome—an outcome that alters the old patterns of feelings and relationships. An effective therapeutic re-experiencing is "safe but not too safe" (Bromberg, 2006), a working of the *therapeutic edge*. It arouses the client to a state of creative emergency (Perls, Hefferline, & Goodman, 1951) while taking into account the client's "window of tolerance" (Siegel, 1999, p. 253) and the intensity of affect and physiological reaction that the client can process without relying on old patterns of self-stabilisation and coping. A secure therapeutic relationship allows the client to almost relive the old neglects and traumas while finding that point of arousal that empowers the client to energise new physical actions. Instead of reactivating archaic patterns of self-protection, therapeutic re-experiencing enables clients to relinquish physiological retroflections, express unexpressed emotions, and make life-changing decisions.

Facilitating memory

One of the prime tasks of doing psychotherapy with their Child ego states is to help our clients translate their physical and affect sensations into language, to gain an awareness and understanding of significant childhood survival reactions and implicit conclusions, and to put their relational patterns into a historical context. A relational perspective that includes attunement to the client's affect, rhythm, and level of development is essential in building an effective therapeutic relationship intended to deconfuse Child ego states and decontaminate the Adult ego. Through phenomenological inquiry the attuned psychotherapist helps to provide a dialogical language that allows internal experience to be formed, expressed, and have meaning. Phenomenological and historical inquiry provides an opportunity for the client's affectively and physiologically charged memories to be put into dialogue with an interested and involved person, perhaps for the very first time.

Once we have established a consistently secure therapeutic relationship and have both explored and resolved relational conflicts as they emerge in various transferences, we often turn our attention to helping the client discover the natural qualities and personal resources that he had as a child, the style of family relationships in which he lived, and the conclusions and decisions that he may have made.

Some examples of the nature of the historical inquiry that we use in facilitating memory with clients who are unable to recall early experiences are:

- Who was there to talk to you about your concerns or joys when you returned from school (or before school)?
- What was the nature of the conversations with your family during dinner?
- What was bath time like when you were three or four years old? Who was there with you? Were you allowed to play in the water? How did you experience the rhythm and touch of the person who dried you?
- What was your bedtime routine when you were young? Who tucked you in and what did you talk about?
- When you were little and wanted someone to play with you on the floor, what would your mother (or father) do?
- When you were old enough to eat some solid food, how did your mother feed you? Was she tolerant of your tastes and behaviour?
- Imagine what it was like to be nursed by your mother.
- Imagine what it was like to have your nappies changed.

Each of these historical inquiries is followed by several phenomenological inquiries such as: What did you feel? How did you respond? Does that have any meaning for you? What is happening in your body while you are telling me that story?

Our historical inquiry is constantly working backward in time. We often begin with questions about the time of adolescence, then we go on to the school years. We interweave our historical inquiry with a number of phenomenological inquiries and selected inquiries about how the client managed each situation. By the time we are asking about preschool years most clients will answer with "I don't remember". We ask them to imagine their experience, to make an impressionistic story since they know the personality of the significant others and how they may have responded in those situations.

We are always working with sensations, fragments of images, impressions, and family stories, what we call "therapeutic inference". It is as though we are co-creating a narrative collage of the client's life story. Each response to the historical and phenomenological inquiries provides one more element to the collage. It may not be an exact photographic representation of what transpired in the client's childhood but our collage represents the client's feelings and impressions.

One client who suffered from a lack of energy and a sense of being melancholy could not even imagine how his mother treated him as a child. He went mentally blank with each historical inquiry. He could only describe how he kept his distance from both of his parents. When his son was born he took the baby to visit his mother. She was uninterested in her grandson and criticised the young parents for holding the baby and not letting him cry himself to sleep. This incident helped my client to realise that his absence of memory was an indication that important relational experiences had never occurred in his family and that his lack of energy and perpetual sadness was a reaction to the absence of sensitivity and affection in his original family.

Each of the historical inquiries listed above can take a whole session or more to investigate the body sensations, affect, reactions, and various associations that occur in the process of answering. Although it takes a half minute to read this partial list of inquiries, it may take a half year or more to investigate the stories that these questions elicit.

Talk is not therapeutic enough

Maria's doctor telephoned and said, "Amaia, please see this woman, we don't know what more to do with her. She has frequent bladder infections and is constantly worrying about contracting all sorts of illnesses. Her distress goes beyond the medical care we can provide her." When Maria arrived in my office she complained about having seen several medical specialists and of having had a "hundred blood analyses". She was angry that her own doctor had sent her to see a psychotherapist.

In her initial session she was certain that a psychotherapist could not help her with her repetitive infections and her other health concerns. She continued to talk about her bladder infections and "strange sensations" in her pelvic area. She was afraid of contracting gynaecological cancer. When asked to describe her childhood she asserted, "I had a normal life, with some incidents that I am aware of, but those don't have any influence on me. I overcame the difficult parts of my childhood." I wondered what had happened in Maria's early life and how it may have had an impact on and in her body (Erskine, 2014b).

It was too soon to make such a historical inquiry since she was intent on talking about both her current ailments and worries about future illnesses.

In this intake session I also asked about her marriage. She gave a big sigh, accompanied by a sad expression, when she told me that he was a "good man that gives me a good enough life". Her answer stimulated my wondering if she enjoyed her marriage or if she felt trapped. She went on to say that they had three children and that her husband had a lot of work in the family's restaurant. She was disappointed that he did not have time to share with her, nor with the children. As I listened quietly she told me that he is a '"very well organised man", and that he had a strong control of the family money. She was not able to buy clothes or anything without his permission. He was not willing to pay for her psychotherapy.

In this first session, and in several following sessions, there were many discrepancies in her narrative and several contradictions between the content of what she said and her facial expressions. I made no confrontations; my intent was to build a secure therapeutic relationship where Maria could find the support and trust necessary to reveal her story—a kind of therapeutic relationship where she could experience full acceptance of her uniqueness and where the therapeutic protection and permission (Crossman, 1966) would create the bridge that could allow her to establish the link between her current symptoms and any past event related to them.

After the first two months of therapy I sought supervision to decide if it was time to explore her obsessions about illness or to try to "decipher the footprints" of possible trauma that may be buried under layers of physical symptoms—symptoms that may express implicit, non-symbolic memory of repeated neglect or abuse and simultaneously distract from feeling the overwhelming emotions related to any possible trauma. As a result of the supervision, I decided to focus my phenomenological inquiry on her affect and body sensations instead of working cognitively, her preferred way of working (Erskine, 2014b).

She reported that at home she would spontaneously become "emotionally swamped" and "tense all over". As usual, she wanted to understand why. I suspected that she was reliving a sub-symbolic physiological memory and that she was being re-traumatised with each episode. I explained the difference between a cognitively focused therapy and a therapy that also included attending to both the body and emotions. We made some clear contracts about:

- Working with emotions and body sensations
- How she could maintain a sense of free choice
- Protection from being emotionally overwhelmed, and
- The therapeutic importance of staying with physiological/affect sensations to discover the unconscious story that was being lived out in her body.

As we did several emotionally focused sessions her childhood stories revealed script beliefs such as, "I'm not worthy", "No one is there for me", "Men are dangerous", "Life is hard and lonely" (Erskine & Zalcman, 1979). Interspersed with the emotionally focused therapy sessions we had a number of cognitively focused sessions where we outlined her script system and explored how she collected reinforcing experiences to confirm her life script (Erskine & Moursund, 1988; O'Reilly-Knapp & Erskine, 2010). She later reported that the combination of the emotionally expressive therapy and the "thinking sessions" helped her to understand her day-by-day behaviour and interactions with people.

In one of our sessions she complained about a painful point on her back. Instead of attending to her frequent questions and fearful antic- ipations about what this could be, I asked her if we could attend to her twisted posture. My hypothesis was that she was having a body memory and that perhaps we may be able to facilitate her awareness and maybe even put her internal experience into words. I wanted her to feel and think about her body rather than fantasise about potential catastrophes. I wondered what she would remember and feel if she was in a comfortable posture. I was reminded that many physical pains are the effect of habitual *retroflections* that are related to emotional/physical distress. Such retroflections, in an attempt to manage emotionally over- whelming situations, interrupt awareness of feelings, needs, and bodily reactions (Perls, Hefferline, & Goodman, 1951).

I asked her to close her eyes, to exaggerate her posture, and to pay attention to what sensations she was feeling. I encouraged her to describe whatever she was experiencing. While she was doing this I had the sense that she had lost touch with her own natural body reac- tions and rhythm and that her retroflections were the only means that she had of managing her implicit memories. "Oohh," she cried. "This is the posture I have had many times when I was eight or nine years old. I had to help my father carry large sacks of potatoes." She cried deeply. "It was terrible. I had to carry these heavy sacks and if I was slow my father would scream at me." While Maria continued to cry she described how she was often forced to do work that was beyond her strength and endurance. She described her childhood as one of "abuse and absence of protection".

This first session of a bodily-oriented therapy opened the door for several other body/affect focused sessions; the result was an unfurling of childhood memories about her father's control and violence (Caizzi, 2012). Over the next several sessions I continued to inquire about her body sensations, affect, and related associations. She told me a number of stories about her early family life that she had never talked about, not even to her sisters. She told me about a "weak mother" who "never protected me" … "she even participated in father's hitting all of us". Maria said that by comparison her husband's control of money and his lack of affection seemed like a "good deal".

When I inquired about her experience of our therapeutic relationship she reported that she was having a "totally new experience" of having "someone who is interested in me" and "who helps me to remember things I had never thought about". My use of phenomenological and historical inquiry became central in our sessions during this phase of our psychotherapy. It seemed clear to me that the functions of Maria's body symptoms were to simultaneously distract her from internal turmoil while unconsciously revealing her history (Erskine, 2008).

The body-oriented therapy we were doing was usually without touch; my emphasis was on increasing Maria's awareness of her affect, physical sensations, and related memories (Erskine, 2014a). When Maria's body and sub-symbolic memories were acutely disturbing she would spontaneously reach for my hand. By holding on to my hand, sometimes with direct eye contact, the intimacy of our relationship provided an emotional re-stabilisation. I was offering my protection, attentiveness, interest, and full presence—the qualities of relationship that the little girl missed from a mother who "never protected me". This relational re-stabilisation provided sensory-motor reorganisation—a re-experiencing rather than a reliving (Allen, 2010).

She reported that she periodically became "a crying little girl … with no words and strange body sensations" when her husband was angry at her. She realised that her bladder infections often happened when she was feeling scared and alone, often after a conflict with her husband.

However, near the end of this first year of therapy, she reported that the pain accompanying the bladder infections was less. She was no longer taking time in sessions to worry about her future health. Instead, she became increasingly aware of three issues: painful and frightening memories; denial of her parents' neglectful and abusive behaviour; and disavowal of her unhappiness in her marriage. My therapeutic task at this point was to keep her aware of her history without her moving into emotion-filled stories that were potentially re-traumatising. There were a few times when her stories would become rapid, her breathing would escalate, and she would lose contact with me. On these occasions I asked her to slow down the pace at which she was talking, to look into my eyes, to breathe deeply, and to feel the story that was in her body while relating it to me. My intention was to increase the interpersonal contact as a new form of emotional stabilisation and regulation.

After a year and a half Maria decided to stop the therapy. She said that she was no longer worrying about her health and that the psychotherapy was helpful because it gave her a sense of "feeling stronger". She could not afford to continue because she and her husband were often arguing about her coming for psychotherapy and he would not allow her to spend any more money. I assured her that if she ever decided to return I would be available. Two years later, after getting a divorce and her father's death, she returned to therapy.

The combination of her divorce and the death of her father provided the stimulus for us to focus on her previously unrecognised feelings of anger at both her husband and father. She had explicit memories of several family arguments in her teenage years where her father hit her, told her "You are nothing", and called her "a piece of shit". She realised that she had always avoided being near him. I used the empty chair method (Perls, 1969) to help her express her anger and to facilitate her having a sense of impact. In the midst of this work Maria was surprised to be saying, "I hated my father so much and I miss him so much." I again used the empty chair method to help her accept and resolve her grief. We focused on Maria telling the image of her father about her longings, sorrow, resentment, and affection; she was saying a genuine "hello" to her father—a session of truth telling—in preparation for an unqualified goodbye to him (Erskine, 2014b).

During this phase of psychotherapy there were three extended sessions where I did psychotherapy with Maria's introjected father. In this work it became clear to Maria that she had four specific parental injunctions: "Don't trust anyone"; "Don't ever show your feelings"; "Life is for strong people"; and "Work hard and don't ask for help". We explored the effects of growing up with such injunctive messages, how she both complied and rebelled against the messages, and the importance of her own expressions of self-definition. It is significant in that much of Maria's self-criticism stopped after the three sessions of therapy with her Parent ego state. As part of the Parent ego state therapy we took time for her to respond from her Child ego state. In this Child–Parent dialogue she understood how her father's injunction had influenced her behaviour and attitude to life. (Please see both John McNeel's and Ray Little's chapters in this book for additional descriptions of the interpsychic dynamics between Child and Parent ego states. Detailed accounts of the theory and methods of Parent ego state therapy can be found in several publications (Dashiell, 1978; Erskine, 2003b; Erskine & Moursund, 1988; Erskine, Moursund, & Trautmann, 1999; Erskine & Trautmann, 2003; Mellor & Andrewartha, 1980; Moursund & Erskine, 2003)).

One day Maria phoned and urgently asked for an additional appointment. She had had a car accident. As part of her medical treatment she had a gynaecological examination. During the examination, later at home, and even in our session, she was flooded with overwhelming emotional and physical sensations. In our session Maria reported facts of the accident and medical examination but her intense emotional expression indicated a traumatic reaction. Was this merely a reaction to a minor automobile accident or was Maria unconsciously reliving some traumatic experience from a previous stage in life? If the latter, I did not yet have enough information to know at what age. I knew that physiological survival reactions and life shaping decisions can occur at any age in response to trauma (Erskine, 1980). It was clear that Maria was inundated with emotions and tense in her body. Even though she was repeating parts of the story she was unable to make interpersonal contact. She was absorbed by internal turmoil. I realised that it was quite likely any cognitive comprehension would not resolve this reliving of a trauma.

I remembered Berne writing that it is a sign of trauma if two ego states are cathected simultaneously. "The repression of traumatic memories is possible, only through repression of the whole related Ego States. These Ego States remain preserved in a latent state, waiting to be cathected" (1961, p. 19). He references Penfield's research to describe how two Ego states can occupy the consciousness simultaneously as two distinct psychological entities: one in the present, the other in the past where the person again feels the emotions and interpretations of the original experience (ibid., p. 17). Berne writes of "two Ego States, one oriented toward the current external and psychological reality, the other a 'reliving' (rather than mere recall) of scenes dating back as far as the first year of life, with great vividness … and the patient feels himself to be back in the situation and experiences the affects in all the original intensity" (ibid., p. 19).

I slowly inquired about Maria's internal experience. My attunement to her rhythm was important. I wanted her to feel secure with me and to have the freedom to express all that she was feeling. As I provided moments of silence she again began to describe her experience in the doctor's office: "He said, 'Take off your underpants.' Ehhh!! I want to kick him in the balls," she yelled. "It was hard to contain myself. What shit is in this man's head to talk to me that way?" Now Maria was screaming even louder, "Men are dangerous." Her emotional reaction seemed more intense than the actuality of the current event. She was like a child reliving a frightening story and partially an adult angrily reporting the incident. Two ego states were cathected simultaneously.

I thought it would be beneficial for her to do some age regressive therapy but first I thought it necessary to re-establish the security of our interpersonal connection and to establish a solid Adult ego understanding of both the external problem and her childlike internal turmoil. I spent the rest of the session questioning Maria about her experience with the gynaecologist. I did not want to minimise the reality of her adult feelings and perceptions about the gynaecologist's insensitivity and intrusiveness. She needed to express her anger as a grown woman before we engaged, if ever, in any supportive age regression. My focus in this session was on validating her anger at the gynaecologist's insensitivity and his failure to have a female nurse present with him in the examining room. Our conversation was woman-to-woman. If need be, I intended to address her Child ego state in a following session.

I began the next session by talking about the importance of clarifying our therapeutic contract (Berne, 1963, 1966; James & Jongeward, 1978; Steiner, 1974; Stewart & Joines, 1987). I wanted to establish a clear contract in order to ensure therapeutic safety and her agreement about doing any possible age regression. We talked about the advantages and possible adverse effects of doing emotionally charged age regression, how she could have choice and control over stopping the regression, and the importance of discovering a new and reparative ending to the traumatic story that she would be re-experiencing. We agreed on booking a longer session for the age regression for two reasons: first, so she would have more time to fully re-experience the old trauma accompanied by a new sense of reparation; and, second, so we could have the time to talk about her emotions and any new reactions or understandings of her Child ego state's traumatic experience.

We spent the first twenty minutes of our next session re-establishing our relationship and reviewing our therapeutic contract. Then I encouraged Maria to close her eyes and to remember the experience with the gynaecologist, to feel what she was feeling when he told her to take off her underpants. She began to shake. She was feeling some intense physiologically based emotions. My mind started to wander and I imagined how comfortable it would be to just work behaviourally or cognitively and to not feel the emotional impact she was having on me. My countertransference was actively taking my mind away from the deep emotional and physical work that Maria so desperately needed. As she shrieked, "Oooh, my God! It's the same situation," I suddenly returned to sensitivity—sensitivity to Maria's agony, my therapeutic commitment, and my sense of ethics. I resonated with her childhood need for security and choice and reassured her that I was with her and would remain so. I gave her the choice of stopping or continuing. She grabbed on to my hand and uttered that she wanted to continue. Like talking to a frightened child, I used a soft voice to encourage her to go fully into the experience, to feel her body and all her emotions, to fully "know what you know".

Maria began to whisper, "I'm in bed with my little sister. We live in a boarding house. I am six or seven." She started to cry and shake. I said, "I'm staying right here with you. You can feel and remember what happened." Maria's upper body was trembling while her legs were coiled to her chest. She began to scream, "He is here … he is here." I responded with, "Let yourself know who it is." Maria's cry merged with anger, "He is a bad man … the one that always looks at my sister and me in such a terrible way." I added, "You can let yourself know what happened." Maria was choking on her words, "He comes into our bedroom." I attempted to reassure her, "Maria, this is very hard for you, but this is just a memory, you can keep going."

Maria cried, "Take off your underpants ... take off your underpants, he keeps saying. I can smell him ... he stinks ... bad man ... I want to scream but no one is going to hear me. I can't call Mommy ... at the far end of the house ... boarders in between ... I must be quiet ... be quiet. No one is here for us. I don't want my father to come ... he's mean ... he hits. I don't want him." She screamed, "This bad man has a knife ... he will cut my sister." I encouraged her with, "Do what your body wants to do, Maria. Your legs are moving." Maria began to kick and claw at the sofa with her fingernails. She screamed, "Get away from us. Don't touch me ... get your hands off me!" With that she ferociously bit the cushion as though she was biting the man. I encouraged her to continue biting and moving her body. She kicked fiercely and screamed, "I won't let you touch me ... get your hands off me! ... Off ... OFF! ... Mooommm! Momma help ... Momma help us!"

When she called for her mother it was evident that something had changed internally; she had achieved a new experience. She was now able to both protest and call for help. She was expressing the human need to make an impact and to be protected; she deactivated her physiological retroflections—rather than being physically inhibited her body was active in protest. In response to her call for help I reached out and wrapped my arms around her. I held her as she sobbed. After a few minutes her body relaxed, and we were quiet together for several more minutes. Then we talked at length about what had happened that night, her becoming numb and tightening her pelvis and legs, her needs for protection and nurturing, how as a child she protected and stabilised herself rather than relying on her parents to provide protection and stabilisation, and how she could respond differently today. The result of this regressive re-experiencing was an evident calmness and relaxation of the tension throughout her body. In subsequent sessions over the next few months it was clear that she had a new sense of trust in her own perceptions and an understanding of her previous physical symptoms. The bladder infections stopped.

When facilitating a therapeutic age regression it is essential that the psychotherapist allow her body to resonate with the client's various movements, tensions, and bodily expressions while simultaneously being attuned to the client's rhythm, affect, and level of development. Such body-to-body resonance and attunement provide essential somatic and affect clues that are necessary for the psychotherapist to adequately protect the client from becoming overwhelmed with affect and body tensions. If the client begins to feel overwhelmed while experiencing an age regression it may be a sign that he has reached a level of *affect tolerance*—that moment when the client's neurological system can no longer safely process the intensity of the affect/physiological experience without re-traumatisation.

Just before the client reaches the point of affect tolerance we either invite the client into doing something physically active, such as protesting or calling for help—a re-experiencing rather than a reliving. Or we make use of here-and-now interpersonal contact and may engage his Adult ego by using Eric Berne's therapeutic operations of explanation and interpretation, methods designed to decontaminate the Adult ego from the intensity of the Child ego state's emotionally laden patterns of self-protection and self-stabilisation (1966).

If the client is ready for more intense age regression it is essential that we co-create a situation where he *almost relives* the original trauma in order to work within the same neuronal pathways of the original trauma. However rather than reliving and repeating the same old forms of self-stabilisation, together we find a way to create a new ending to the client's experience—a *therapeutic re-experiencing*. This may involve a relationally oriented therapy with the Child ego state, active movements of protest, or experimentation with new ways of self-expression. We may provide either explanations suitable for a young child or validation to facilitate what Berne calls "deconfusing the Child" (Hargarden & Sills, 2001). A high quality of interpersonal contact between client and therapist is essential. In the original situations the events became traumatising because of the absence of a reliable, consistent, and dependable other who could help the child regain affect stabilisation (Erskine, 1993; Stuthridge, 2012). What we are describing here is psychotherapy with a confused, frightened, neglected, or oppressed Child ego state and it is essential that the client senses the full protective presence of the psychotherapist.

This therapy had five stages: first, re-establishing the security of our therapeutic relationship (Erskine, Moursund, & Trautmann, 1999); second, decontaminating and strengthening the client's Adult ego (Berne, 1961); third, providing Maria with permission to know and value her own childhood experience (Allen & Allen, 1972); fourth, maintaining a relational presence that made the age regression safe and reparative (Erskine & Moursund, 1988; Moursund & Erskine, 2003); and fifth, continuing with several sessions after the age regression that focused on

Maria's Adult ego processing of her childhood experiences and how they influenced her adult life.

Remembering (Therapeutic)	Reliving (Retraumatizing)	Reexperiencing (Therapeutic)

1. Relational security
(*Potency*) Clear contracts, affect and developmental attunement to build a secure therapeutic relationship before, during, and after possible regressive work.

2. Awareness of internal conflict   *Therapeutic understanding*
(*Punishment*) Arousal of affect and body reactions. Facilitate internal and external contact, assessment of possible punishment, provide protection and validation.

3. Support memory and affect arousal
(*Permission*) Cognitive analysis of the internal conflict. Adjust contract: either adult ego state decontamination via explanation and interpretation or supportive age-regression.

4. Reexperiencing the original scene
(*Protection by providing choices*)
Facilitate regression to original childhood experience.
Emotional and cognitive reorganization.

5. Supportive age-regression   *Therapeutic Reparation*
(*Presence*) Facilitate expressing the unexpressed, activating inhibited gestures, articulating needs, and expressing self. Always checking the contract, providing options, respect, and security.
Deconfusion of child ego states, redecision (cognitive & behavioral), or diconnecting rubberbands (affect & psychological). If therapeutic presence, protection, and security are missing then traumatic-reliving may occur.

6. Post activation contact & relaxation
(*Potency & Protection*) Intergation of physiology, affect, and cognition, so that behaviour is by choice in the current context and not activated by fear pr compulsion.
Resolution of the internal conflict evident in calmness, awareness, spontaneity and intimacy.

Figure 1. Therapeutic age-regression.

Age regression: depending on the psychotherapist

Stella was slouching on the office sofa, her knees drawn up to her ears. For the past three minutes she had been whimpering and gnawing on the skin of her left thumb. She was reliving the experience of being a preschool child whose mother was screaming at her and telling her that she was "wicked" and such an "undeserving child". My heart ached for her. I (Richard) wanted to comfort her, to bring her back to the here-and-now, to somehow make it all OK.

Yet it seemed too soon for me to intervene; I waited for a change in her breathing. For this age regression to be therapeutic she needed to stay in her early childhood physiological/emotional experience for a moment or two longer, to fully feel the intense discomfort, but not for too long. It was essential that she *almost relive* the trauma of the relational abuse to activate the same neurological circuitry that was activated in the original series of traumas that she had lived as a child. It was also essential that this regression have a different outcome, one in which she *re-experienced* the trauma and her self-protective strategies while also activating an entirely new experience—a reparative experience that would establish a new neurological circuit.

After eighteen months of addressing Stella's childhood relational experiences cognitively, through *therapeutic inference*, it was necessary to support Stella *re-experiencing* how she, as a young child, managed her mother's rage. Yet I was concerned that she did not have the internal resources to do anything other than to *relive* this relational trauma. If I left her to relive her intense affect any longer she most likely would be re-traumatised in this therapy session and would reactivate the old *self-stabilising strategies* that constituted the "palimpsests" of her life script. "Palimpsests" refers to the physiological, sub-symbolic, and procedural forms of memory that form the unconscious relational patterns and experiential conclusions that are the core of life scripts. The palimpsests are the child's pre-language coping strategies that emerge after the "script protocol", the earliest traumas in infancy (Berne, 1961, pp. 116–126).

In a soft voice addressing a frightened child, I said, "I am right here with you." After another half minute of silence I said, "I know it hurts when mom screams at you … the only relief is to hide." She nodded her head in agreement. Her whimper changed to a cry. After another minute I added, "It seems like mother did not comfort you. You needed someone." Her breathing changed and her crying quieted.

At this moment we had gone far enough into the regression; she was about to exceed her level of affect tolerance. She was intensely afraid of being punished for crying. It was the time to re-engage with her. "Do you experience me being here with you?" I asked. She nodded a "yes". I went on with, "What is it like when I am here with you?" She answered slowly, "I can let myself feel ... I can dare to remember ... hiding is not so important." These *relational inquiries* brought Stella's focus back to the security of our therapeutic relationship. We then continued to talk about our relationship and contrasted it with her relationship with her mother, both when she was a child and as an adult today. We talked about my being present for her and how this was so emotionally different from when she periodically regressed at home and would lie on her bed and cry for hours. The contrast between the client's relational experience with the psychotherapist and past relational disruptions helps the client to integrate a new value of self and a new sense of being-in-relationship (Erskine, Moursund, & Trautmann, 1999).

As I inquired about the physical sensations and affect she experienced during the age regression, Stella was gradually able to put her body sensations into words and to form an association between her somatic/affect experiences and an image of her mother yanking her out of the bathtub and slapping her little body. This memory had remained unconscious and non-symbolic for many years because there had been no one to help her form the physiological/emotional memory into a concept or words. Over the next two sessions, as we reviewed her age regression in detail, Stella was able to put into words an additional aspect of her personal identity—she was articulating another chapter in the narrative of her life.

On the day that this regression occurred, Stella had spilled a bottle of water on my carpet. Although I assured her that the wet carpet was not a problem she spontaneously began to curl up and whimper—a regression to a much earlier age. Winnicott (1974) implied that the resolution of preverbal traumatic memories was only possible through a *dependent therapeutic relationship* that often involves an age regression. Margaret Little (1981, 1990) went on to describe the significance of *dependence* in facilitating age regression and, moreover, viewed it as a way to resolve sub-symbolic emotional disturbances. Lorraine Price's (2014) qualitative research and review of a vast number of psychotherapy publications provides credence to the idea that there are significant therapeutic benefits emerging from a supportive, therapeutic regression wherein the client can trust in the dependability of the psychotherapist. Bowlby says that security is developed in a child through the caregivers' ongoing availability and emotional responsiveness, consistency, and dependability, where such caregivers are experienced as "stronger and/or wiser" (1988, p. 12).

For an age regression to be therapeutic and beneficial to the client rather than re-traumatising, the relationship with the psychotherapist must also be secure, attuned to the client's affect and level of development, consistent, and dependable. In the example provided here, Stella's regression was stimulated in two ways: the first was her innate urge to use the security of our relationship to be healed from trauma; the second was the accidental spilling of the water that precipitated the unconscious, sub-symbolic, procedural memory of being hit and yelled at by her mother when she, at the age of four, had splashed bath water on the floor. These two factors made it possible for Stella to have an age regression that was healing.

When this age regression session occurred, Stella had been in therapy once a week for eighteen months. When she entered therapy she described her life as "... living on an emotional roller coaster, sometimes very competent and sometimes a crying baby. I have no sense of who I am". She declared that she had no memories before the age of ten. I suspected that her "crying baby" was memory—memory that was physiological, emotional, and relational—memory that was sub-symbolic. Historical inquiry revealed little in the first months of psychotherapy. I relied on attunement to her rhythm and affect while continuing to think about her emotional volatility from a developmental perspective.

During our first year together I focused on creating our therapeutic relationship as secure, reliable, and dependable—a relationship that would stabilise and regulate her "emotional roller coaster". In the year leading up to this session my therapeutic goal was to create a therapeutic relationship that would foster a restoration of her diminished sense of self. I focused on inquiring about her phenomenological sensations, feelings, and associations. As a result Stella began to have some specific memories; often these memories would begin as painful sensations in her body along with an urge to withdraw and cry alone. In response I explained ego states and transactions. We also spent part of several sessions attending to the emerging transferences that included Stella's anticipation that I would ridicule her or rage at her.

Through therapeutic inference we were constructing a mosaic about her early life and the neglect and physical abuse that she experienced in her early years. I often addressed the child in her, as Eric Berne describes when he writes,

> The ego state can be treated like an actual child. It can be nurtured carefully, even tenderly, until it unfolds like a flower, revealing all the complexities of its internal structure. (1961, p. 226)

I (Richard) have chosen a case from my clinical notes to illustrate a therapeutic situation where I intervened in such a way as to draw the client out of the age regression at a point that I surmised would be most beneficial. Ideally, Stella's age regression could have continued to the point where she would have protested against her mother's brutal treatment. However, Stella did not have sufficient internal resources yet to actively protest, to fight against her mother's hitting, or to defend against her mother's ridiculing definitions of her. She had reached her level of affect tolerance. I stopped her from going any further because she was on the edge of intense fear—fear of the potential punishments from her internal mother—and another retreat into her "internal hiding place". This was not the end of supportive age regression in Stella's therapy, but it was enough for that day.

Reparation of Stella's relational trauma was dependent on the psychotherapist's provision of a secure relational alternative—a psychotherapeutic relationship that was consistently attuned to her affect and developmental needs. With other clients it may have been beneficial to support their remaining in the age regression longer for the purpose of expressing the unexpressed and activating what was inhibited, such as screaming for help, pushing away, hitting or kicking in protest, truth telling, or defining one's self.

Conclusion

The case examples of Maria and Stella were chosen to illustrate the comprehensiveness of an integrative and relational Transactional Analysis in contemporary psychotherapy. The effectiveness of such an in-depth approach to Transactional Analysis is in its emphasis on the psychotherapist working affectively, physiologically, cognitively, and behaviourally to facilitate an internal integration of Child and Parent ego states into an Adult ego. Much of our therapeutic work is relational: working with and within the transference; inquiring about the client's phenomenological and historical experiences; attuning ourselves and responding to the client's affects and rhythms from a developmental perspective; and, providing the client with an awareness of the self-reparative or self-stabilising functions of his intrapsychic dynamics and behaviour.

As cited earlier, Berne stated that the optimal situation for the reintegration of the personality involves the phenomenological experience of the Child ego state becoming vividly revived in the mind of the client. Much of the Child ego state therapy that we do involves a number of elements: phenomenological and historical inquiry to stimulate a vivid awareness of affect and physical sensations; providing the security, consistency, and reliability that allows clients to feel what they feel and to know what they intuitively know; supporting the client's awareness of implicit and sub-symbolic memory; and, validating the client's early affect and relational experiences. Often this involves working with "therapeutic inference" to facilitate the client's forming a personal narrative out of the myriad affects and internal sensations, fragments of implicit and procedural memory, family stories, and observations of current family dynamics.

With some of our clients it is necessary to support an age regression and provide a reparative re-experiencing of early neglects or traumas. This requires an awareness of the client's level of development and a sensitivity to working at the client's edge of affect tolerance—to take the client into the regressive experience deep enough to re-experience the traumas in a new and healing way yet not so deep as to be re-traumatising. In this chapter we have emphasised the importance of relational dependency on the psychotherapist as the foundation for the client to vividly re-experience implicit and pre-symbolic memories in the resolution of trauma. Foremost in all of our therapeutic discourse and interventions is our premise: *healing occurs through a contactful therapeutic relationship*.

CHAPTER EIGHT

Evolving theory and practice with the self-destructive individual

Tony White

Introduction

This chapter examines recent developments in the theory and practice of therapies with self-destructive clients. They include those people who are either suicidal or who engage in repetitive destructive alcohol and drug use. However, people can display self-destructive behaviour in many ways and these are also covered in this chapter. The emerging ideas to be described have evolved over three decades of work, but what is more important they have crystallised in the past four or five years through discussion, writing, and experimentation with alternative modes of practice.

The nomenclature used in this chapter includes the Free Child ego state and the Adapted Child ego state. The Free Child ego state (FC), at times referred to as the Natural Child ego state, was originally articulated by Berne (1972) and has been developed by many others since, including Stewart and Joines (2012) and Woollams and Brown (1978). Berne developed this aspect of personality theory to explain the child at birth with his labyrinth of emotions, needs, drives, and so forth that naturally occur in us all prior to the development of a life script. This aspect of the personality remains with us for the rest of our lives in varying degrees.

However, at birth a child also craves a life script. He seeks to develop a story that he can use as a template for living life. Without such a story the child would remain an imbecile, incapable of selective perception or the ability to ignore certain stimuli and attend to other stimuli. He would have to take in all stimuli and therefore constantly be overloaded and incapable of basic information processing. The life script in this way allows him to develop into a normally functioning mature adult.

In his personality theory Berne used the concept of the Adapted Child ego state (AC) to explain this and it is here where the AC assumes its great importance. As Berne (1972, p. 31) says, "Each person decides in early childhood how he will live and how he will die, and that plan, which he carries in his head wherever he goes, is called his script." The AC explains, in terms of personality theory, the result of that decision making process. It is the response to parental directives that allows the child to develop the life script. Berne (ibid., p. 32) states, "A script is an ongoing life plan formed in early childhood under parental pressure." The child seeks out the parental pressure just as much as the parents apply the pressure, and the Adapted Child ego state was Berne's way of theoretically explaining the result of this process. The Adapted Child ego state is essential in understanding how the life script plays out in a person's life.

Don't exist decision

In the Transactional Analysis literature one does not have to look far to find a theoretical explanation of self-destructive behaviour. The works of H. S. Boyd (1972), Drye, Goulding, and Goulding (1973), Goulding and Goulding (1979), and Mellor (1979) on injunctions and early decisions present the idea of the "Don't exist" early decision. They argue that some children early in life make a decision that can lead to suicidal behaviour later in life. They in fact propose a set of seven such decisions (sometimes referred to as the suicide decisions):

1. If you don't change I will kill myself.
2. If things get too bad I will kill myself.
3. I will show you even if it kills me.
4. I will get you to kill me.

5. I will kill myself by accident.
6. I will almost die (over and over) to get you to love me.
7. I will kill myself to hurt you.

Since this theory was originally presented many have subsequently described and developed the ideas. For example L. Boyd (1986), Joines and Stewart (2002), Mellor (1979), White (2008, 2011). A substantial body of work on the "Don't exist" decision exists in the literature. Recent emerging developments have sought to add to the theoretical understanding in two ways. First, what does making a suicide decision mean in specific psychological terms? It is proposed that a person who makes such a decision comes to the conclusion that suicide is a viable solution to a problem. Later in life when certain environmental conditions appear, such as financial collapse or divorce, the person can then consider suicide as a possible solution to his difficulties. The individual who has not made the suicide decision does not have the belief that suicide is a viable solution to a problem. However, it is not that he decided suicide is not a possible solution; instead the question is never asked in his own mind. Or it may fleetingly be considered but is quickly discarded. The non-suicidal person does not have to resist the pull of suicide in difficult times; instead it is something he just doesn't consider as a possible behaviour. The individual who has made the suicide decision is, in essence, adding to his behavioural repertoire with one extra possible behaviour. Those who don't make the decision do not make such an addition.

The second emerging development is an expanded knowledge of the suicide decision making process. Progress has been made in this area such as classifying the seven suicide decisions into two types depending on the natural temperament in the individual. This has resulted in understanding early decision making as a hierarchy of decisions, not simply a single decision made by the young child. With regard to suicide decisions the development of two hierarchies has evolved (see Figures 1.1 and 1.2).

We all are born with some form of temperament. The bipartite model of fight and flight is used to explain the different kinds of suicide decisions when basic temperament is included in the theoretical understanding. In Figure 1.1 the basic temperament of flight is followed by a learned core belief of "I'm not OK". If the person develops a core belief of "I'm OK" then no suicide decisions will result. Combining the

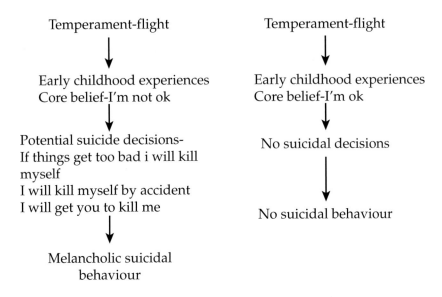

Figure 1.1.

flight temperament with the "I'm not OK" belief, the stage is then set for the person to make melancholic suicide decisions such as indicated in Figure 1.1. Melancholic suicidal behaviour results from that person who views suicide as a means to quietly die or leave this world. He tends to view himself as a burden to others and thus his suicide is an attempt to release others from the difficulties he causes in their lives. It is an attempt to "go out" with as little trouble and fanfare as possible.

This is different to the type of behaviour one finds with the angry, punishing suicide (Figure 1.2). The basic temperament in this case is fight. These people do not go down without a fight and this is reflected in their suicidal behaviour. Combined with an "I'm not OK" core belief the stage is set for suicide decisions that result in suicidal behaviour designed to hurt others, as Case study 1 shows.

Case study 1

The subject is a fifty-five-year-old woman with a long and volatile relationship with her husband involving many disputes and arguments. There have been a few separations over the years but at the point of her suicide they were living together and married. She plans the

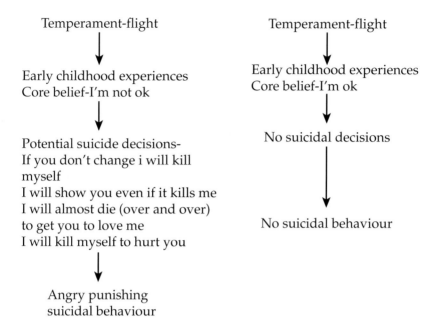

Temperament-flight

Early childhood experiences
Core belief-I'm not ok

Potential suicide decisions-
If you don't change i will kill
myself
I will show you even if it kills me
I will almost die (over and over)
to get you to love me
I will kill myself to hurt you

Angry punishing
suicidal behaviour

Temperament-flight

Early childhood experiences
Core belief-I'm ok

No suicidal decisions

No suicidal behaviour

Figure 1.2.

suicide such that she will be found by one of her daughters and not the husband, which is indeed what happened. With her is a long suicide note stating how badly he has treated her over the years and how he has finally driven her to suicide. Clearly this is designed to punish and hurt the husband and possibly even cause some kind of estrangement with his two daughters. This suicide is designed to have ramifications long beyond her death. She is also a woman of some substantial financial wealth and she has designed her will to also cause hurt to her husband, leaving him only a small amount and the two daughters the vast amount of her estate. This again is punishing behaviour that could also cause subsequent legal difficulties between him and his two daughters.

Case study 1 is not the behaviour of a suicidal person who wants to quietly die with as little commotion as possible, out of respect to those she has left behind. She is wanting to cause psychological and relationship damage long after she is gone. This formulation allows for a deeper understanding of the suicidal individual and that suicide is not a uniform act from person to person. Most suicides result from the individual making the suicide decision early in life, as shown in Figures 1.1 and 1.2. Having stated that, suicides are not uniform in the motivations people attach to them, as explained here. Fortunately this usually is not difficult to ascertain. One simply talks with the suicidal individual and quite quickly one begins to hear which kind of suicidal act the person may endeavour to make—suicide as a melancholic act or an angry punishing act. This also has implications for suicide risk assessment. If it is known the person will tend to use suicide as a punishment one is alert to an increase in relationship disharmony with those the person is angry at and may wish to subsequently punish.

Eros and Thanatos

Another area of emerging thought has come in the way suicide is understood as an overall concept. For many years suicidology has tended to be myopic and singular in its view of suicide (Edwards & Pfaff, 1997; Lange, 2013; Marcus, 2010). It has mainly been picture straightening by restating and reconfiguring the same concepts and statistics over and over. Despite this backdrop emerging ideas in suicidology have led to formulating the concept of a "normal person suicide", thus breaking the conventional boundaries of how we view suicide in general.

Most suicidal people are very unhappy, distressed individuals who have felt tormented for some time and see no other solution than to end their lives. Clearly they are in great pain, often with depression and anxiety which tears at their very core. Most of us understand suicidal people to be like this. However, as we look at people in general, meet with them in psychotherapy and discuss their lives there emerges another significant group. There are those who will voluntarily and repeatedly place themselves in situations where the likelihood of their death significantly increases: people who voluntarily enter a war zone, those who repeatedly engage in very high risk sports like some mountain climbing and BASE jumping, or those who take up motor racing or work with dangerous wild animals. People who do these sorts of activities, we hear from time to time either die or suffer some significant physical damage.

In many cases when one talks with such people one finds them to be quite well adjusted, to have quite normal lives with families, to have good jobs, and to be future focused in significant ways. They are not like the suicidal person who is full of pain and angst and sees no future for himself. This leaves one with a dilemma. Any person who repeatedly behaves in the same way over an extended period of time is displaying some aspect of his psychology. People do not do the same thing over and over again through an extended period of time unless that reflects features of their own psyche. If they repeatedly and voluntarily put themselves in highly dangerous situations that reflects a belief they have about themselves. Part of them is voluntarily "dancing with death". In this way it could be argued they are suicidal and indeed some do die from the activities they have voluntarily sought out over an extended period of time. Interestingly, Erskine in his chapter of this book talks about homeostatic strategies. He notes that people use repetitive behavioural patterns to provide themselves with, amongst other things, identity and a sense of integrity. If they have a repetitive pattern of high risk behaviour that would reflect, according to Erskine's views, a sense of their identity and who they are which supports the concept being presented here.

How can this be? What sort of theoretical explanation can one provide for this group of people? At our institute these things were discussed, but we have been left befuddled for some time. Upon inquiry, it is obvious these people had not made the suicide decision. How can one behave in a suicidal type of way and not make one of the seven suicide decisions described above? Eventually, after some time we stumbled upon an answer when reading the book, *A Layman's Guide to Psychiatry and Psychoanalysis* (Berne, 1957).

In this book, Berne discusses at some length the concepts Freud presented on the life instinct and the death instinct, sometimes called the libido and mortido. Eventually it was psychoanalyst Paul Federn who coined the terms *Eros* and *Thanatos* for the life instinct and the death instinct (Ikonen & Rechardt, 2010). In Greek mythology Hypnos (the god of sleep) lived with his half-brother Thanatos (the god of non-violent or peaceful death). Technically, this may have been a poor choice of terms by Federn as many a suicidal or destructive act can be of a violent nature. Indeed it is the Keres, the sisters of Thanatos who are the goddesses of violent death. However, be what it may, the term Thanatos has been coined and is now widely used to identify the death instinct.

As Ikonen and Rechardt (2010) note, over many years there has been considerable debate for and against the concept of the death instinct or Thanatos. However, Eric Berne openly embraced and agreed with these concepts as primary drives or instincts and maintained that agreement until his very last book (1972, p. 399), where he states, "The writer, for example, besides having repeated and confirmed the conventional observations of Freud, also believes right down the line with him concerning the death instinct, and the pervasiveness of the repetition compulsion."

In his first book Berne (1957, p. 60) also talks about these drives at some length. He notes, "The two most powerful urges of human beings are the creative urge and the destructive urge." The creative urge, or Eros as it is sometimes known, results in procreation, loving, generosity, and so forth. He refers to this as a drive that results in constructive goals and one finds its most concentrated expression in sexual desire. On the other hand there is another drive that can result in hate, cruelty, anger, and hostility and this is sometimes known as Thanatos. Eros is the energy of the life wish and Thanatos is the energy of the death wish. Berne also talks about the directions in which Eros and Thanatos can be expressed. About the life instinct he states, "Some people direct their love mostly towards others, and others direct it mainly towards themselves. The direction of various quantities may change from time to time" (1957, p. 62). He goes on to discuss the death instinct: "Similarly, one can be very hateful toward others, the most aggressive act in this case being murder; or one can be very hateful toward oneself, the most aggressive act then being suicide."

This "discovery" of Berne's theorising about the death instinct made the link that had been long searched for. At last we are provided with a substantive theoretical explanation of how a reasonably happy, well adjusted individual could display suicidal behaviour. To explain this we must first go back to the suicide decision. A child makes the suicide decision in response to some adverse parenting in childhood. The decision is made in response to some parental directive. It can be seen as an adaption to authority in this way and thus is theoretically described as a function of the Adapted Child (AC) ego state (see Figure 2).

As an adaption to a parental directive, the suicide decision only occurs in a small group of people: in a mild form perhaps five per cent, and in a strong form perhaps two per cent. However, Thanatos and Eros are not a result of a parental directive. We all have them from birth; they are a natural part of human psychology. As a result, as indicated in Figure 2, 100 per cent of people have these and they are a function of the Free Child (FC) ego state. They are not an adaption to authority, but are natural inborn drives which we all have.

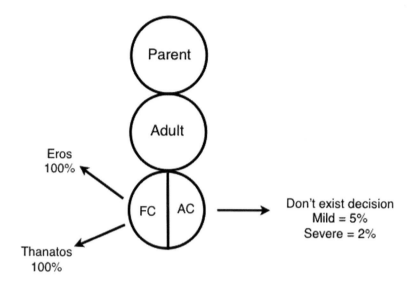

Figure 2.

While this allows a sound theoretical explanation for that group of people who are well adjusted and still display suicidal behaviour, this unfortunately creates more problems than it solves. If the drive of Thanatos allows some people to put themselves in situations where there is a significant risk of dying, and some do die, is that a form of psychopathology? Recall, this is not an abnormal state. It is a function of the Free Child ego state, not a result of maladaptive parenting, and as a result one can't say it forms part of a hamartic life script even though some of them do end up dead by their own hand. If these acts are deemed pathological are they meant to be treated, and if so, how do you treat something that is a normal function of the Free Child ego state?

This begins to cause us to question the very definition of psychopathology. Dictionary.com (2014) defines psychopathology as "a pathological deviation from normal or efficient behaviour". Rycroft (1977, p. 3) defines pathology as "the abnormal processes inferred to be responsible for the manifest symptoms", and then defines psychopathology as "the study of abnormal mental functioning" … "the theoretical formulation of the abnormal workings of some particular person's mind" (p. 131).

Key in these definitions is the abnormality of mental functioning of the mind. If this is so, what is described here could not be defined as a form of psychopathology. Behaviour resulting from the drive of Thanatos is a function of the Free Child and hence not an "abnormality" of mental functioning. Yet one can have an individual behaving in a high risk way such that his life could quite possibly end. Perhaps this raises an anomaly in the definition of psychopathology. Most often those individuals who engage in such high risk behaviour would see no abnormality at all. Generally they say they are happy people who knowingly engage in these activities but only take "calculated risks", which allows them to rationalise the dangers in their minds. If they perceived the true dangers they may not engage in the activities. There have been hundreds of people who have attempted to climb Mt Everest and have miscalculated their "calculated risk taking" and died on the slopes of just that one mountain. Current estimates put the total at around 250 deaths.

Thanatos in everyday life

What has been discussed so far relates to a small group of individuals, who, it could be said, behave in an extreme way. As Figure 2 shows, we all have the drive of Thanatos and thus we will all display, at times, destructive behaviour. Eric Berne (1957) noted the death instinct can vary in the direction it is expressed and the intensity of the drive which will also vary from time to time. Those who engage in high risk behaviour could be said to have an intense or strong drive of Thanatos at that time, whereas the majority do not and thus display destructive behaviour in a less intense form.

The list of less destructive acts is long and varied and includes: cigarettes, alcohol, medication non-compliance, not getting medical treatment when indicated, poor quality diet, poor physical condition, overeating, undereating, playing games in relationships, unsafe sex, full body contact sports, and so on endlessly. These are less directly physically destructive than the behaviours described previously. Nonetheless they are destructive and thus could be seen as an expression of Thanatos that we all possess (as shown in Figure 2). Psychotherapists see these types of behaviours over and over again in their everyday work. It seems reasonable to suggest there is clear behavioural evidence for the contention that the destructive drive of Thanatos exists in all of us.

This evolving idea provides an exciting new perspective for the basis of many psychotherapies. When a client presents such behaviour, most often the psychotherapist will seek to understand it as some kind of psychopathology. All psychotherapies have some kind of definition of what is abnormal and what is normal. As soon as the problem is defined the therapist will call on her theory behind the psychotherapy and seek to understand the cause of the problem. These theoretical explanations are many and varied. Once the cause is defined the therapy can proceed. Often psychotherapists will view some kind of adverse parenting as the cause of the problem. The theory will explain the problem presented as a consequence of dysfunctional parenting received in childhood. For example in Transactional Analysis problematic parenting results in the formation of a life script which can then explain the cause of the current problem behaviour. Berne (1961, p. 117), in discussing the life scripts of females who marry alcoholic men states, "Many such women were raised by alcoholic fathers, so that the infantile origins of the script are not far to seek." It is probably safe to say that the vast majority, if not all psychotherapies, have this structure for understanding the problems presented by clients.

However, Figure 2 shows we all have a destructive drive which can result in all sorts of problematic behaviours. Some of these behaviours are not the result of adverse parenting but are a natural part of us. If the problem behaviour presented by the client is the result of Thanatos then it is not a form of psychopathology. It is simply a reflection of the Free Child natural part of the personality. If the therapist goes seeking examples of adverse parenting in childhood to explain the problem behaviour, then the therapist has taken a significant wrong turn. The presenting problem is not the result of any maladaptive childhood experiences but a normal part of their Free Child ego state. As a result any therapy provided, based on the incorrect assumption of the cause of the problem, is going to be ineffectual to some degree if not wholly so.

Even so, this idea creates further problems. Without a doubt, problem behaviours presented by clients are sometimes the result of adverse parenting. When this is the case the problem is not the result of the Free Child but is an adaption to a parental directive and thus a function of the Adapted Child ego state. In suicide the parent gives the injunction of "Don't exist"; the child then decides to accept the injunction or not. If accepted then he has made the suicide decision. Of course there are many other injunctions such as "Don't be important", "Don't feel", and "Don't belong". These can all form as a result of maladaptive parenting and a child's adjustment to such parenting.

Theoretically they are explained as an adaption to a parental directive and as a result psychotherapy seeks in some way to realign or alter the client's perception of the childhood experiences such that he is not adversely affected in his present day life.

If a client presents playing the game of "Uproar" (Berne, 1964) in a destructive marital relationship how does one ascertain if that is the result of adverse childhood parenting or a result of the natural drive of Thanatos? Furthermore, if it is a consequence of Thanatos what does one do about it, if anything? If it is a natural human drive then it is not an abnormality and hence there is nothing to treat, even if one wanted to. What does one say to the client? "It's a natural part of you, so live with it"? If one is working with a client and the symptom is especially resistant to change that maybe a sign it is the drive of Thanatos.

Suicidal ambivalence

Based on this theory, what therapeutic method can flow from it? To answer this first requires the theory of suicidal ambivalence to be

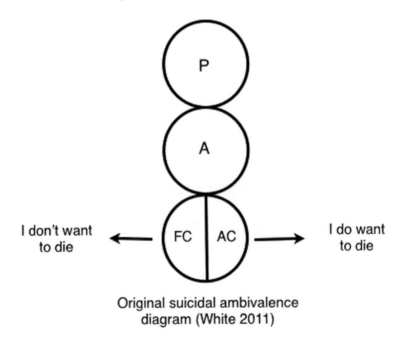

Original suicidal ambivalence
diagram (White 2011)

Figure 3.

articulated. In two previous books (White, 2011, 2013) I presented the concepts of drug use ambivalence and suicidal ambivalence. Suicidal ambivalence is diagrammed as such in Figure 3.

This diagram shows two different aspects of the personality representing two different urges, leaving the individual in a state of ambivalence: two urges desiring two different things at the one time. Clinical experience shows most people can understand this diagram and experience it personally, quite easily. In this theory the desire to die is represented by the Adapted Child ego state and the desire to live is represented by the Free Child ego state. Regardless of the theoretical explanation most people can quite easily isolate these two aspects of their personality and experience them in a two chair situation. In one chair they can experience the AC part of the self and in the other chair they can experience the FC part of the self.

However, it now needs to be added, the evolving theory described in this chapter requires the original diagram to be altered. This is presented

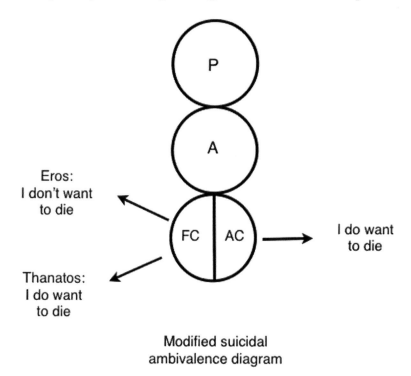

Modified suicidal
ambivalence diagram

Figure 4.

in Figure 4. With the introduction of Eros and Thanatos, a change is required to the suicidal ambivalence diagram.

Diagrammatically we can now see there are two sources of suicidal ambivalence. Every person experiences one kind of suicidal ambivalence as a function of the inborn drives indicated in the Free Child ego state. The natural drives of Eros and Thanatos leave each of us in a state of suicidal ambivalence. We all have self-destructive urges and we all have constructive urges existing in us at the one time. In addition there is also a small group of people who have made some kind of suicide decision and this is a function of the Adapted Child ego state. Hence, for a small group there is also a state of suicidal ambivalence between the AC and the Eros part of the FC.

Case study 2

The subject is a forty-year-old man with a long history of prison time and addiction to cocaine and heroin. Previously he had made a few suicide attempts which indicated he did view suicide as a solution to his problems. From an abusive and neglected background it was evident he had made the suicide decision and hence we have ambivalence between his AC wanting to die and his FC Eros wanting to live. In this instance he was feeling very despairing and was considering plunging a fishing knife into his abdomen.

He gets himself into highly emotional states where there is very little Adult ego state thinking and on this occasion he did eventually force the knife quite deeply into himself. He then reports the pain from that brought him out of his emotional state so he could cathect more from an Adult ego state and indeed realised the reality of what he had done. When this occurred the drive from the FC Eros took over: he phoned his mother and she took action which got him to hospital and saved his life. This was a serious suicide attempt that could have quite easily killed him.

This case study is designed to show how different urges behaviourally manifest and highlights other features of the suicidal ambivalence. Most, if not all suicide attempts are "half hearted" and reflect the two drives, to live and to die. The AC part of this man is seeking to plan an attempt that will be completed, whilst at the very same time the FC part of him is seeking to usurp or sabotage the very same suicide attempt. This leads to odd, contradictory behaviour as is shown in the case study. Some will misdiagnose the situation and conclude he is using the suicide attempt as a form of attention seeking from his mother. They reason that if it had been a "real" suicide attempt, he would not have contacted his mother and he probably would have died. While this can indeed happen, in this case it was not so. Instead the pain of the stab allowed him to switch ego states out of his very regressed Child into his Adult. When this happened there was a shift in the psychic energy of his ego states. This allowed the FC Eros to take more executive control in the personality and the resultant life saving behaviour was exhibited. It was not attention seeking behaviour but a reflection of the two opposing forces residing in him at the one point in time.

Case study 3 provides a unique insight into a man's ambivalence, illustrating the thinking and switches in ego states during an actual suicide attempt. Initially there is a preamble that was written some days after the suicide attempt. That is followed by a brief journal written as the suicide attempt progressed. The following was written by the client. My comments are in parentheses (White, 2011, pp. 207–210).

Case study 3

Preamble

Confidentiality is a major hot button issue for me …

> *I work very hard to keep my privacy. I don't have any close friends and especially not at school. I can't trust anyone. If someone gets too close they might find out how crazy I am …*
>
> *I know it's paranoid, but I have to protect myself. No one else will. This reactivated and exacerbated all of my fears about my privacy being violated, anger towards health professionals who have been sloppy with confidentiality in the past, anger towards people who have used my personal information against me. I had just an overall sense of powerlessness, anger and feeling overwhelmed. I can't put it into words that do it justice so I'm just going to stop trying. Point is I was extremely upset.*
>
> *I was having cycling panic attacks. I'd taken my maximum daily dose of klonopin and it felt like I hadn't taken a thing. So what next? Clearly the logical step is to take a bunch of painkillers, right? Of course. So I did that.*

(My comment—a distressing event has occurred, the breaking of his confidentiality. This leads to a number of conditions such that the suicidal decision can be acted upon:

1. Thinking—I have to protect myself. No one else will.
2. Anger towards others.
3. Sense of powerlessness, anger, and feeling overwhelmed.
4. Cycling panic attacks occur.
5. Next logical step is to attempt suicide.

This could be reflective of the suicide decision: "If things get too bad I will kill myself").

Day of the suicide attempt

This is a series of notes written by a twenty-eight-year-old male while he was making a suicide attempt. He had received his file notes from a hospital where he had once been a patient. He felt that some of the things written were unfair and breaking confidentiality.

The suicide attempt involved placing a whole packet of nicotine patches on himself and taking a large quantity of Klonopin, an anti-anxiety prescription medication along with Motrin, an over the counter painkiller.

9–2-09 2:07 pm

having really bad cycling panic attacks
klonopin not helping
I'm really freaking out a ton over this the idea that there careless with the
super personal info is just too much to handle
How can I get help when doctor patient confidentiality is a lie.

(Comment—at this point the person is angry at the breaking of confidentiality which has led to the thought that he is unhelpable and no one can be trusted. These are the conditions necessary for the suicide decision to be acted upon and the Adapted Child aspect of the personality is strong).

3:36 pm

I've cried so much I don't think I have any more left
taking a 2nd klonopin in 1 day
only done that like 2 times ever b'fore.

(Comment—at this point the person has decided on the suicide attempt, one and a half hours after the initial angry reaction. In the next two hours the rest of the medication is taken. One can already see the ambivalence beginning with the statement— "only done that like 2 times ever before"—which indicates some trepidation at what he is doing and the Free Child becoming stronger).

5:40 pm

this has escalted extrordinarially yuckily
i dunno what the fuck is going on
how can i get help if i cant trust them.

(Comment—possible anger still present and a restatement of the conditions necessary for the suicide attempt. That is being unhelpable and not being able to trust anyone thus indicating that things have reached the point of being too bad).

6:31 pm

feel so nausiated
i dunno what im doing

(Comment—confusion indicated and no restatement of the conditions necessary for the suicide decision to be enacted. This could indicate the Free Child desire to live is becoming stronger).

7:49 pm

I'm such a fucking idiot
i took too much of motrin
put a whole package of nicotine patch on me then i slept for a while
then was like fuck i don't wanna go to the hospital and this isn't enough
to kill me.

(Comment—the Free Child ego state is now strong enough to lead to direct survival behaviour. No restatement of conditions for the suicide decision to be active).

took off the patches
make myself vomit up the motrin
i didnt get it al but got out as much as i could
still feel crazy nausiated
when i was vomiting some blod came up
not a ton
but stil Iworry some
not like i vomit regurally
hadt done it in years
must be the motirn
dizzily walked ot store ot buy moutwash and salt to rinse
i feel like shit
ovrheating
took off my clothing
don't have a fever
im realyl bloated dunno why
fuck im an idiot
all over this cofidentiality shit.

(Comment—five and a half hours after the episode started there has been a shift in ego states from the Adapted Child to the Free Child. Whilst under the influence of the Adapted Child he was stating the circumstances necessary to enact the suicide decision. By the end of the process the conditions necessary to enact the decision are discounted thus reflecting the more powerful influence of the Free Child in the personality).

In case study 2 there was quite a quick change in ego states and hence quite a quick change from being influenced by the AC to the FC. In case study 3 the same change occurs but over a number of hours. However, the same suicidal ambivalence is being displayed.

Therapeutic practice from suicidal ambivalence

With the concept of suicidal ambivalence described one can move to the therapeutic practice that evolves out of this new theoretical understanding. There are a number of approaches one could use with this new understanding. The most obvious is providing the client with an opportunity to experience these two aspects of himself. With experiential understanding can come awareness and integration amongst other things, such as building relational contact.

Fortunately this is not hard to do as one draws on the empty chair technique originally described in Gestalt therapy (Latner, 2000; Nichol & Schwartz, 2008; Schacter, Gilbert, & Wegner, 2011) and then from redecision therapy as explained by Goulding and Goulding (1979). Two empty chairs are placed in front of the client, one representing the Free Child and the other the Adapted Child. As is shown in Figure 3 the ambivalence can then be experienced by the client. The client may first sit in the FC chair and begin talking from that aspect of the personality. The actual content depends on the issue at hand. For instance, if it is an issue of suicide he will be talking about the drive or urge to live as opposed to the urge to die. Alternatively it may be a destructive drug use issue where the ambivalence is between the FC desire to live and the AC desire to use drugs or alcohol destructively.

As we see in Figure 4 the two chairs may in fact be representing the FC Eros and the FC Thanatos (not the AC). However, at this point we assume it is the FC Eros and AC in the two chairs as it is unclear, at this juncture, if one can do therapy with the FC Thanatos at all. The client identifies his destructive urges and his desire to stay alive and be healthy and begins to experience this as he sits in the various chairs and enters into dialogue with the guidance of the therapist. Case study 4 provides an example of this. In this case the client was using alcohol destructively.

Case study 4

A forty-year-old male who drinks two bottles of wine each night of the week. He has done this for the past four years.

THERAPIST: Be the part of you that wants to drink. What does he say and feel?

CLIENT: I like it … I like the feeling it gives me and I work hard all day and it is my present to myself at the end of the day. It's my little party with myself. All my friends don't drink or only drink a bit, they look like they are getting old.

T: Say more about that.

C: We all used to drink together but now they don't drink much at all … I have not got old like them. I like this about myself. I feel good being young in mind … but my body is getting older and that is not good for the drinking.

T: OK that is the AC, so switch chairs and be the part that does not want to drink or drink so much.

C: Compared to others I drink a lot. Much, much more … I worry about the health effects. I have had all the blood tests and my liver and so on are fine but I worry that this will hurt me later in life. I don't like feeling like crap the next day. This gets me a bit angry at myself.

T: You feel anger at yourself?

C: Yes, when I get up in the morning feeling like shit, I get angry at me (said angrily) … each morning I promise to not drink tonight but by mid-afternoon I look forward to my little party that night. Sometimes I feel very sick but I still go to work. The odd time when I don't drink when I wake up the world looks much brighter and clearer. I am surprised by it but it shows how it affects me and I don't like it.

T: Which part is the stronger part?

C: I'm not going to stop yet … it is now 70%–30% wanting to use. It used to be 90%–10% wanting to use. I know if I just let myself go I will get more and more sick of it. If I try and stop myself I will only use more. I need to be very careful with the Rebellious Child in me as that will not stop drinking if I tell it to.

This is a reasonably short exercise and at times it can go on much longer. However, it shows the basics of what is being achieved. This is the first time this man did this and hence he is obtaining an experiential understanding of himself. One could then invite the client to integrate these aspects into the personality. The client is asked to state that he accepts both the FC and AC as part of himself. Most find the FC part easy to do but accepting and integrating the AC part of the self can be much more problematic. Indeed some find this very difficult to do. For example, a person with a significant addiction who is currently clean can have considerable trouble accepting even the idea of integration, let alone actually going through the process of verbalising and experiencing such an integration. However, with experiential understanding comes awareness, which can then lead to an integration of parts of the self into the sense of who one is.

The other interesting aspect of this exercise is the ability of people to cite the percentages for the AC and FC. Most can do this readily and will feel confident in their choice. This was initially surprising as it was not expected. However, it seems many people are quite attuned to themselves in this way. This exercise allows the client to access these percentages from his unconscious and bring them up into the conscious. Again this allows self awareness and also is important information for the psychotherapist to have. With the suicidal it is a good way to monitor the current level of suicide risk as people can cite percentages for those also. This exercise can be used repeatedly over time and thus one can monitor the changes in the percentages of their suicidality.

In addition the therapist gets to observe the client experiencing at first hand these two parts of the personality. Diagnostically this is most helpful. All the body language is directly observable and one can see where the energy currently is. In the FC chair the person may struggle to say anything whilst in the AC chair they may be quite animated and outspoken. This allows the therapist to directly observe what is happening in the psyche of the client in relation to these two aspects of the personality.

However, what is more important, in the AC chair one has a quite unique therapeutic situation. In that chair the person has stripped away all aspects of the personality except for his own destructive urges. Sitting directly in front of the psychotherapist is the core of the destructiveness in the person, which is a very desirable circumstance to have. It allows the therapist to relate directly with that. It allows the therapist to build up relational contact with it directly, by conversing with it. This is an unusual therapeutic situation and one with considerable therapeutic value. Very few people have ever experienced this— another person relating directly with the core of his destructive urges, which are usually out of awareness or securely hidden away from the rest of the world.

Clinical observations to date show that after a period of a few weeks or months of building relational contact with the destructive core there tends to be a pacifying effect. It does not disappear but tends to become less "vocal" and influencing in the personality. Most often a therapist would have tried to restrain it, contain it, or modify it in some way. In this approach the destructive core experiences being related to directly. Instead it is invited to express itself and talk with a sympathetic other. The effect seems to be like a small child who is being naughty because he is not getting any attention. When he starts to get attention he tends to become less naughty and does less attention seeking behaviour. He is pacified in this way. To date the same effect has been observed in most circumstances when one is afforded the opportunity to relate directly to the core of the client's self-destructive urges.

Case study 5

This was written by a thirty-five-year-old post anorexic woman who still has some eating difficulties. She describes her AC or FC Thanatos, which she has named the e.d. monster (eating disorder monster). The naming was not done as a result of any therapeutic intervention; instead it was spontaneously named by her many years before. She had on her own, identified her self-destructive drive to such a degree that she had named it. My additions are in parentheses.

> The part that is nice is the part that is trying to live, survive, be positive. In recovery this part of me is "winning". I am successfully living, I am a functioning human.
>
> If I wasn't "winning" the e.d. monster or anorexic part of self would be. In a sense I would be slowly killing myself e.g. (for example) not eating, purging, isolating, ruminating, obsessing, that is how I know it has control.
>
> But then there is day to day living which is the e.d. (monster) voice constantly telling me "I am fat" and everything that I eat I feel guilty about and I go through a conversation in my head with the e.d. (monster) about if I should or should not eat it.
>
> My first clear memory of the e.d. (monster) voice is about 15/16 years of age. It would say, "You are fat", "Life would be better if you were skinny". It wants me to be skinny and it is always looking and comparing self with skinny girls.
>
> It had a positive function. It helped me deal with life as a teenage girl and the distressing emotions, loneliness, feeling different and feeling not good enough.

At the moment it feels angry because it is not winning (haven't purged for 3 months).

The e.d. (monster) voice is always there so it is very strong in that way. It is not threatened by therapy because it knows it will always be there with everything I eat.

I realise now that the ever present nature of the e.d. (monster) is less. When I was in the eating disorder clinic it was really there all the time. There is now some freedom from that when I wake up in the morning for example. In the clinic it was there every time I woke up in the morning, now some mornings it is not there.

The self-destructive aspect of the client (e.d. monster) had developed relational contact with the therapist over the previous few months. At no point does the therapist seek to challenge it, contain it, or modify it. Indeed this client reports the e.d. monster does not feel threatened by therapy. The therapist acknowledges its power and seeks to develop a coexistence with it through the therapeutic relationship. As we can see there has been a reduction in the recent purging and its ever present nature is reportedly less. One could describe this as a pacifying effect on this self-destructive aspect of the personality.

Conclusion

This final therapeutic approach is currently in a state of evolution and development. It is seen to have considerable therapeutic potential for dealing with the suicidal and those who are behaving self-destructively. To have the very core of a person's self-destructive urges sitting directly in front of the therapist is quite an unusual therapeutic situation that merits much more theorising and therapeutic experimentation.

Also central to this chapter is the evolution of the idea of the Free Child Eros and the Free Child Thanatos. This means the Free Child contains one source of the destructive drives in the individual. This means all people will, at times, behave in self-destructive ways which is a natural state implying it is not a form of psychopathology. This raises questions which are yet to be answered. Is it psychopathology? If it is deemed so, can it be treated? If one believes it can, then how? If the destructive behaviour is not a consequence of adverse parenting in childhood, how does one treat that?

CHAPTER NINE

Psychological games and intersubjective processes

Jo Stuthridge & Charlotte Sills

In this chapter, we describe some of our thinking about working with the transferential dramas that Berne (1964) referred to as "psychological games". We propose that the therapist's participation in a game can become an important avenue for "hearing" the client's unspoken communication.

Clinical experience has led us both to discover the inescapable presence of *ourselves* in the therapy room. We both spent many years in training and personal therapy learning how to eliminate our personal script proclivities from our professional lives. However, we accept that self-awareness is a lifelong task, that therapy is never complete, and that a therapist always arrives in the room with her vulnerabilities and script in addition to her expertise. Indeed, we have become interested in how this mutuality of "flawedness" has the capacity to foster growth in a therapy relationship, especially in relation to those moments when two scripts collide in a game.

How do games emerge between two minds? How do we communicate with another person outside awareness? And what can we do about it? How do we use ourselves and our subjective experience to resolve games? We have both been wrestling with these questions from different theoretical perspectives and have reached a shared conviction that resolution of a game often requires a genuine internal shift within the therapist, which can lead to growth for both parties.

Berne's game theory attempts to explain complex intersubjective dynamics, dynamics that bridge the space between client and therapist, between speech and action, thinking and feeling, mind and body, and also conscious and unconscious realms. These dualities are increasingly being dissolved within contemporary psychotherapy (Aron, 1996) and we believe that game theory, arguably the centrepiece of Berne's (1961) "social psychiatry", can usefully contribute to this endeavour. Developments in neuroscience (Panksepp, 1998; Schore, 1994), infant research (Trevarthen & Aitken, 2001), and clinical experience have underscored the centrality of reciprocity and relatedness in human development. They have also highlighted the importance of affective and somatic forms of organisation and the interdependence of these with cognition and behaviour (Bucci, 2001; Damasio, 1999). Chaos theory (Gleick, 1987) encourages us to think of a therapy relationship as an evolving inter-subjective system, in which small gestures can amplify into profound pattern shifts in the client's life. The therapist is no longer viewed as a neutral, uninvolved observer, but rather a separate human subject who uniquely and unavoidably participates in a volatile interactive process. Shifts in the dyadic system invariably mean both client and therapist are changed.

Relational Transactional Analysis views the therapy relationship as an encounter between two psyches with each partner contributing consciously and unconsciously to this process. Patterns belonging to both client and therapist emerge in the consulting room and become the intersubjective vehicle for exploration and understanding. From this perspective, countertransference, mutual enactments, and games are no longer seen as unfortunate but rather as an important source of data.

Berne understood games as defensive; however, these days we can think about these processes in broader terms. Games can involve the replay of, or defence against early experiences which were in one way or another limiting to the person's capacity to process and integrate what was happening to and inside him or her. Games contain both the deepest level of relational expectation and unmet need, and also attempts to avoid the pain of these early experiences. However, they can also be understood as the enactment of unworded experiences;

the communication of something that has never been formulated in language and can therefore only be expressed through gesture, affect, and action.

When a game occurs in the therapy room, it is the most vital, vibrant, experience-near revelation of the client's unspoken truth—and often that of the therapist. Games allow for the possibility of reliving early experiences, bringing here and now reality to bear on them, and also weaving new meanings. In this light, games are not something to be avoided but to be welcomed by the therapist.

In this chapter we offer a framework for understanding and working with consulting room games.

Early game theory and methods

Berne originally defined a game as an "an ongoing series of ulterior transactions progressing to a well-defined, predictable outcome" (1964, p. 48). A subtle provocation from one person hooks a defensive anxiety in the other, nudging or prodding him to react in a way that confirms his transferential expectations. Berne believed that the primary function of games was concerned with psychic stability or "homeostasis" which he described in terms of four main factors: "... 1) the relief of tension, 2) the avoidance of noxious situations, 3) the procurement of stroking and 4) the maintenance of an established equilibrium" (ibid., p. 19). In a later definition ("Formula G") (1972, p. 23) he emphasised the importance of a sudden "switch" in roles.

English (1977, p. 243) challenged Berne's focus on a switch, suggesting that this only occurs as a desperate measure when one player fears the other might stop playing. She suggested that the primary motivation for playing the game is in the process itself, the aim of which is to obtain strokes in the familiar, predictable ways that script dictates. Zalcman (1990) pointed out that English's explanation is "more plausible and less fatalistic than Berne's" (p. 7). Schiff offered a yet more life-affirming view: "We view games as a desperate attempt on the part of a struggling individual to re-create an environment in which archaic problems can be reenacted and resolved" (1977, p. 71).

Over the next three decades game theory described a proliferation of new games. Games outside the consulting room were often described as bidirectional two-handed interactions, with both players equally involved (Berne, 1964; Hine, 1990). However, inside the consulting room, a more one-handed approach prevailed. Transactional analysts became adept at confronting the invitation or "the con" (Berne, 1964) and derailing the potential game, ideally at its first appearance. The implication was unavoidable that it would be shameful and a sign of incompetence for a therapist to be "caught" in a game.

In more recent years, the use of confrontation has been questioned due to its potential for shaming, the risk of increasing defensiveness, or, worse, a slide into despair (Woods, 2002). Many therapists have become interested in exploring alternative ways to work with games (Deaconu & Stuthridge, 2015; Hunt, 2011; Shadbolt, 2012; Woods, 1996, 2000, 2001).

We hope to build on these ideas and develop game theory as an intersubjective model describing multilevel communication between two intrapsychic worlds.

How do games emerge between two minds?

"It is a remarkable thing that the Ucs [unconscious] of one human being can react upon that of another without passing through the Cs [conscious]" (Freud, 1915e, p. 194).

Freud's statement is quite remarkable for its time. The question of how unconscious communication occurs between two minds, as in a game, has puzzled psychotherapists ever since. The everyday bewilderment of how we engage others in repetitive patterns to confirm our worst nightmares often brings clients to therapy. Concepts like mutual enactment (Jacobs, 1986; McLaughlin, 1991, 2005), projective identification (Bion, 1962; Grotstein, 2005; T. Ogden, 1994), and theories concerning "thirdness" (J. Benjamin, 2004; T. Ogden, 1994) which have emerged from psychoanalysis are attempts to explain these mysterious interpersonal phenomena by extending intrapsychic theories into the realm of interaction. These ideas have all made important contributions to the growing interpersonalisation of psychoanalysis (Aron, 1996; Brown, 2011).

In contrast, Berne's game theory is first and foremost an interpersonal theory—it describes what happens between people. Beginning with the assumption that there are often two conversations taking place side by side, one verbal (social level transactions) and one non-verbal (psychological level transactions), game theory attempts to explain the mechanics of how transference and countertransference are actualised in relationships.

Berne (1961) developed game theory working with therapy groups. He noticed how group participants acted like a "casting director" (ibid., p. 118), unconsciously choosing game partners, with "considerable intuitive acumen" (ibid., p. 119) to play the parts required by his script. "When his casting is complete he proceeds to try to elicit the required responses from the person cast for each role" (ibid., p. 119). We suggest that in individual therapy the client unconsciously scans the therapist as a possible game partner, intuitively looking for vulnerabilities that meet the character descriptions in his script.

One person unwittingly nudges the other into a particular feeling state employing a range of ulterior transactions, including verbal ploys, tone of voice, pitch, rhythm, syntax, actions, behaviours, and sensori-motor transactions such as breathing, posture, or facial expression. The game that emerges is a product of two intrapsychic worlds, only the "currency" (Berne, 1964, p. 63) tends to reflect the client's agenda. The client's ulterior transaction meets with the therapist's whole internal cast of characters (which might be considered affects, self-states, Parent and Child ego states, whole or part objects), which, to continue with Berne's theatrical metaphor, are "waiting in the wings for a director's call" (Stuthridge, 2015a). The client unerringly targets the particular quality in the therapist required by his script. Depending on the degree of game, the characters on stage may represent symbolised and repressed aspects of each player's psyche or more dissociated elements that have yet to find a name and costume. An aspect of the therapist's mind best suited for the part then steps forward to take centre stage. The therapist has unconsciously accepted a role and the drama begins. While there is some freedom to ad-lib, in each new scenario the roles are prescribed by the scripts of each player and lead inexorably to a replay of an old emotional conviction.

In this light, games and enactments can be understood as an "intersection between two scripts" (Stuthridge, 2012, p. 245). Client and therapist each become actors in the other's script. A game is jointly constructed by the therapy couple and experienced by each person according to his or her own internal story. Every therapy couple is unique and while a client might play the same game with three therapists, with each, the familiar moves will take on a different flavour and specific nuance.

Three degrees of games

We think that that Berne's (1964, p. 64) model of three degrees of games provides a framework for recognising and utilising the therapist's experience (or countertransference) in a way that can provide useful direction. Berne defined:

1. A first degree game as "one which is socially acceptable in the agent's circle" (ibid., p. 64). (For example, in the therapy context: every transaction the therapist makes is greeted with "Yes I understand that but …". The therapist begins to feel irritable and hopeless).
2. A second degree game as "one from which no permanent irremediable damage arises, but which the players would rather conceal from the public" (ibid., p. 64). (The client gets upset towards the end of the session, complaining that nothing is working and the therapist lets her stay five minutes longer. She forgets to discuss the incident in supervision).
3. A third degree game as "one which is played for keeps, and which ends in the surgery, the courtroom or the morgue" (ibid., p. 64). (The client misses the next session and phones from the emergency room having taken an overdose).

Berne's pithy definitions are powerful and yet they remain at the level of behavioural outcomes. Sometimes, while the therapist is aware that "something is going on", it is extremely difficult to know how to proceed. Confronting the client's behaviour may shift away from the therapist's discomfort and uncertainty and can lead to closing down on important meanings for the client. We think that looking at a deeper level is important. In other words, we are interested in exploring various levels of ulterior transactions that reveal vital features of script, as well as the intrapsychic and interpersonal dynamics behind the manifest behaviours.

Britton (2007) proposed that enactments occur on several levels, an idea which we think can shed new light on Berne's three degrees of games (Stuthridge, 2015a). Britton's concept draws on Bion's (1963) theory that the mind contains differing levels of symbolic functioning, from inchoate raw sensory data, through to complex symbolic processes that create emotional meaning from perception. We paraphrase Britton's levels here:

1. Enactment as the unconscious expression of organised thought (experiences that we can bring to awareness and think about).
2. Action as an alternative to thinking and feeling, and;
3. Action as "evacuation of a psychic state" (2007, p. 6) or ridding the mind of unformulated affect.

In relation to games, we see the term "action" here as including physical behaviours and a wide range of ulterior or non-verbal transactions that are used to "do something" to another person in order to extract a predictable reaction. These might include concrete events like missing a session but also silence, gestures, or subtle shifts in tone, or words used as acts to exert pressure on another person (Aron, 2003). "Action" would also include the passive behaviours described by Schiff et al. (1975) as escalating attempts to "shift responsibility" for resolution of the problem to someone else (ibid., p. 7), starting from extreme apparent inaction, and rising to incapacitation such as fainting or violent emotional or physical outbursts.

Each level or degree of game represents differing degrees of reflective capacity and abilities to symbolise experience in the moment. Thus first degree games might be considered an externalisation of symbolised thought (similar to Britton's first level) or the external manifestation of an internal dialogue that can be brought to awareness. They are, therefore, familiar patterns of gaining strokes and defending against uncomfortable experiences. Second and third degree games concern experience that has never been fully symbolised (felt, recognised, named) or contained as internal conflict. Second degree games defend against deeper unconscious levels of script that threaten to "break through" into unwanted awareness. Third degree games usually concern the parts of the self that have never been experienced, often due to trauma or deficit. This is illustrated by Hargaden and Sills's "the undeveloped self" (2002, p. 24). In other words, first degree games are more likely to involve meanings we have known but would prefer not to, while second and third degree games can involve meanings we attempt to repress or have never known. These unlanguaged meanings are the "inarticulate speech of the heart" (Van Morrison, 1983, cited in Hargaden and Sills, 2002, p. 45) and might include a whole range of processes such as D. B. Stern's (2003) "unformulated" and Bucci's (2001) "unsymbolised" experiences or Bollas's (1987) "unthought known".

Each degree includes the two levels of conversation defined by Berne as an exchange of ulterior transactions. However, there are key differences between each degree, in terms of the extent to which the content of the communication is symbolised. This concept differs somewhat from Cornell's (this volume) understanding of the distinctions between degrees, particularly in that his focus is more on intrapsychic processes while we are more interested in the way they manifest interpersonally.

The difference in experience between each degree is reflected in the therapist's countertransference. In first degree games there is a reasonable degree of symbolic functioning present and countertransference is accessible at a conscious and cognitive level. We know what we are feeling. In addition, the meaning of what is being communicated can often be detected through verbal clues. For example the infamous use of "Yes but" (Berne, 1964), or verbal invitations (cons) such as "If it weren't for you ...", or "Oh I do wish ...". Berne's (1964) and Dusay's (1966) methods which relied on cognitive interventions work well with these games.

In second degree games the experience evoked in both participants is likely to be unlinked to symbolic capacities. Ulterior transactions contain significant incongruities between the social and psychological level messages. According to Berne's (1966, p. 227) third rule of communication the outcome of an ulterior transaction is determined at the psychological level. Thus, the non-verbal transaction induces the unwanted affect in the other person. This "action" becomes a substitute for thinking and feeling. Countertransference can usually be felt as an affective disturbance but it is difficult to decipher cognitively. That is, we can feel something is wrong without knowing what it is. The meaning of what is communicated is more often detected through the therapist's unconscious associations as images or daydreams.

Third degree games involve highly toxic affect and experience that has never been symbolised. The aim is to rid the psyche of feelings that are unbearable, not just unwanted, through "psychic evacuation" (Bion, 1963). Berne associated these tragic outcomes with "tissue scripts" and client histories of child abuse (1972, p. 111). The other person typically feels bombarded, invaded, disconcerted, and destabilised. Countertransference is felt viscerally and the therapist's reflective capacities are usually decommissioned in the moment.

We both feel that the words of Gabbard and Ogden (2009, p. 423) chime with our experiences. "It has been our experience that when the analyst is off-balance he does his best analytic work." We wobble on our metaphorical chairs and sometimes fall off when a game process engages our own script, and our dissociated or repressed parts of the self join the fray. These moments can lead to effective therapy in that they insist on a deep level of emotional involvement in the process, which is perhaps the only way to hear a client's unspoken story.

Engaging with games in the consulting room

Early transactional analysts expected to avoid involvement in games, and to address them in the moment. Dusay (1966) offered four ways to respond: 1) play along in service of the larger goal; 2) ignore the game; 3) offer an alternative game (to de-escalate a situation), and 4) expose the game by naming it, often with humour.

These pragmatic ideas, alongside the overarching intention to identify the unmet need, are primarily used to establish social control over the client's behaviour. They are described in action by, for example, Goulding and Goulding (1979).

Phenomenological inquiry offers another important approach to working with games once the therapist is aware of the ulterior dynamics. This approach (Erskine & Trautmann, 1996) requires the therapist, inquiring into the client's phenomenological experience, to detect the client's invitation to enter a game and to employ close tracking of what is happening for him. It might be seen, perhaps, as a more empathic way of confronting the first con or crossing the transaction. For example, the therapist might say, "I notice that you looked away as you said that. What was happening for you at that moment? How are you feeling as you say that? What was it that I said that made you feel that way?", and so on.

Cornell (2015) building on the work of (Cowles-Boyd & Boyd, 1980) offers a creative option with the "game-play shift", in which a therapist uses play and humour to subvert a potential game.

These strategies, like Dusay's (1966) methods, rely on the premise that the therapist will recognise a game as it arises. However, we contend that so much of our script is nonconscious that in any close relationship, there is a risk that script will emerge. The therapeutic relationship with its periods or moments of closeness and vulnerability can "open the edges of script pressures" (Cornell, personal communication). Indeed, we would go further and propose that some deeply held relational patterns are so embedded—simply held in our viscera—that they can *only* be brought to awareness in this way. Therefore, in a sense, being available to play is vital.

When both parties are locked in their scripts, resolution often requires one person to contain both roles within one mind. We think it is the therapist's duty to "go first", and "surrender" (J. Benjamin, 2004, p. 8) to the truth of her own involvement. This usually means reclaiming a disowned aspect of her experience before she can understand the game and risk making a different gesture. We offer here some suggestions for how we might do this, exploring the three degrees of games in more detail with a focus on the differing countertransferential experiences.

First degree games

As Berne observed, first degree games can be played in public without much shame. Both therapist and client may recognise the sense of familiar discomfort and, if the game proceeds to a pay-off, the accompanying wave of recognition: "How did I get here again?" The relational enactment, though not in awareness, is one that is amenable to thought. With this idea in mind we consider two further approaches to working with first degree games:

1. *Analysing the countertransference* (by "countertransference" we mean the whole of the therapist's experience in the therapy relationship): Recognising that it is often only after a session, in reflection or with a supervisor, that we may become aware of a game, we carefully explore our responses. We draw on the work of several writers who have offered useful questions for inquiring into our countertransference (Hunt, 2011; Mazzetti, 2013; Novellino, 1984; Stuthridge, 2015b in press).

1. Notice our own feelings and countertransference.

    - What am I feeling towards the client? And how do I feel before, during, or after the session?
    - What do I want to do?
    - How do I want my client to see me?

2. Reflect on the implications for our own script.

    - What do I know about this experience for myself?

3. Reflect on the implications for the client's script.

- Why now … and why this client?
- Why does the other person want me (unconsciously) to feel what I am feeling?
- Who have I become for the client?
- How does this current drama relate to the client's past?

4. Think about what to do next.

- Offer an interpretive comment as one possible meaning among others.
- Comment on what is happening in the relational space.
- Or simply allow the new understanding to inform us, knowing this will change the emotional field.

With conscious reflection, using questions like these as a guide, the therapist's subjective experience in the game becomes a pathway to understanding the client's nonconscious communication.

2. Karpman's (1968) drama triangle: In a development of Karpman's concept, Sills (2007) has described how games occur through the negotiation with others of three capacities: power, love, and vulnerability. When an individual is limited to one (script driven) position in that intersubjective engagement, those aspects turn into the negative roles of Persecutor, Rescuer and Victim. The game is played between two of the positions, producing deadlocked complementarity (J. Benjamin, 2004) and the third position is accessed only as the switch in the game, which leads to the script pay-off.

This can sometimes offer a way through to deeper understanding. Ideally it will be through conscious choice. The therapist becomes aware that she is caught in some form of rigid relational pattern, but is not able to free herself because of the pressure of her own script not to acknowledge certain parts of herself—often represented in the third position on the triangle. She uses the framework of the drama triangle to help her think about what is happening. The missing capacity or skill (Choy, 1990) offers a new way of viewing the dyad.

For example, a therapist recognises that she is in Victim-Persecutor complementarity, what Racker (1968, p. 140) called "paranoid ping-pong", where there might either be open hostility or perhaps a competition under the subtle guise of interesting exploration, with both parties vying to have the power to be right, to define the other and free themselves of blame. After reflecting in supervision, she comments with compassion to them both, that "It seems that we both are determined to be right in this conversation—I am wondering whether it was dangerous to be wrong with your mother." Another therapist realises that he is desperately trying to be the Rescuer of his mother, as he takes responsibility for healing his "powerless" client. Thinking about the strength in the avoided Persecutor position, he decides to put a boundary on the client's e-mails.

The Persecutor-Rescuer bind can take various forms. In the example below, a particularly malignant and unhelpful dance takes place, in which the therapist allows herself to be attacked viciously in the name of allowing the client to have her true feelings. In a sense, she is "identifying with the persecutor" (ibid., p. 163).

The examples above demonstrate the therapist becoming aware of the game dynamic, and using Karpman's triangle to open up a space and dissolve the bind of dyadic complementarity.

However, it may only be via the switch and the final pay-off that the therapist becomes aware of her participation in a game, when the feeling of shock and surprise, the "cross-up" as Berne (1974) called it, breaks through the deadlock and introduces something different. The danger here is simply a shift to a different complementarity; the opportunity is that at that moment, the whole field of play becomes clear to the therapist, who can then regain her capacity for mentalising and contribute to the development of meaning and thought.

Robert

Over several months in therapy, Robert, a chief executive with a history of unhappy relationships both within and outside work, had begun to access his feelings and risk moments of vulnerability. After the Christmas break, Eddie, my (Charlotte's) supervisee, decided it was a good moment to review their work together. He was shocked when Robert sneeringly told him that he thought the therapy was a waste of time and he didn't want to listen to someone asking him "How do you feel?" all the time. In that moment, Eddie felt as if a bucket of water had been thrown over him. Frozen, he simply agreed to Robert's demands, empathising with his need to take charge of the process and merely suggesting that they give each other feedback more regularly.

In supervision, Eddie reflected on what had happened, addressing some of the questions about his countertransference outlined above. He knew that he wanted to be seen as the robust, understanding therapist. But he realised that he had actually felt hurt, frightened, and humiliated in the session and he recalled his schoolday experiences of having to show that he was "tough" in order to avoid being bullied. As Robert had taken the Persecutor role, Eddie had avoided feeling vulnerable by Rescuing, being understanding, and interested in Robert's thoughts. He began to realise that this had been the subtle dynamic since the beginning, as he had accepted and empathised with his client's bursts of abrasiveness. He recognised that his own response might very well be saying something about his client. At the next session, Eddie said, "I was thinking about last session and what was happening between you and me. It brought to mind some of the stories you told me about your father. I wondered if your father made you feel scared and ashamed when you were little." Robert began to talk about his experience with his bullying father and his decision never to let anyone see him as vulnerable. The growing closeness in the therapy relationship had begun to "open the edges" of his script and the break had given him just enough time to start rebuilding his defences.

We move now to thinking about the second and third degree games, whose provenance in recognisable script is harder to capture.

Second degree games

In second degree games, action functions as an alternative to thinking and feeling. The action takes the form of a psychological level transaction that is incongruent with the accompanying social level transaction and might include anything from overt behaviour such as arriving late at a session, a phone call at the weekend, to very subtle shifts in tone, facial expression and posture, or words with coded meanings. These actions all involve some element of symbolisation but there is usually no thinking subject present. That is, there is no connection between the action and the sense of "I". For example, Jo's client in the vignette below who turned up late, exclaimed, "It wasn't me!" explaining how it was her husband's fault she didn't make it on time. It was only after this happened on several occasions that she became curious that it might indeed be she who was coming late after all, and further that this might have some meaning.

The therapist's countertransference is neither as nameable as in the first degree game, nor as disconcerting, overwhelming, and destabilising as in the third degree. Frequently, there is simply a sense of unease, discomfort, and disorientation. The therapist's behaviour—anything that might veer from the norm—is often the first signal that a game is in progress (Renik, 1998).

Strategies that rely on conscious understanding, as outlined in the previous section, are not immediately available when working with second degree games. In exploring ways to work with these less conscious interpersonal dynamics we have found that the therapist's free floating associations, such as visual and auditory images, memories, or daydreams often provide important clues. Imagery, generated either by client or therapist can provide a link between conscious and unconscious realms and between client and therapist, thus forming a route to understanding what is being communicated.

Berne's early work on intuition and his concepts of the "primal image" (1955) and "ego image" (1957) focused on this realm of unconscious interpersonal communication. He described the primal image as "pre-symbolic representations of interpersonal transactions" (1955, p.67) which leads to the "primal judgement": "the understanding (correct or incorrect) of the potentialities of the object relationship represented by the image" (ibid., p. 67). He says intuition is "a more or less distant derivative" (p. 67) of the primal image and can be useful in diagnosis. Interestingly, Berne cautions that the primal image is influenced by "the percipient's own problems" (p. 87) and "particularly subject to distortion" (p. 93) by the therapist's script. However, he seems to have more faith in the "ego image", which, perceived by the therapist, is described as "specific perceptions of the patient's active archaic ego state in relation to the people around him" (p. 102), in other words, an image of an actual child with historical basis. He considered the ego image to be a vital therapeutic tool. He suggests, further, that in everyday life, interpersonal relationships are likely to be based on "mutual intuitive understanding through partial ego images and primal images even though these may never become conscious" (p. 115).

Berne also refers to the ego symbol (pp. 113–115) which he describes as a picture, metaphor, or symbol, often offered by the patient himself, which indicates how he feels and is a guide in therapeutic technique. Clearly Berne was experimenting with spontaneous images as intuitive forms of induction between client and therapist.

A similar idea was developed in more detail by Otto Isakower, a Viennese analyst who, interestingly, like Berne, was analysed by Paul Federn (Brown, 2011, p. 28). Federn's interest in phenomenological ego experiences is evident in both Berne and Isakower's work. Berne cites Federn's work as the theoretical basis for his ideas on ego images.

Isakower described how auditory and visual "images that come spontaneously to the analyst's mind during the session should be taken seriously as data for understanding the patient" (Spencer, Balter, & Lothane, 1992, pp. 248–249). He argued that images occupy a transitional space between unconscious and conscious realms, and as such can provide a way to decode unconscious communication.

Although later writers (Bollas, 1987; T. Ogden, 1994) have taken this idea very seriously, drawing on Bion's (1963) notion of reverie, Isakower's work, like Berne's work in this area, never attracted much interest at the time. Brown (2011) suggests that this might be because of political influences that marginalised those who didn't tow the mainstream ego psychology line and also ongoing suspicion about the therapeutic use of countertransference.

Bucci, a cognitive scientist, offers another way to think about nonconscious interpersonal processes. Her theory of emotional communication argues that imagery provides a halfway house between verbal symbolic and sub-symbolic communication, embedded in motoric sensory and somatic systems. In brief she describes a three step process for working with the therapist's countertransference:

1. Arousal of experience dominated by sub-symbolic elements, the sensory, somatic, and motoric components of the affective core.
2. Representation of experience in symbolic form as a visual or auditory image (non-verbal symbolic).
3. Conscious reflection on the meaning of the metaphor (verbal symbolic) (2001, p. 54).

The therapist's capacity to symbolise experience and link incongruent affects then fosters the client's ability to integrate dissociated or split off experiences.

We are proposing that at moments in the work when the therapist senses that she might be embroiled in a second degree game, objective analysis, phenomenological inquiry, and conscious analysis of countertransference all risk being skewed by the therapist's unconscious participation. Instead, images that arrive in the therapist's mind, usually uninvited and unwilled, can offer possible pathways to deciphering the game. The therapist allows herself to notice any odd phenomena that pass through her, from images, to words, to snatches of song. She then associates to and feels with this experience, letting its meanings come to her.

Karpman's (1968) triangle can also be used here, through playing with imagination. For example, the therapist might ask herself what would it be like to be stuck on a desert island with this client? Would we be camped at either end of the island, or trying to kill each other, or having an erotic getaway? Allowing fantasy can sometimes find a route through to identifying the game role.

Julia

Julia was an impressive woman in her late forties who was both charming and formidable in equal measure. She was like a glittering chandelier that other lesser lights revolved around ... me (Jo) included. She had a stunning career but came to therapy because her twenty-year marriage was a source of misery. The relationship was a businesslike arrangement; they led separate lives, slept in separate rooms, and often bickered. Julia had developed a somewhat manic lifestyle that seemed to be built on a rigid denial of desire for love, sex, or food. She exercised and counted calories obsessively.

Julia said she had a "happy childhood", a statement roundly asserted although backed by slim evidence. She described parents who were proud of their youngest daughter but emotionally remote and self-interested. A rough picture emerged of a child who had learned to subjugate her own needs, seeking praise in the absence of love.

Despite her extroverted nature Julia felt emotionally unseen by others and she would test people to see if they cared, then watch them fail. We began to understand this as a script repetition of her experience with her self-absorbed parents.

A game pattern emerged between us around repetitive enactments with lateness to sessions and missed sessions. Julia would religiously turn up four or five minutes late. My attempts to address these issues were curtly dismissed: "You're barking up the wrong tree." There was always a good reason; the accountant, the car, or her husband. She would predictably cancel one or two sessions following my breaks. Through talking she eventually acknowledged these patterns were unusually consistent, but the meaning eluded us. At one point she said, "What's good for the goose is good for the gander," confirming my sense that a tit-for-tat dynamic was clearly in play.

I had a nagging feeling that I couldn't see where we were going or what we were doing but I didn't delve too deeply. I was vaguely aware that I was avoiding a script dystonic feeling of "not seeing" or knowing. I was also no doubt avoiding the whole issue of cancelled sessions, along with Julia's somewhat intimidating manner.

The events that brought the game more clearly into view began with a session when Julia showed up a minute early and almost sat but more grazed the edge of a chair in my waiting room. I noted this because it was so unusual. There was a sense that the work was hotting up just as we were approaching a summer break.

I said, "You were *almost* sitting and *almost* waiting for me instead of me waiting for you, … as if you are almost ready to be here?"

She said, "It nearly killed me." As we explored this further Julia struggled to find words: "I know I'm fighting something … something inside … I don't know what." She seemed to tiptoe around a dangerous feeling. The session was tense, close, and tender. The room felt too hot. The following week I was away at a workshop and predictably, Julia cancelled the next session.

Her first transaction when we next met was, "It took all my strength to come out here today."

Her talk began to move from one thing to another across different topics. I tried looking for a thread, and saw none. I felt as though I was following her while she edged further and further away. Her talking traversed places, time periods, and various relationships … the content fell through my fingers like sand.

I said, "It seems like you are distant today," and Julia immediately became tearful. "I take one step forward and two steps back … I come out of my shell then retreat."

I wondered out loud if this might be what the missed sessions were about: "When I miss one week you miss the next two. You cancelled last week and it's as if you are not quite here today." She said, "It is hard to come back … it makes no sense …"

She paused a while, then said, "I've never felt this vulnerable before. I'm full of bluff and bravado everywhere else … but for fifty minutes here I feel seen."

I felt that something important was happening but I still couldn't see what it was. At this point the feeling became troubling. I sifted through my notes looking for clues but these conscious attempts to understand led to dead-ends.

In a quiet moment, what jumped out at me was the image of a jack-in-a-box. This picture conjured up the jolly face Julia showed the world, her buoyant entertaining presence, and also coiled springs, hidden things and tightly repressed desires. I remembered a comment that Julia had made weeks earlier, "I've lived with a giant lid on me all these years and I want to come alive. I can't stand being like this for the rest of my life but I'm terrified of where this might lead."

I faced the next session with Julia, not sure what I might say. She began by telling me she had watched a documentary on sex, knowing I would be as surprised as she was. When sex came up early on in our work, Julia would promptly dismiss it as something that needed doing occasionally then crossing off, like an item on a grocery list. This time, she explored her reactions to the documentary with cautious curiosity. She wondered about attraction to women, "coming out" and homosexuality. Mostly she marveled at the way she had cut off sexual feelings over a lifetime. Despite my awareness that Julia avoided sex, my collusion in this process suddenly struck me. Perhaps for the first time, I was available to listen.

The following week Julia arrived ahead of time. I noticed her hands and feet moving expressively as she ventured, "I think I'm out of the box ..." and I guessed, "Jack-in-the-box?" "Yes! " she exclaimed, "that was the picture in my mind."

She said the last session had "opened up a world of possibility" and she was sleeping better. She described, through tears, a process of opening up and shutting down as she left each session, "I used to close the door and forget... I shut down." In the weeks that followed the transferential relationship became alive with all the dangers inherent in sexual desire, and also emotional need and visibility. The shame and terror that had silently driven the persistent enactments were also revealed more fully.

On one occasion I was a few minutes late in starting a session and after 5 years of me waiting for Julia, she waited for me. I asked how it felt and she said, "In the past it would have been unbearable. I would have hidden behind a magazine." I asked, "What would you be hiding?" and softly she replied, "The part of me that needs someone."

Julia began to see that leaving me waiting, was like the myriad ways she rejected her husband, ensuring that this repellant scary needy feeling remained out of mind and safely lodged in others.

The jack-in-the-box became a shared symbol for all that could not previously be spoken; unspeakable desires, vulnerabilities, longings and fear, which had lain dormant and coiled within her. In the absence of words, she communicated these feelings through enactments around lateness and missed sessions. The jack-in-a-box, a non-verbal symbol in Bucci's (2001) schema, formed a bridge between the subsymbolic realm of affect and verbal understanding. Our conversation became rich, relaxed, intimate and laden with new meanings about retreating and coming out, being seen and not seen, aliveness and deadness. The shift in the intersubjective field was internalised by Julia as an increasing ability to think and feel, "In the past these feelings would have spun me out … but actually I don't have to do anything … I can think now."

As we talked, I realised that I had played the part of the unseen child for years, feeling peripheral to Julia's life when she missed sessions or turned up late, but I had also become the unseeing parent. I had been dazzled by Julia's vivacious front and there was a part of me more than willing to ignore sexual desire and neediness. Our scripts had dovetailed to create a jointly constructed game pattern.

These events with Julia illustrate how games can be understood both as repetitions of the past and gateways to novel experience, particularly intimacy. The enactment communicated the first clues to unspeakable desires that had never been symbolised in feelings, thoughts, or words. Resolution required a shift in me, a turning towards, instead of "turning a blind eye". The mutual loosening of script constrictions ultimately produced profound changes for her.

Jill and Terry

My (Charlotte's) supervisee, Jill, a trainee, described her client Terry to me. He was in a good deal of emotional pain since his wife had died, and his loss clearly triggered the pain of his early years. I learned that his mother had died when he was a young teenager and he had been brought up by his local neighbourhood gangs. From occasional references to punishments and to his father's violence, Jill surmised a life on the edge of society and the law. Frequently, when Terry seemed near to his distress, he politely asked if they could stop now. Jill got into the habit of going to make them both a cup of coffee at that point. Her reasoning was that it kept Terry from leaving the session, yet offered him some respite. I invited her to describe what it was like to sit with Terry; "Absolutely fine," was Jill's sanguine reply. I asked her to experiment in the following session with noticing her own feelings and perhaps asking Terry if they could both stay a little longer with his. Jill agreed to do this. She also acknowledged her own lifelong script of steering clear of painful feelings.

Driving to the session later in the week, Jill reflected on her "steering clear". She experimented with looking inside herself: how was she feeling about the upcoming session with Terry? She was startled to notice how very anxious she felt; and then, tracking her own process carefully, the almost conscious self-talk: "Don't think about it." She stopped the car and sat thinking and feeling about Terry, herself, and the unmistakeable resonance between their stories. Although her childhood had neither the terrible losses nor the violence of Terry's, she recalled the desolate loneliness of having a depressed mother and being bullied as a new girl at school after her parents had to move district. She realised that her action of leaving the room to make coffee for them when Terry got distressed had served the purpose of allowing her to "steer clear" and protect herself as well as him from his pain. Knowing this about herself, she began to wonder, "Why now, with this client?"

Jill restarted the car and "steered thoughtfully" to the session, feeling compassionate and available. She prepared herself to address differently that moment when Terry would say, as always, "Can we stop now?" However, she was astonished when, this time, he started to talk and share his feelings of almost unbearable loneliness, staying with the session to the very end.

In this example the trainee therapist's action is the first clue to the enactment which we explored in the supervision. Her action of leaving the session to make coffee carries a symbolic meaning that she is not aware of in the moment. The dynamics of this game are based on collusion, "Let's not talk about it". As Hine (1990) suggested, a switch is usually pulled by the party with the lowest threshold for tolerating tension. Without her realisation, a switch from either client or therapist could have resulted in the therapy, to continue the metaphor, "stalling".

It is interesting that the therapist's revelation occurs in the moment of stopping her car. In this moment she is no longer "steering clear" and we wondered if the image found its way, "unbidden" (D. B. Stern, 2010) to language and conscious verbal knowing in this instant.

Third degree games

Clients prone to third degree games often come from backgrounds of severe trauma and neglect. Concrete thinking and a poor capacity for reflective functioning can be part of the legacy that trauma leaves in its wake (Fonagy, Gergely, Jurist, & Target, 2002). Traumatic experiences of overwhelming pain and intolerable stress combined with a lack of adequate mirroring from a caregiver can cause the mind to become fragmented. Experience that has never been thought about or symbolised remains as pockets of dysregulated and dissociated experience (Schore, 2003). The narrative part of the brain, which provides the sense of chronology, fails to function, so that past and present become one (P. Ogden, Minton, & Pain, 2006). Unintegrated experience is then endlessly re-enacted in the present rather than archived in the past, providing ongoing reinforcement of the rigid closed script system (Stuthridge, 2006).

In third degree games both therapist and client must often withstand replaying the parts of the abused child or the abuser, as this experience, internalised in Parent and Child ego states, is reactivated. The incongruity between these aspects of the self can be severe, and psychic stability often depends on keeping one aspect or other out of mind.

The function of a third degree game is to rid the mind of affect that is unbearable, unthinkable, and unspeakable—often in a moment when it threatens to become conscious. An exchange of ulterior transactions arouses an analogous affect in the other person.

In the midst of this interaction the therapist usually loses her ability to think or reflect on her experience. Cornell (this volume, p. 89) suggests that in a third degree game, client and therapist "live the problem together". The therapist's focus in the moment is often on simply surviving the game. After she has survived and regained a capacity to think, there is an opportunity to transform the raw sensory experience into symbolic thoughts and coherent self-narrative. Working with the countertransference of third degree games usually involves an attempt to translate visceral or somatic experience into symbolic meaning. Neither conscious thought, nor associations and imagery are generally available as in first and second degree games.

Dean

Dean was an ex-gang member with a long history of violence towards men and women. I (Jo) felt that he took some pleasure in relaying garish stories of his exploits to me. He came to therapy because he knew his history of severe abuse had somehow "fucked up his life" and he wanted to keep custody of his daughter. Over the first two years it became apparent that he was experiencing disabling panic attacks and periods of severe dissociation, in which he would lose hours of time, coming around to find himself in a foetal position under a bed or dangerously close to a heater. In broken snippets, devoid of feelings, he disclosed a horrific history of childhood sexual abuse and neglect. He had been fostered by a woman who tortured him by applying electric cattle prods to his genitals. She was also the only adult figure in his life who he felt had ever shown him affection and care, creating an attachment that was both needed and feared.

Dean often filled sessions with colourful accounts of skirmishes with the police, his gang associates, and ex-partners. These events were told as if he was always in the right and others were stupid and deserving of his contempt. He explained to me his various theories about life at length. Any response I made other than affirming his views would mostly be greeted with "You don't get it". I think he was right, I didn't really get what was happening between us but I had become fond of him and his growing trust in me felt precious. We had developed sufficient intimacy for a game (Berne, 1964).

This event began with Dean talking about an interaction with his six-year-old daughter the previous evening, in which he had severely disciplined her. The details were disturbing to hear and he told me he felt nothing when she cried. He was self-righteous and justified his harsh approach, telling me she deserved to be punished. I heard in the transference a warning.

Cautiously and respectfully I began to explore the moment with him and as we talked he began to feel less certain about what had happened. I sensed an opening in his rigid defences and *probed* further: "What did you see in your daughter's face?" Dean's words slowed, he became thoughtful, and very gradually a quiet sense of empathy for his daughter emerged, conveyed through a softening in his voice and body.

Then in quick succession, Dean recalled a memory of abuse from his own childhood, along with intense feelings. He realised with sickening insight that he had frightened and humiliated his daughter. Feelings of shame and childhood terror began to overwhelm him. He became anxious and agitated, squirming on the edge of his seat. Sweat appeared on his brow and his eyes darted towards the door. I was acutely aware of the rising tension in the room.

Suddenly he snapped. He looked up and glared. In a fast about-turn, he barked at me that it was different with his daughter and she deserved to be punished. "You don't get it," he repeated over and over, his voice rising steadily in volume. I began to feel afraid that the situation could get dangerously out of control. Dean jumped up from his seat, came towards me in a threatening manner, paused while he stood over me breathing heavily, then abruptly turned his back and walked out. I was left feeling severely shaken.

Dean made no contact and it took me two weeks to recover adequately to think about what had happened and what to do next. Initially I felt his behaviour had been "abuse", not "use" of an object in Winnicott's (1968) terms and I wasn't sure I wanted to continue.

The image of my "probing" only appeared as I found myself using the word to write up notes, in an attempt to make sense of the session. The word pulsed with electricity on the page and connections between the incident and Dean's past suddenly fell into place in my mind. I realised that he may have felt my "probing" as a violation: too intrusive and too painful as it connected him to intolerable feelings. In this moment I became the terrifying sexual abuser; the trusted woman with the cattle prod. As feelings of terror and humiliation threatened to overwhelm him, he pulled a switch to evacuate the toxic affect, evoking terror in me.

I decided to write him a brief note saying firstly that I wanted to see him again and secondly that he seemed to get stuck with me at times, either being frightened or frightening. He came back the next session and said, "Now you've got it." He told me that this was the story of his life; knowing terror as a child, and how to terrify others. In the session he could see that he had moved quickly from one state to the other. He said he had left because he was afraid he would hurt me. Dean's unfolding story was of course more complex than this incident reveals; however, it marked a point at which we began to create shared meanings. He was able to symbolise his experience with me and link it to his past. As Dean began to contain split-off states of mind such as fear, rather than evoke it in others, the dissociative experiences lessened. He developed some ability to turn the horror of his childhood into a story that could be thought about and remembered rather than enacted in the present.

Conclusion

Games are essentially crucial scenes or acts in the drama that take place in the consulting room theatre. Each therapist and client arrive at the therapeutic meeting with their own cast of characters who then engage with each other to perform all the great mythical themes: to fall in and out of love, to separate, compete, destroy and divorce, seek reparation, and discover gratitude. This jointly constructed performance is experienced by client and therapist according to his and her own unique personality, past and script.

We are suggesting that, rather than aiming for the grail of neutrality, the therapist embraces her unique personality and uses this experience to understand the client and foster his growth. Having an acceptance of her own involvement is often key to freeing up the interpersonal knots, or games that inevitably emerge in a therapy process. The therapist's own growth might be considered a bonus.

These knots in the interpersonal field may be repetitions of the past or clues to emergent new experiencing. In unravelling the knot, new possibilities for living and relating that have never previously been felt or formulated arise. Games are one of the most important ways we have of dissolving restrictive script patterns and opening up new realms of experiencing.

Co-writing this chapter has required a collaborative effort to turn our separate clinical experiences into a shared narrative, a story that makes sense of things. As happens in a successful therapy this story has evolved from concrete accounts of diverse events, which often confused us, into an increasingly abstract and coherent narrative. This creative process echoes the transformation that is possible in a working therapy relationship. Games are first enacted on the therapy stage and then transformed by the therapy couple—as experiences are tossed back and forth between two minds—into symbolic thoughts and a speakable, thinkable story. This intersubjective process can then be internalised by the client, enhancing his capacity for story-making out of life's rough materials.

CHAPTER TEN

Transactional Analysis in the psychotherapy of personality disorders

Moniek Thunnissen

Introduction

One of Eric Berne's aims in psychotherapy was to *cure* patients rather than have them just make progress (Berne, 1972). This ideal is put into practice since 1978 in a short-term inpatient TA-based programme at De Viersprong, Netherlands Institute for Personality Disorders (Thunnissen, 2010). To illustrate how the short-term programme at De Viersprong is structured, I will reference throughout this paper a case study of Robin, a thirty-year-old woman for whom the treatment was quite effective.

Our view on personality disorders

In our view, personality disorders develop out of the interplay between innate genetic and temperament factors, the influence of the family of origin and early life experiences, and what we think of as good or bad luck: external events out of the individual's control.

In the *Diagnostic and Statistical Manual DSM-5* (APA, 2013 pp. 646–649) a personality disorder is characterised by enduring maladaptive patterns of behaviour, cognition, and inner experience, exhibited across many contexts and deviating markedly from those accepted by the individual's culture. These patterns develop early, are inflexible, and are associated with significant distress or disability.

In Transactional Analysis, a personality disorder is characterised by a script with self-destructive messages that influence the functioning of the integrative Adult with negative consequences for work and relationships (Thunnissen, 2015). Erskine (2009) focused on the influence of attachment in personality disorders and distinguished between a personal *style*, which can develop into a *pattern* and ultimately perhaps into a *disorder*. Attachment *style* refers to the general way someone experiences attachment based on early childhood experiences and how that may affect the person's way of being in the world. An attachment *pattern* refers to a more problematic level of functioning in relationships with others. An attachment *disorder* refers to the continual reliance on dysfunctional early childhood internal working models of relationships and archaic methods of coping with relational disruptions.

In a personality disorder, we often see a prevalence of destructive injunctions developed at an early age, which that led to script convictions. As Erskine (2010b) wrote, "Life scripts are the result of the cumulative failures in significant, dependent relationships" (p. 1).

In relation to personality disorders, we can say that people with a personality disorder are often imprisoned in ways of thinking, feeling, and acting that lead to difficulties in relationships with others. Without realising it, they are frequently experienced by others as manipulative, aggressive, entitled, or difficult (Thunnissen, 2009).

The sequence articulated by Erskine as going from style to pattern to disorder is also described but in a somewhat different way by Hellinga (2004). He focused on the role of unconscious mechanisms in communicating with others and described them in terms of degrees of self-fulfilling prophecies:

- First degree: *Selection*. This is something everyone does in the face of the overload of stimuli from the outside world. We select stimuli that fit our frame of reference and ignore what does not. This can be connected to an attachment style.
- Second degree: *Interpretation*. We interpret our experiences according to our frame of reference. For example, when someone we experience as egoistical and self-centred does something nice, our first thought might be, "What does he want from me?" Our interpretations reveal

our life position: constructive, inferior, superior, or hopeless. This can be connected to an attachment pattern.

– Third degree: *Manipulation*. When selection and interpretation fall short, we use manipulation. This can be connected to an attachment disorder. Unconsciously, we may show a predictable sequence of interactions that we learned at a young age, and ultimately we receive our familiar psychological pay-off. For example, a woman with a good deal of experience of abuse, neglect, and abandonment meets a man who really loves her. She can hardly believe it and constantly expects that he will leave her. However, he remains trustworthy and loving. Then she starts challenging him without being conscious of why she is doing so. She fails to keep to their appointments, is unfair in their interactions, and finally has sex with his best friend. When he breaks off the relationship she complains, "I knew it, men are not trustworthy and I don't deserve a stable relationship."

Everyone creates his own "SIM card" of selection, interpretation, and manipulation, that is, self-fulfilling prophecies by which each of us navigates the world. This SIM card helps us to reconfirm our convictions about ourselves, others, and the world. Because we are often blind to our own frame of reference but sharp-eyed about the disadvantages of others' frames of reference, group psychotherapy is eminently suited to discovering each others' SIM cards and pointing out how interpretation and manipulation work to preserve a defective frame of reference.

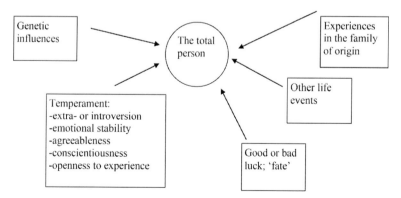

Figure 1. Influences of the developing personality.

The three months inpatient programme

We chose Transactional Analysis as the foundational method for the three-month short-term programme, and in the following sections I will explain the reasons for doing so. A short-term programme for patients with severe personality problems needs to meet certain standards to be effective. First, the programme should be coherent and well thought out. Therapists and patients should have a clear goal and an idea of how they might cooperate to reach it, and the staff—which at our centre included a psychotherapist and a psychiatrist, nurses (who were called *sociotherapists*), and movement and art therapists—should be knowledgeable and work closely together so the different elements of the programme reinforce each other. Taking time with staff to tune in and reflect on what happens in the patient group and any parallel processes between staff and patients is essential. Because personality disorders involve longstanding, often rigid patterns that have shown their usefulness in the past (which is why we also call them *survival decisions*), it is often difficult for patients to let go of their familiar styles of behaving, thinking, and feeling. The therapy programme can stimulate this process when it offers structure, holding, and clarity.

Another advantage of an inpatient setting is that temporary regression can be tolerated. Patients can function for a while at a more primitive level at which corrective experiences are possible (for more on the psychotherapy of temporary regresson see Richard Erskine and Amaia Mauriz-Etxabe's chapter in this book). Since personality disorders develop in relationships with parents and other significant people, working with and in the therapeutic relationship and offering corrective experiences is essential in the therapeutic approach to personality disorders. We call this the *reconstructive milieu* of inpatient psychotherapy (Janzing & Kerstens, 2012; Thunnissen, 2001; 2015).

The whole setting and milieu of the psychotherapeutic programme is aimed at discovering links between past and present and changing dysfunctional patterns. This means that working with the transference is significant: the entire staff and the institute as a whole begin to play a role in the transference-countertransference process with each patient. Patients repeat their familiar ways of behaviour, feeling, and thinking in their here-and-now interactions with staff and other patients (see Ray Little's chapter in this book). Dealing with this process can be challenging. Staff members need to demonstrate enough coherence in their behaviours to become trustworthy, stable transference objects and to show that with them, processes of splitting and projection will not prevail. On the other hand, it is necessary to let the transference develop to a certain extent so that patients' patterns become clear both to them and to the staff, and changes can then be made. An advantage of a heterogeneous staff is that patients have a choice in their transference objects: someone may, for example, not feel at ease with a psychotherapist but find a confidant in a nurse.

Programme therapies

To construct and maintain the coherent, reflective milieu, the staff meets twice daily to discuss each patient's progress in various therapies. Sometimes patients experience the staff as all-knowing mothers or fathers. For example, when patients discuss something in early-morning group psychotherapy, the therapist in movement therapy after the coffee break already knows about it. At the beginning, this sometimes creates distrust and fear in patients, but after a few weeks it usually changes into a feeling of being contained by a group of benevolent people who strive for the same goal, which is for patients to feel better and have more fulfilling lives.

Basically, the programme consists of three therapies each day: group psychotherapy, one of the non-verbal therapies (art, movement, puppet therapy, or archery), and sociotherapy. In puppet therapy, patients create their own puppet(s) from cloth (often pieces of cloth they bring from home, like material from an old dress or sweater). For some men, it is the first time they have handled a needle and thread, and they often feel awkward and vulnerable (they can also use glue or staples). Gradually, most patients find pleasure in the process and may create quite elaborate puppets: a dragon, a bird, and often the little boy or girl they were or wanted to be. During puppet play, they begin playing in a real puppet theatre, often shy and anxious at first but gradually becoming more daring. Puppets frequently have already formulated patients' redecisions, and through them patients may experiment with new behaviour long before they are ready to engage in such behaviour themselves.

In archery, patients shoot with bow and arrow at a goal about twenty-five metres away. For most people it is the first time they have done something like that. To shoot well, they need to combine balance and strength and to take a proud, firm stance. This is often hard for women who try to hide their breasts or for men who feel insecure and lack self-esteem. In the first weeks, they often succeed in shooting only a few metres, and the arrow hits the ground with a miserable little curve. By the end of three months, they are often standing proudly and shouting a triumphant "Yes!" as they hit the target.

In sociotherapy patients discuss their household duties and how they experience living together in the house where they stay during the treatment programme. Duties such as shopping and cooking are divided up, so housemates have to decide who is doing the shopping, what are they cooking, and how to make do with the budget. Some patients have little experience of household chores or cooking and wait until they are served or until the irritation of other house members pushes them into the kitchen. Others reflexively draw all the household work to themselves until they are confronted by group or staff members about their rescuer behaviour. In addition, two or three housemates share a bedroom, which can be quite a shock for the more avoidant patients. This also can result in corrective experiences such as talking about body care products and make-up, tampons and contraception, and trying on each other's clothes or shopping on a free afternoon. With the sociotherapists, patients also have a daily forty-five-minute contract meeting during which they discuss the progress they have made with their therapeutic contracts. The therapeutic contract is one of the elements of Transactional Analysis that is essential in the programme.

Transactional Analysis as a therapeutic model

When the three-month inpatient programme described here was developed, Transactional Analysis was chosen as the basic therapeutic method. Similar to Eric Berne's development in moving from psychoanalysis to Transactional Analysis, the founders of our programme wanted a model with an active therapist, one that was interpersonal and not just intrapsychic and in which patients were involved as active participants in their treatment. We found all of these prerequisites in the Transactional Analysis model.

For example, the language of Transactional Analysis made patient participation easy. Each patient was introduced to the basic principles of Transactional Analysis, including strokes and hungers, ego states, transactions, games and script, the life positions, and the repetitive patterns of drivers and injunctions. All the therapists in the programme used TA language to explain certain group events or intrapsychic dynamics. Patients learned to use Transactional Analysis language as a tool to understand their own and others' behaviour and to make changes. During the first week of treatment, each patient made a therapeutic contract about what he or she wanted to change. Often the first sentence of the contract formulated the old behaviour that the person wants to stop, and the second sentence an alternative behaviour with more freedom and choice.

Within Transactional Analysis, we chose the redecision model developed by Robert and Mary Goulding (1978, 1979) as the model for therapeutic change. In redecision therapy, concepts from Transactional Analysis and techniques from the Gestalt approach are combined into an effective therapeutic model. The core idea of the redecision model is that children make decisions early in their lives to obtain strokes from their parents and to survive in adverse circumstances. These decisions represent the child's best attempt to deal with the main themes in his family and to find an answer to the questions, "Who am I, who are the others, and what am I doing here in this world?" The Gouldings argued that people are capable of making a different decision at any time in their lives, one that goes against the grain of the original early limiting decisions.

The child's decisions are based on early messages from parents, which the Gouldings summarised in a list of injunctions, such as "Don't be", "Don't be important", "Don't succeed", "Don't be close", "Don't be a child", "Don't grow", "Don't be sane", "Don't belong", and "Don't feel, think, or do" (for more details see John McNeel's chapter in this book). These messages are given by the unhappy, disappointed, angry, scared, jealous, traumatised, or needy Child ego state of parents who also try to survive in an often difficult, confusing world. Although injunctions can be powerful, the child always has the choice to accept, change, or reject the message and in that process, he fantasises, invents, and misinterprets. For example, when his father dies, a child might believe he magically caused the death and may decide never to be close to anyone again.

Injunctions are complemented by counterinjunctions from the Parent ego state of the parents. The counterinjunctions—such as "Be strong", "Please me/others", "Be perfect", "Hurry up", and "Try hard" (Kahler & Capers, 1974)—are restrictive and, if adhered to, prevent growth and flexibility. They often develop into rigid commands: never show your emotions, never ask for what you need, always strive for perfection, hurry up until you drop dead, and take every task without ever saying no. Together, these early injunctions and counterinjunctions, which people are often not aware of, may prevent living a happy and fulfilling life.

The simple and clear language of the redecision model often is a real eye-opener to patients. They recognise how they restricted themselves in their life course and became stuck in rigid patterns. Formulating their contract often is the first, often deeply moving experience of how life can be different. This is often followed by a struggle between the wish to change and the internal pressure of the old script messages. In the verbal and non-verbal therapies and experiences with other group members during unstructured time at the house, patients often discover unknown blind spots in their behaviour, thinking, and feeling. For example, someone who experiences herself as a quiet, cooperative person with a lot of Adapted Child energy might find it quite shocking and confronting when group members comment on the harsh internal Critical Parent they see trickle through from her. The discovery that each game has at least two players can be painful (Thunnissen, 2001). Patients complain about their disinterested partner or neglecting parents but then must face their own adapting, rescuing, rebellious, or destructive behaviour. Forgiving others and themselves, and taking responsibility, is often the main process of the second half of treatment.

The first interview with Robin

During the first interview Robin immediately began with a number of horrible stories from her past. She had abused alcohol from a young age (her parents and many other family members were alcoholics). She had been sexually abused by her maternal uncle from her childhood until her adulthood. She was convinced her parents knew of the abuse, and encouraged it. She fled to Spain, returning to Holland a year before the interview. Through an acquaintance, a minister of the church, she obtained a grant from his church that enabled her to go to school and live in a house with other students. She chose the short-term (three-month) treatment programme so that she would not lose the church grant and her chance to study and her place at the student house.

In the first interview, I saw a sloppy young woman with a tangled shock of dark hair behind which she often hid; her sweater, jeans, and sneakers made her look rather boyish. Her demeanour was stiff, although I could see and feel her emotions beneath the surface. The modest way in which she described her traumatic history evoked my empathy. Of her affects, anxiety was the most prominent, probably to cover underlying strong feelings of anger, sadness, and despair.

Already in our first meeting the diagnosis of borderline personality disorder was emerging. It was clear that she had many bad objects in her inner world, especially her father, her mother, and her uncle. There were good objects as well, especially her grandfather and the minister who took her in. Although the staff of the short-term programme thought that longer treatment would be better, we decided to accept her in the inpatient treatment of three months followed by aftercare.

Despite the severe trauma she had suffered and the pathology she manifested, we saw a number of positive factors as well. She showed psychological mindedness and self-insight and was clever, honest, attentive, and thoughtful. She was able to engage in relationships with honest, well-meaning people like the minister of the church. She demonstrated humour and perseverance as well as a great longing to change her life. Her power to survive and to live was strong.

Robin's diagnosis and contract

Robin grew up in a chaotic environment, full of alcohol abuse and violence. The only positive relationship she had when she was young was with her grandfather, a relationship she seemed to repeat with the eighty-year-old minister who protected her and helped finance her studies. Her anxiety was predominant, under which anger, despair, and a deep sadness were hidden. Nevertheless, we also saw a powerful drive to live. Her distrust, understandable given her parents' unpredictable behaviour and failure to protect her from her uncle's sexual harassment and abuse, clearly hindered her in intimate relationships.

We recognised at least six symptoms of borderline personality disorder as described in the DSM-5 (APA, 2013): impulsivity, affective instability, inappropriate intense anger, recurrent suicidal threats, marked and persistent identity disturbance, and chronic feelings of emptiness and boredom. In interactions with borderline patients, we often see primitive defence mechanisms such as splitting, projection, and projective identification. Splitting (also called black and white thinking or all-or-nothing thinking) involves a failure in a person's thinking to bring together both positive and negative qualities of the self and others into a cohesive, realistic whole. In projective identification, the person unconsciously denies certain feelings in the self and projects them onto others who, also unconsciously, identify themselves with the projected feelings.

With such an overwhelming number of symptoms, it is hard to find a start in the treatment. The despair the patient feels can easily infect the psychotherapist and lead to therapeutic nihilism. In a focused treatment such as our three-month programme, it is important to choose such a focus so that the healing power of the treatment spreads from the focal area into other parts of the individual's personality. That is the challenge when making the treatment contract with such patients: what do we choose as the focus of treatment so that the three months are as effective as possible for the patient?

Robin began in the therapy group with a detailed story of her past while showing no feelings. Group members felt increasingly oppressed and choked as she talked. They began feeling all the feelings Robin herself was trying to avoid (e.g., anger, sadness, despair, etc.), an example of projective identification. To make this process conscious, I asked Robin what she was feeling. "Nothing," was her honest answer. She was genuinely amazed to learn how many feelings her story engendered in other group members.

I wondered if she was too scared at that point to make a therapeutic contract. Robin did recognise her fear but acknowledged that numbness or not feeling at all was a mechanism she used to defend herself against overwhelming negative feelings. I proposed that she take a few more days to explore her feelings and to ask herself what they were and what she wanted.

Robin agreed and was shocked at what she discovered. Her first reaction in many situations was often, "I don't care, what do you want?" The mechanisms of numbness and adaptation were so strong that she was no longer even aware of them. And when she took time to tune in to her own needs and feelings, she was terrified of the violence of her despair, rage, and deep sadness.

In the next group session, Robin began with her story about the previous few days and what she had discovered about herself. However, the same day a patient had dropped out of the group, and that was the priority for the group that day. Robin did not acknowledge this, and without making an effective contact with the group, she continued with her story. I decided to make a non-verbal confrontation: I turned my chair with the back to Robin, in this way imitating her behaviour of not listening to what was happening in the group. Robin stopped for a few seconds, then, hiding her shock and anger, continued talking. At that point, other group members intervened: they were amazed by Robin's stoic behaviour. In contrast, whenever I had turned my back on one of them as they were talking, they had felt angry, excluded, and ashamed. Then Robin whispered in a small, thin voice, "I only know how to fight." A deep silence followed.

Then her contract became clear: "I will stop fighting. I will show myself, and you can touch me." This contract focused on her most prominent counterinjunction ("Be strong") and gave her permission to be and to feel (her most important injunctions) and to get in touch with others (aimed at the injunction "Don't belong").

Early countertransference in working with Robin

One essential aspect of Robin's was the development of her transference towards me as the psychiatrist/group psychotherapist, towards a female sociotherapist, and towards the institute as a whole, including the buildings, the group, and the programme. Robin's most important injunction was "Don't be". When this injunction is in place, most other injunctions follow from it, so it is essential for the person to make a redecision about it. Often this is a gradual process with different steps during which the developing transference, the protection offered by the inpatient milieu, and the feeling of belonging to a group are essential.

In Robin's case, a few weeks after the start of treatment, I had a week's holiday. In the first group session after that break, Robin spent an hour telling one story after another about the horrible sexual abuse by her uncle, her loveless childhood as an unwanted child, and the alcohol abuse and violence of her father. The group reacted with anxiety, horror, and rescuer behaviour. I registered strong countertransference feelings: to my amazement, I hardly felt any compassion towards Robin but did feel disgust because of all the horrendous experiences. I also felt excluded because Robin began blurting out her stories without making any contact with me after not having seen me for a week. I wondered what the message of her behaviour was and decided to cut through the stories to ask, "What do you want to say to me, right now?"

Robin stopped, clearly startled, and then burst into anger. She said she felt utterly deserted by me when I dared to go on a holiday just when she was beginning to trust the staff and the group. In the days before my return, she had nightmares about killing others or being killed and felt despair about her treatment, feeling that it would lead to nothing. She shouted, stamped her feet, and waved her arms, a fireball of anger. I kept looking at Robin and felt myself softening and tears welling up in my eyes. When she finally stopped shouting to catch her breath, I softly called her name. Robin looked me in the eye and burst into tears. I asked her to come near me and we sat on the floor, Robin in my arms sobbing like a small child. The group was silent and respectful.

Developing countertransference in working with Robin

A few weeks later, Robin again wanted to bring up something in the group. I interrupted her because another group member started a story at the same moment. Robin did not have another chance that morning because others asked for attention and she did not bring up her subject again. Just before the session ended, I asked how she was feeling, and Robin said that she felt like other group members were more important than she was. She denied that her frequent loud coughing during the session represented any meaning other than that she had a cold.

Later that day, in the living room, an older female sociotherapist who also was an important transference object for Robin, asked what happened in the group session. At first, Robin denied any feelings of anger and hurt, but when the sociotherapist looked puzzled and inquiring, she admitted that she felt angry at first and later increasingly sad about not getting the attention she wanted. Instead of retreating to her familiar "Be strong" position (I don't care, of course others go first, I don't need anybody), she could feel her longing, her need for connection, and her disappointment and sadness when she did not have her needs fulfilled. The sociotherapist stroked this insight as well as Robin's ability to contain her feelings instead of acting them out or projecting them onto others.

This pattern, of having destructive thoughts at the moment Robin got in touch with her Child needs and feelings, repeated several times over the next weeks. At first, she was not able to use her Adult to understand

and analyse or her Nurturing Parent to tolerate the complex feelings; instead, she was just overwhelmed by her feelings. Gradually, however, she was able to tolerate and even to express the feelings of which she had been so afraid.

In the last group session before the break, we discussed how every group member was feeling. Robin was withdrawn and did not participate in the group. In the last five minutes of the session, I complimented her on her behaviour. She looked at me distrustfully but a bit curious. I explained that I saw her behaviour as a positive sign: group members had become important to her and she would miss them. She was beginning to feel a sense of belonging, which was scary to her. She was surprised at this explanation and still a little distrustful.

During the week between the two periods of treatment, Robin felt alone in her house. She felt inclined to fall back into old, self-destructive behaviours but decided to do something new: she phoned me for a consultation. She was surprised and confused when I stroked her for this new initiative, and she succeeded in not drinking or harming herself during that week. However, she was glad when the week was over and she could return to De Viersprong.

Robin's work in group psychotherapy

Being part of a healthy group was a totally new experience for Robin. She never knew the cosiness of a home, the experience of attentive listening by and to others (in her family, shouting and disregarding each other was the culture), the pleasure of cooking meals together, and the sharing of intimacies with sisters or friends. At first she was suspicious of anyone who was friendly towards her, like a scared animal in a cage. She struggled with whether she was in or out: "Am I part of this group or, rather, do I want to be part of this group? Do I want to get involved, become attached, and let myself be known by others?"

At one point, the atmosphere in the group had been tense for a few days. Many negative strokes were exchanged, and group members had entrenched themselves behind walls of cautious politeness without any intimacy. During a group session, I brought up the topic of the group atmosphere, and some members exchanged positive strokes. However, just as things were becoming more relaxed and friendlier, Robin brought up an annoying incident between herself and another group member from the day before. Immediately the old icy atmosphere was back. I wondered why Robin referred to this incident just then, and immediately she said: "I quit." Asked what she meant, Robin said she understood the destructiveness of her behaviour and wanted to stop it. I felt that there might be another layer of meaning in her comment and asked whether at a psychological level she might be suggesting that she was thinking of quitting treatment. Robin laughed, both trapped and relieved. She acknowledged that part of her wanted to run away when it got too tense or intimate.

Slowly Robin loosened up a little and made awkward attempts to connect with others. Of course, she easily fell back into her old pattern of distrusting others and quickly felt attacked by questions from others, which she experienced as intrusions or criticism. She often chose the chair next to me in group and watched closely what everyone did during sessions.

In the second half of treatment, Robin began competing with group members from a more secure base. She quarrelled during meals about food portions, sometimes ran away angry and slammed the door. She behaved like an adolescent, testing boundaries with her rebellious behaviour. However, it looked healthy and vital and quite different from the isolated position she took in the beginning. She developed into an important group member for others, often being supportive when others did individual work in the group and active when a general group theme was discussed.

At the end of treatment, Robin said, with some embarrassment, that a few times when she felt afraid during the night, she had moved her bed closer to another female group member's bed. They were both scared that the staff would criticise this, so they carefully returned the bedroom to its normal order in the morning. This was a first step in tolerating closeness with others, and, just like a child growing up, Robin began exploring closeness with other females. Sexuality still seemed far away for her. Although at the end of treatment she could tolerate some jokes about sex and even told some dirty jokes she learned during the time she worked on a farm.

Decontamination work with Robin

After a stormy group session with a group member who often suddenly became angry, Robin said (the only one in the whole group to do so) that she was not afraid of his anger. Her own thoughts were full of anger: either she wanted to hurt someone else or she expected that she would be abused. She was convinced that her thoughts could harm others. I invited her to voice some of her thoughts and see what happened. Robin resisted vehemently, and it was clear how scared she was. With support from the group members, she experimented with uttering some curses aimed at her father and confronted my co-psychotherapist whom she experienced as cynical. To her surprise, nothing bad happened; the co-psychotherapist even thanked her for her comments and invited her to say more. She received strokes from group members who were glad that she was revealing herself. This seemed a beginning of the development of trust.

A week later she continued. It became clear how she projected her own anger onto other people, making them into a negative Critical Parent to which she reacted from Adapted Child. I proposed an exercise in which she stood in the middle of the circle, looked carefully at a group member, and described what she saw, thought, and felt. Robin chose one of the men in the group and looked at him. She began talking but she could hardly offer a neutral description. She saw a "threatening big man" towards whom she must "behave strongly, otherwise he would get her". She felt scared looking at him and was convinced he could not be trusted. I drew her contaminated ego states (Figure 2): contamination means that the person mistakenly experiences the emotions or attitudes of Parent or Child ego states as emanating from the Adult ego state.

Robin agreed it showed the way she perceived the world. She began checking out her fantasies with the man and could hardly believe that he (who was so big!) meant her no harm. She asked for my permission not to believe immediately what others say that differed from her angry and scary fantasies.

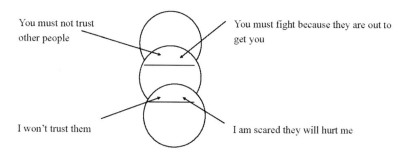

Figure 2. Robin's contaminated ego states.

In the weeks following this group session, Robin experimented with expressing her negative thoughts about men in the group, and each time she was surprised to find that they did not disappear, run away, or hit her but rather made contact and were interested in why she thought as she did.

Ego states in the work with Robin

In the last few weeks of the programme, Robin struggled with questions such as "What next? What am I going to do after De Viersprong? What will my future look like?" I proposed exploring these questions using the five-chair exercise in which five chairs are put in a half circle, each representing an ego state: on one side the Natural Child and the Adapted Child, on the other side the Nurturing Parent and the Structuring (Critical) Parent. Because the Natural Child and Nurturing Parent are closer to the person's core, they are placed closest to the Adult. The Structuring Parent and Adapted Child develop more in interaction with the outside world, so they are placed farther away. The chair for the Adult is placed at the head of the ego states (see Figure 3). (For a more elaborate description of this exercise see Stuntz, 1973).

Robin's initial thought about what she was going to do after De Viersprong was, "You must continue with your studies!" We decided that was her Structuring Parent so she sat in that chair. It was easy for her to speak from that position: "You must be grateful for the chance you got to study and for the grant from the church; you must keep your

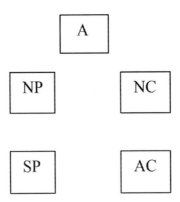

Figure 3. Ego states as represented in the five-chair exercise.

promises; you are obliged to show that you are worth their efforts."
I invited her at that point to move to the Adapted Child chair to see
whether from there she agreed with her Structuring Parent's commands. She was completely in accord with all of its "sermons". But she
was scared that she would not be successful, and at that moment she
laughed a cynical gallows laugh, a laughter that serves to reinforce the
person's script decisions (Berne, 1972, pp. 335–338).

Then I saw something happen in her body: one leg began moving in
a kicking way, and she seemed less at ease in the Adapted Child chair.
I asked which ego state she was in, and she jumped up and moved
to the Natural Child chair. She blurted out that she would love to go
back to Spain where she had been happy, working on a farm and being
outside much of the time. Then she fell silent, unsure how to continue.
I invited her to move to the Adult chair, and she acknowledged that
she faced a real dilemma between two contrasting wishes. We both
remarked that her Nurturing Parent was absent, and when she moved
to that chair, she felt numb and speechless. The only things she heard
in her head were the harsh comments of her Structuring Parent and the
anxiety of her Adapted Child.

I asked her again to return to the Adult chair. Because treatment was
going to last only a few more weeks, I decided on a supportive, structuring strategy and asked what would be the wisest thing to do right
now. With the support of the group, Robin said that it would be wise
to go back to her house and study, and to use the next year to become
clearer about what she really wanted in terms of a job, a career, and a
place to live—and go back to Spain for a month during the holidays to
see how she felt there at that point in her life.

Robin says goodbye

When the last week of treatment approached, Robin showed some old
behaviour patterns. In the group she often acted like a co-therapist,
helping, interpreting, attending to others but neglecting her own needs.
Towards me she was distant and at one point overtly angry. I asked her
what had happened, and she complained about minor things: a session that was moved to another time, an appointment that one of the
sociotherapists forgot. I looked at her, wondering what the real reason
was, and when she looked back, she burst into tears. She realised that
the group and treatment programme were the first places in her life in

which she had felt welcomed, like she belonged and was allowed to be herself. And she was now faced with having to leave in a week, to say goodbye to group members and staff. How could she manage, and how could we do this to her?

I stroked Robin for her openness and remarked on her new behaviour of expressing her primary feelings of sadness and anxiety instead of acting out in anger. She understood that she could take her good experiences with her and use them to build a good life after treatment.

In the end, Robin took her leave from group members and staff in a clear, personal way. It was obvious that she had never said goodbye in a good way before. De Viersprong gradually became an important place for her in which she felt, for the first time in her life, unconditionally accepted. She experienced belonging and closeness with others. In evaluating her treatment contract she said that the moment she stopped fighting (the first sentence in her contract), she could then put the second sentence (showing herself and getting in touch with others) into practice.

The importance of puppetry in Robin's treatment

One of Robin's most significant experiences during treatment was in the puppet play. She made a male puppet, Robbie, onto whom she projected her will to live and survive. Her puppet was a kind of cowboy, with a hat and leather trousers, who was sturdy and adventurous. Gradually less and less shy, Robbie went into the big world, had adventures with other puppets, fought with some of the other male puppets, and made advances towards one of the female puppets.

The most difficult moment for Robin in saying goodbye was probably when she took leave of Robbie, who had been so important to her during treatment. Robbie had said and done what she herself did not dare or was not allowed to do when she was a child. Through him, Robin's Child wishes found a clear place in her inner world again. The non-verbal therapist gently took Robbie from her, holding him on her arm like an infant, and in tears Robin said goodbye to that symbol of the development of her Child.

Evaluation of Robin's treatment

In the first part of treatment, her borderline mechanisms, such as projection, projective identification, and splitting became clear and then gradually lessened. After decontamination of her Adult, Robin could experience her violent emotions in the safe atmosphere of the group and the therapeutic milieu, and they grew weaker. She was increasingly able to set limits, keep Adult control, and create space for another course in her script.

In the second part of treatment, Robin began experimenting with intimacy. Once she felt she had a right to be part of the group, to belong, and to exist, her feelings grew more ordinary. Ambivalence took the place of splitting, she took better care of herself, and she set clearer limits. She developed the beginning of a Nurturing Parent and could tolerate more of her Child feelings. Saying goodbye presented a final test of the stability of the changes she had made at De Viersprong, and she passed gloriously.

Conclusion

In this chapter I described an intensive treatment process with a patient with a borderline personality disorder. It was clear that Robin's treatment was not finished after the three-month inpatient programme. Nevertheless, she made an important switch in her life position, and started living instead of surviving. Thanks to the extensive cooperation within the staff, the use of Transactional Analysis as the model of psychotherapy, and the holding which the programme offered, Robin could make substantial intrapsychic changes which offered hope for her future.

CHAPTER ELEVEN

Social-cognitive Transactional Analysis: from theory to practice

Maria Teresa Tosi

"The mind works with motivations that affect both self-regulation and the regulation of the interpersonal field."

—*Mitchell*, 1988, p. 10

Introduction

"The last terrorist attack will not stop me from taking the plane. Twenty years ago I did not take the plane because I was so scared after a terrible accident due to a terrorist attack. I know what it means to feel free and I do not want to forfeit my wishes any more. Now, if I'm afraid to take a plane, I consider which realistic dangers are in a situation and which ones are a figment of my imagination and then I choose what to do. When I was eight, I often heard my grandfather saying: 'If you are born round, you can't become square.' That fascinating sentence became like a cornerstone for me, meaning, however, 'You can't change'. Now I know it is possible to change."

Noemi said these words at the end of her therapy that she started because of a serious obsessive compulsive disorder. She felt compelled to carry out many rituals in order to calm down when she was feeling scared about her or her relatives' illnesses.

The tendency to control herself in a destructive way when she was in contact with strong emotions was apparent in many ways. She referred to a story of abandonment when she had had to face sudden traumatic events. Originally the rituals were a magic strategy she found to reassure herself when no adults were present and she felt overwhelmed by fear.

The "control issue" was reinforced by several messages she received during her life. For example, "You can't change" was both a family and cultural way to stigmatise people. For her it represented also an easy and simple vision of the world that could direct her behaviour. She had not separated psychologically from her beloved mother, a strong and protective woman, whose rules and teachings became her internal guide throughout her life.

"Control" had the function of regulating Noemi's development both in a protective and destructive way. For example, in many events Noemi's mother guided her with love. Noemi behaved in order to be a good student and to be respected by teachers and classmates. These experiences were characterised by a positive loving and controlling attitude that helped her integrate in social groups. However, in a child-hood traumatic situation when she felt abandoned and scared, she discovered that she could reassure herself by performing some actions. So here "control" assumed a painful feature. Moreover the distressing experience of being lonely in frightening events led to a tendency to isolate herself and not to look for emotional help when she was facing difficult moments in her life. Also her beloved mother became openly controlling when, in adolescence, she started to have romantic relationships that her mother did not approve of. "Being free" was an experience well represented in her fantasy as a wish that she could not realise.

Exploring the world, feeling safe, and creating intimate bonds are experiences far from being easy for Noemi, while being well integrated in social groups is a common experience for her.

The therapist's experience with this patient is of being needed and avoided at the same time, because Noemi does not know how to regulate the affective distance with the other. So, for example, she regularly arrives late at sessions, always having an excuse to justify her delay and she redefines any attempt to talk about that issue. In Noemi's eyes the therapist can become both a controlling figure that can be reliable or rigid and an abandoning figure not available when she is in trouble.

Social-cognitive Transactional Analysis (SCTA) has helped me to frame this clinical case right from the first sessions because it offered me a specific lens through which I could reflect on Noemi's way of presenting herself to me and telling her life story. Therefore Noemi's "redecision work" (Goulding & Goulding, 1979) was much facilitated by that approach.

The categories of freedom and control, pleasure and pain, the developmental issue of individuation, the attachment theory, and the relational theory of ego states are typical categories used by SCTA to understand human behaviour in a complex enough way.

Social-cognitive Transactional Analysis

Social-cognitive Transactional Analysis defines an approach devised by Pio Scilligo and his collaborators, in particular members of the Research Lab on the Self and Identity (LaRSI). This approach has been developed in Italy over forty years of research and theoretical reflections on a social and cognitive model of Transactional Analysis (a process that is still ongoing).

Theory and practice should influence each other as the latest trend in research on psychotherapy indicates (Migone, 2006). In research the clinical practice can be valued as an initial "lab" in order to understand which processes seem to be correlated to a positive outcome. SCTA proposes some tools that hopefully will allow this fruitful dialogue. Confirming Transactional Analysis theory with scientific evidence and enhancing the effectiveness of clinical practice would give a sound basis to TA that could open up new areas of work and keep a constant dialogue with the main theoretical developments and research based on approaches similar to it.

Scilligo also wanted to ground SCTA on an anthropological view that considers each person capable of responsible choices despite being affected by her personal, physical, and interpersonal history. He suggested the use of various research paradigms because he was convinced that:

> … interventions based on scientific assumptions entail the risk of valuing the objective over the subjective, surrendering to hedonism

at the expense of the right to be treated humanely, equating spiritual and material aspects, ignoring that man is a social being, is not alone and certainly not mainly a monad so that the uniqueness of a person cannot be sacrificed to the assumptions of universalism. These polarities should be kept in mind in the belief that the human solution always needs the dialectics of ying and yang, the dialectics of subjective and objective and all the other polarities typical of human acting. (2004, p. 17)

This long quotation allows us to see the basic vision that inspired the construction of SCTA and is found in the model's different levels of abstraction.

The effort of Scilligo and collaborators has also been to offer a theory of personality and a psychotherapy model that could preserve the main concepts of Transactional Analysis and its basic philosophy while accounting for the complexity of human behaviour and development. If we look at the theories that explain human behaviour in SCTA a fundamental role was played by the studies of social cognitive psychology (Andersen & Chen, 2002; Baldwin, 1997; Mischel & Shoda, 1995) for understanding the processes of learning and building the self.

In addition, SCTA recognises the essential contributions of relational psychoanalysis (Mitchell, 1988) and Bowlby's (1969, 1973, 1980) research that have profoundly influenced all contemporary psychotherapeutic approaches with their vision of a "dyadic mind". Berne was a pioneer in this sense because he anticipated the importance of relationships for human development. The unconscious dimension is highlighted, according to contemporary theories, on implicit processes (Tosi, 2008).

SCTA includes also the research on adult attachment carried out by Mikulincer and Shaver (Mikulincer, 2007; Mikulincer & Shaver, 2003). Lastly, the valuable theoretical and clinical contribution of Lorna Benjamin (1974, 1996), a contemporary theorist of the interpersonal approach, allowed SCTA to represent ego states according to the model of structural analysis of social behaviour (SASB) that she devised.

Summarising, we can say that SCTA integrates different theories on human development and represents a development of the redecision approach (Goulding & Goulding, 1979) and of Bernian social psychiatry (Scilligo, 2009; Tosi, 2011). Social psychiatry (Berne, 1964) represents one of Berne's most innovative contributions due to its capacity for significantly linking interpersonal and intrapsychic processes. Readers interested in a more complete description of the theoretical growth of SCTA are referred to the articles published in the *Transactional Analysis Journal*, in particular those by Scilligo (2011), De Luca and Tosi (2011), and the various publications in Italian whose references can be found in the mentioned articles.

This chapter discusses some relevant influences of the main SCTA principles on psychotherapeutic practice as I saw them in my long clinical and supervisory experience. It is therefore my personal elaboration of an approach that in my opinion provides new tools at the relational and methodological level rather than in terms of technique. After an introduction to the main theoretical concepts I will describe the therapeutic approach of SCTA by means of examples and reflections that show how these theoretical principles help shape clinical practice.

Ego states in SCTA

Scilligo's research focused on the concept of ego states that is a central tenet of TA. Many models of ego states can be found in Berne and later authors (Trautmann & Erskine, 1981), and Novey (Novey, 1998; Novey, Porter-Steele, Gobes, & Massey, 1993) grouped them into two distinct models—the three ego states model and the integrated Adult model (De Luca & Tosi, 2011). In SCTA we found it necessary to define ego states anew because we considered Berne's definitions very helpful in clinical practice and not useful in clinical research. We paid specific attention to the construction of explanatory definitions and operational definitions that are necessary for research.

I have mentioned the relational models as the basis of SCTA and now I will explain how the concept of schema seemed especially useful to Scilligo to conceptualise ego states. In SCTA ego states are "complex schemas of emotional, cognitive and behavioural nature" (Scilligo, 2009, p. 73) that define "a cluster of mediation processes that build an interface between the external world and the behaviours acted by the individual in a circular process of adjustment and assimilation" (Scilligo, 1986, 2009). These mental schemas have an intrapsychic and interpersonal nature and include explicit (conscious) and implicit (unconscious and pre-verbal) processes (Scilligo, 2009). As a matter of fact Berne also gave an elegant and simple definition of the ego state, which resembles that of a schema: "A consistent pattern of feeling and experience directly related to a corresponding consistent pattern of behaviour" (1966, p. 364).

In other publications (De Luca & Tosi, 2011) we explained that the definition of ego states in SCTA makes use of the concept of schema derived from cognitive psychology, in particular according to the "parallel distributed processes" of McClelland, Rumelhart, and the PDP Research Group (1986). The concept of schema has been widely used in psychology under different names, like Horowitz's person—schemas (1991), or Bowlby's internal working models (1973). We can think of ego states as active social-cognitive processes, or schemas, continually being recreated in the dynamic interaction between the individual and his environment. According to this view, ego states are continuously evolving during life (Tosi, 2010), even though sometimes their very strong connections can create rigid correlations, making them unresponsive to actual environmental stimuli, while in other cases the connections are so weak or loose that the schema is not activated even when necessary or adaptive.

This conception allowed SCTA to overcome the distinction between structure and function in the definition of ego states that had created various theoretical and methodological problems in Transactional Analysis, such as the risk of reifying the concept and moving away from the current conceptions of the functioning of the mind. Erskine (1991, p. 67) well explains that the analogies used by Berne to describe ego states sometimes have become specific entities. I remember patients talking about their Child as if it was a "homunculus" in their head.

The concepts of schemas and prototypes allow us to organise the concept of ego states as a process and therefore, ultimately, as a function. We could say that SCTA expands Berne's original three ego states model (Novey, 1998) that considers Child, Adult, and Parent as three prototypical ego states always evolving during life. However, in SCTA the theory of ego states is not complete if in trying to explain its formation and origin we do not take into account the three evolutionary dimensions together with the developmental dimension and the theory of attachment that Scilligo used for their definition.

In summary, Scilligo (1998) redefined ego states as complex schemas on three levels:

- A more general conceptual level related to the evolutionary condition of human beings (existence, survival, continuation of the species).

- An intermediate level of explanation related to the affective and interpersonal aspects of behaviour outlined by the structural analysis of social behaviour model (L. S. Benjamin, 1974), and;
- A third analytical level related to the evolution of human development in biological and psychological terms towards a more complex type of individuation.

I will briefly describe the three evolutionary dimensions (Ceridono, Gubinelli, & Scilligo, 2009; Scilligo, 2006) and the developmental dimension based on Mahler's work (Mahler & Furer, 1968). Lastly, I will show how these four dimensions, which can be found also in L. S. Benjamin's structural analysis of social behaviour (1974)—related to existence, survival, and the continuation of the species, in addition to development—characterise ego states.

The capacity to reach for pleasurable situations and avoid painful situations is an initial given and represents an important way to self-regulate affects. This is the pleasure-pain dimension that refers to the love-hate polarity because we obtain pleasure through love and pain through hate. In the theory of ego states we call this dimension *affiliation*. The capacity to respond passively or actively to context stimuli is the second basic genetic given for children, and human beings in general, as it allows us to actively change the context or to change our response to it. This skill develops with experience and becomes more and more complex with the evolution of cognitive functions. This dimension is related to the passive-active polarity and we call it *interdependence*. The third dimension, related to the continuation of the species, is the *relational* or *power* dimension that concerns the capacity to exert power on the other assuming a transitive position, or to focus on oneself in the relation assuming an intransitive position. A fourth *developmental* dimension assumes that persons evolve during life and develop increasing levels of complexity and individuation.

I will show now how ego states are characterised when we cross the dimensions of affectivity and interdependence and we obtain four quadrants and four different types of ego states: the ego states characterised by love and activity are called "free"; those characterised by activity and hate are called "rebellious"; those characterised by hate and passivity are "critical", and those characterised by passivity and love are "protective" (Fig. 1).

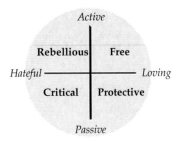

Figure 1. The four quadrants.

The relational dimension is represented by the interaction of the Relational Parent and the Relational Child with an additional third dimension called the Self (Fig. 2).

The distinction between different positions taken in relationships and the operational definitions of the Relational ego states and the Self ego states derive from Benjamin's research (L. S. Benjamin, 1974, 1996). The complete model of the structural analysis of social behaviour can be found in her many publications (L. S. Benjamin, 1974).

Here it is enough to specify that the Relational Parent is in a transitive position. As an example, imagine a parent who says to his child: "Your ideas are interesting." The Relational Child answers complementarily in an intransitive position: "I like to express my personal opinions."

Three surfaces to represent the behaviours
Labels for the four quadrants

Scilligo assigned a label to each of the four quadrant:
Free (give power + friendly)
Rebellious (give power + hostile)
Critical (take away power + hostile)
Protectve (take away power + friendly)

Relational Parent	Relational Child	Self

Rebellious ↑ Free	Rebellious ↑ Free	Rebellious ↑ Free
Invoke hostile authonomy / Encourage friendly authonomy	Take hostile authonomy / Enjoy friendly authonomy	Neglect, reject self / Accept, enjoy self
Hostile power / Friendly influence	Hostile comply / Friendly accept	Put down, oppress self / Manage, cultivate self
Critical ↓ Protective	Critical ↓ Protective	Critical ↓ Protective

Figure 2. Relational and self ego states.

The Self ego states describe how the person treats herself prototypically as a result of the most significant relational experiences she has had over her life.

Clinical example

This example can help us understand and locate the Relational positions described above. In exerting a loving power aimed at limiting the patient's destructive behaviour, a therapist says to the patient who skips sessions: "If you want to take care of yourself, you need to come with continuity to your therapy sessions" (Relational Parent position, Protective).

In the same situation a therapist might prefer a different option and say: "I wonder what is happening in our relationship when you skip sessions without informing me." In this case the therapist gives power to herself freely ("I wonder ...", Relational Child position, Free), gently acknowledges that the other has an active role ("skipping session without informing the other", Relational Parent position, Free) and waits for the other to explain freely what is going on.

The therapist might also choose to offer an interpretation of her patient's destructive behaviour, activating a transitive relational position characterised by not too high control levels and a positive affective tone, and saying: "When you skip sessions I think that you are trying to stimulate in me a behaviour similar to that of your father when he left you alone in moments of distress." Relational nuances of this kind are frequent and relevant both in helping situations and in affective relationships.

I think that an essential practical implication of this theory is that SCTA allows us *to calibrate interventions* because of the high precision of its dimensional analysis of ego states, which helps us to keep in mind both the transactional complexity of therapeutic relations in the various stages of treatment and the specificity of any co-constructed relation.

The taxonomy of behaviour that is offered by the structural analysis of social behaviour (L. S. Benjamin, 1974) and by the SCTA model of ego states is a way to offer a validated operational description of human behaviours and should not be confused with a behavioural approach to psychotherapy. Operational definitions of concepts facilitate research in psychotherapy. For example, in psychoanalysis Luborsky and

Crits-Christoph (1990) offered an operational definition of transference that allowed us to do research on that construct. Any type of behaviour, conscious and unconscious, verbal and non-verbal might be categorised with the SCTA ego states model. However the four dimensions described, the social-cognitive and the attachment and object relations theories allow to understand *why* persons develop specific ego states profiles.

Relational ego states

SCTA ego states include different mental representations: Relational ego states and Self ego states. The relational dimension is used to describe dyadic relationships in a continuous process of giving and taking power to oneself or the other, consistent with the view of ego states as schemas evolving in time. The transitive transactional position is called Relational Parent, while the intransitive position is called Relational Child. The reason for this choice is simple and represents a step forward from Bernian Transactional Analysis.

This model highlights in fact that an actual parent in transactional exchanges with his or her child is typically in an active caring and/or control position, in both cases with a positive or negative affective tone. The same can be said of the child who is typically in the position of receiving his parents' care, being more or less active or passive, loving or aggressive in reaction to them. On the other hand, these positions should be seen as *prototypical*, which means that any person, child or adult, in any relationship can take a different relational position in the transactional exchange.

Again, here we can see SCTA's effort to explain the complexity of human development in the whole lifespan through the lens of transactional dynamics.

To understand the hierarchical levels that define ego states we can analyse the behaviour of the mother of a five-year-old child who activates different relational processes that can stimulate the construction of a solid self. For example she takes care of him and says, "Put on a sweater because it is cold," so we can consider her as a Relational Parent who protectively controls her child. When her son makes a drawing showing satisfaction, she might say, "What a beautiful picture you drew!", proposing herself according to SCTA as a Relational Parent

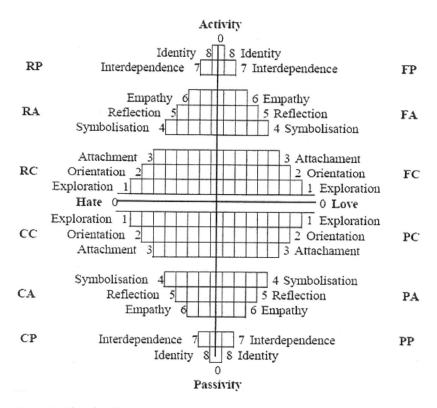

Figure 3. The developmental ego states.

acting from her Free Child (see the developmental model in Fig. 3). If this mother, who at a certain level always remains a Parent, responds to her child who spontaneously tells her, "Mom, I love you so much!" with "Thank you, honey, me too!", we can say she is changing position and reacting to her son with loving dependence that facilitates intimacy. The mother could also propose herself as a proud Relational Child if she says to her son, "Look at this beautiful cake I made!", adding, as a Relational Parent, "Do you want some?"

I think that the reader can intuitively grasp the rich interplay that characterises all human relationships, and intense affective relationships especially.

Therapists should be sensitive to understand that in the intersubjective field of therapeutic relationships they are also called upon to take several ego states positions flexibly, otherwise they may miss the opportunity to get in touch with their patients' experiences and with themselves. The affiliation dimension is usually recognised as important in the therapeutic relationship, while I think that the rich dynamic related to the power position ("to give to and to take power from the other" and "to give to and to take power from oneself") is less appreciated.

Self ego states

We then have a third position that defines the Self, that is, the outcome of the relevant interpersonal and relational experiences that deeply affect the attitudes one has to oneself. This distinction allows us to see the constantly interactive processes in interpersonal relations at implicit and explicit levels and the relatively more stable processes that characterise how one treats oneself and develops images of oneself. Self ego states are defined by thoughts, feelings, and behaviours that are not necessarily relational but, however, are born in the relationship with oneself, the others, and the world.

Since Self ego states are also "mechanisms for selecting experiences that determine to what information one pays greater attention and how information is structured, attended and used later" (Scilligo, 2009, p. 107), they can give rise to recurrent systems of elaboration of experience similar to the concept of structure. In fact they are continuously reactivated processes that allow an orientation beyond the information found in the context.

The interplay of Relational and Self ego states

We can see two separate relational processes: those related to Self ego states and those related to Relational ego states. In both cases we have potential ego states which, once instantiated, give rise to observable Self or Relational operational models. For each Relational ego state a corresponding Self ego state is activated. In treatment this continuous oscillation from being in relationships as persons in relation with themselves or in relation with others is very evident and the therapist needs to start building a narrative thread that keeps account of both perspectives.

Clinical example

What follows is a simple example of two different interventions that a therapist might choose taking into account Relational and Self ego states. At the beginning of treatment a patient says:

P: I don't understand why I keep getting entangled always in the same disappointing romantic relations with women. I think I found the right one and then she deceives me and I have to leave her!
T: Would you like to understand in treatment how you contribute to creating your painful experience?
P: I don't want to understand anything! I just want to feel better!

In classical Transactional Analysis that patient's reaction is considered a crossed transaction typical of a transference process. Now let's see what SCTA can highlight in that exchange. I think that the patient depicts a relationship to himself (Self ego state) characterised by a slightly hostile distance (he doesn't understand himself), and relational experiences characterised by a certain passive aggression (Relational ego states) and a passive-critical way to consider himself (Self ego state) since he keeps getting entangled in disappointing situations, suffers deception, and feels forced to leave his partner. The woman's mind is probably unpredictable for him. Emotionally the latter part of his narrative seems the most significant. The patient's opening to the therapist seems characterised by a search for the therapist's accepting understanding rather than a contractual request. The therapist's intervention suggests a direction which is related to a possible implicit wish of the patient to understand himself. Even if the therapist addresses the patient in a loving and protective way the patient responds negatively to such a suggestion. As a matter of fact the therapist's invitation seems to come early when compared to the patient's ability to both be in contact with his implicit wishes and to depend on an interpersonal relationship.

At this level the therapist's intervention could be the following:

T: I imagine that it is not easy for you when you don't find a logical explanation either for how you choose a partner or for how a woman behaves with you. It is like treading again a path that does not lead where you want to go.

This intervention "respects" the patient's level of opening and paves the way for a future contract: it introduces a new idea, the importance of finding logical explanations for one's and others' behaviours, stressing also a possible "activity" in the patient's choice of a partner. I could say that the therapist is motivating the client to activate his Adult ego state. The therapist's relating seems also empathic, characterised by a medium degree of freedom and love and does not "press" the patient to a relational collaboration. This second intervention is inspired by Free ego states while the first one is nearer to Protective ego states.

The developmental dimension

We will now see how our developmental analysis will allow us to find the Child, Parent, and Adult closer to the Bernian definitions as further specifications of these basic relational positions that can be referred to being a Relational Parent, a Relational Child, and a Self.

The developmental dimension assumes that persons evolve during life and develop increasing levels of complexity and individuation according to Mahler and Furer's (1968) description. Scilligo describes eight stages that recur cyclically during a lifetime: 1) exploration and acceptance; 2) orientation and approach; 3) attachment; 4) symbolisation; 5) reflection; 6) empathy; 7) interdependence; 8) identity.

As did L. S. Benjamin (1974) in her structural analysis of social behaviour, Scilligo located these eight development stages in the bidimensional space used to define ego states (Fig. 3).

Using factor analysis, Scilligo (2009) correlated the first three of Mahler and Furer's developmental stages with the Child ego state, or Developmental Child: 1) approach-avoidance (also described as *exploration*), 2) need fulfilment (which Scilligo spoke of in terms of *orientation*), and 3) *attachment*. The next three stages were correlated with the Developmental Adult: 4) logic communication (the process of *symbolisation*), 5) attention to self-development (which includes *reflection*), and 6) balance in relationship (most saliently characterised by *empathy*). The last two stages were correlated with the Developmental Parent: 7) intimacy-distance (which can be thought of as *interdependence*), and 8) *identity*.

In Figure 3 we see the Child, Adult, and Parent ego states in a position that is very similar to Berne's concept of ego states but with a new view of Adult.

SCTA (Scilligo, 2009) relates the developmental Child ego state to processes characterised by emotions. In Child ego states thoughts, emotions, and behaviours typical of the first years of life prevail: for example, intuition, concreteness, and impulsivity. To explain Child processes it is important to make use of theories that explain emotional regulation in children.

The developmental Adult ego state, developmentally located at an intermediate level between purely affective and normative processes, represents the processes characterised by more differentiated and structured thoughts, emotions, and behaviours, as a consequence of the full development of Piaget's formal operations (Piaget, 1952). An Adult has developed skills related to being in the physical and interpersonal world, and also skills in abstract observation, analysis, and synthesis related to the perception of oneself and of the interpersonal and physical world. These are typical of adults.

The developmental Parent ego state is characterised by complex thoughts, emotions, and behaviours related to past experiences. It has the function of regulating a person's balance by means of rules, limitations internalised on the basis of the interactions with others, and reflections on oneself and the world. In SCTA it is considered the normative pole of a person.

In his research, Scilligo (2009, p. 179) found that the Parent has a different characterisation from the Child and the Adult that instead have a factor in common, that is, the capacity for orientation and presentation grounded on an adequate evaluation of reality which is based on intuition and generalisation in the case of the Child and the connection between cause and effect in the Adult. Scilligo relates the functioning of Child and Adult to Zelazo's consciousness levels (Zelazo, Hong Gao, & Todd, 2007) that are hierarchically organised. The Parent ego state instead is more developmentally advanced and represents "the capacity to regulate oneself by means of the definition of guidelines for action aimed at reaching goals that have a meaning for the person also in the light of the person's reference values" (Scilligo, 2009, p. 180).

A magnifying lens on the Adult ego state

In SCTA there is a totally new understanding of the Adult ego state, because we think of Adult as a process with certain functions that is affected as much as the other ego states by experiences and attachment links.

Interesting implications of this theory can be assumed not only for psychotherapy and counselling but also in the fields of education and organisation. As a matter of fact we can understand that the full development of symbolic thinking, meta-reflection, and awareness of self in contexts is rooted in well balanced affective and respectful relationships.

Berne used the metaphor of *contamination* to describe the overlapping of Parent and Child ego states with Adult ego states and illustrated it mainly with an analysis of the contents and origin of the patient's narratives. For example, in discussing psychiatric symptoms Berne (1961) describes hallucinations as ego syntonic manifestations of the Parent so that the "contaminated" Adult is in agreement with the Parent's voice. In SCTA, instead, the Adult is analysed in light of the quality of the activated processes. Based on Zelazo's research on consciousness levels (Zelazo, Hong Gao, & Todd, 2007) and on Carver's research on cybernetic self-regulation circuits (Carver, 2004), Scilligo states that the conscious control of thoughts can be functionally attributed both to the Free Adult and the Protective Adult, as both use symbolisation, while the regulation of emotions is made primarily by the Free Adult that is especially activated in the self-reflection process (Scilligo, 2009, p. 173).

Clinical example

The analysis of a dream below is an example of how one can analyse different processes related to the Adult.

Gloria, fifty-five, is asking for therapy because she is living a very difficult crisis in her family characterised by deep conflicts and rifts. "Pain" is a major issue in her life because of the illness of her elder brother who died when she was thirty. Her destructive script decision is: "In order to be loved by my relatives and to show them my love, I can not enjoy life."

After few months of psychotherapy, for the first time she brings a dream to the session and she wants to work on it. In the dream, she is sitting on a sofa in a lovely country house surrounded by a garden. Her aunt is sitting just on the opposite side. A beautiful dancer, dressed in white, crosses the room and jumps out of the window in the empty space. At this point Gloria wakes up, feeling surprised and curious of her dream meaning. When she narrates that dream I feel concerned for her and, also, I feel excited and very interested because I think she is bringing something crucial for herself that she wants to work through with me.

Gloria explores the diverse symbols of that dream. Briefly, she gets in contact emotionally with "the country house"—her "self" open to others, harmonious, elegant but also empty inside, because there are conflicts among the house inhabitants. Her aunt: a detached part of herself, the "self" which resembles her mother. The dancer: the "self" that wants to feel light and to become free of burden. Gloria in the dream: a passive "self" that looks at what is happening without taking a stand.

Exploring the dream Gloria develops a narrative that links the various selves. She especially understands that she creates her own void as a consequence of her difficulty in putting boundaries to the expectations of others and in taking her wishes into account. So "the dancer" represents her wish to develop her free self that is not supported by loving care. She deeply understands the importance of giving some protective options to herself, instead of acting out potentially destructive ones ("jumping into an empty space"). She also relates the destructive risks to the self that is passive in the dream. At the end of that session I ask her: "So, which important message do you want to take for yourself from this dream?" She answers: "I seem very capable, but actually I'm not."

I feel surprised by her answer and start to reflect on the quality of her self-reflection. Is she aware of her own problem and evaluating herself in a loving way? Or is she evaluating herself in a hateful and controlling way? Is she considering concrete options that are respectful both of her wishes and context? Or is she taking into account only "some" meanings sprung from the exploration of her dream, disregarding the full meaning of her dream through which she was recognising wishes, difficulties, and conflicts? (Fig. 4)

Considering both the content of Gloria's answer and the non-verbal process, I think that she presents a thinking process characterised by some emotional distance from herself (freedom + hate), which resembles that of a Rebellious Adult. My hypothesis is that we have a good therapeutic alliance through which she is able to explore herself in a process characterised by empathy and openness, as long as she is in the relationship with me. However, when my final question prompts her to develop her own direction, she reverts to a process that is not supportive and positive towards herself.

My hypothesis is that she is still frightened by the possibility to develop protective options for herself in her context, that is, a Protective Adult, which is defined through sentences such as: "I develop my competences, I want to understand what is happening around me and I find a way to protect myself with love." If I consider my hypothesis I should develop the therapeutic alliance towards a more careful attention to her implicit wish to have a protective guide. I know from her story that she was the "perfect child", the daughter without problems who should compensate her parents for all the pain they suffered for their son.

A few sessions later I start the session telling her that I was reflecting on something important she said the session before (she was talking about the relationship with her husband), which, from my point of view, we need to explore more. She feels moved because I thought of her. After this session she starts to put up protective boundaries and to find options that take into account her wishes and others. So, it seems to me that my hypothesis about the quality of her self-reflection was right and that my careful attention stimulated a similar process towards herself.

Adult ego states

The operational qualities of the four Adult ego states

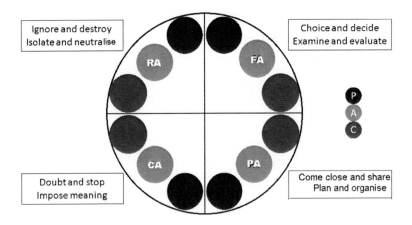

Figure 4. The Adult ego states.

Transference processes

In Berne's Transactional Analysis the difference between P_1 and P_2 has a relevant explanatory and clinical value (Berne, 1961). P_1 is an archaic self-normative process developed by the child and considered a subsystem of the Child ego state usually associated to pathologies in the adult. The case of Noemi, at the beginning of this chapter, shows a typical example of P_1 that exerts a magical self-control in order not to feel overwhelmed by her own fear, in the absence of protective parental figures. Some authors (Hargaden & Sills, 2002; Moiso, 1985; Novellino, 2004) stressed the importance of working with transference/countertransference processes in psychotherapy especially when P_1 is split into a "good" and a "bad" part due to the defence of splitting, as this defence did not allow the development of a P_2 capable of regulating affects harmoniously. P_2, instead, represents the most evolved and complete Parent ego state of all three Child, Adult, and Parent subsystems.

In SCTA normative modes characterised by strong hatred or love are represented near the poles of the Relational Parent's affects. The significant other that abandons, attacks, threatens will be coded as a Relational Parent that acts from a Rebel or Critical Child and indicates that, for example, an actual parent approaching a child in a way that is seen as highly hostile is in fact activating a Child aspect of himself or herself. If then this actual parent (or another significant person) alternates very aggressive to very loving behaviours and the child cannot perceive the logic of this alternation, or if the actual parent presents aggressive and loving behaviours at the same time, as it is happening in some kind of abuse, we think that it is more likely that the child internalises split off modes of managing and seeing himself and the other. It is important to see that the Relational Parent-Relational Child-Self should be considered as different positions of the same pattern, although they have different representations, so that transference processes can alternate the use of all the parts in the pattern.

Clinical example

Rita, twenty-five, requests therapy because of very unstable affective relationships and in particular because of the fact that she was left recently by a much older partner. She already underwent various treatments which all ended with her dropping out angrily.

In the relationship with me she tends to idealise me and she tries to please and to control me through rapid improvements in mood that she attributes to our therapeutic work. These moments alternate with others when she feels very depressed and desperate. Every instance of lack of empathy on my part, or of persons close to her, triggers violent and angry reactions. From an aetiological point of view her developmental story is characterised by an attachment style and experiences typical of borderline pathology (see the interesting research of L. S. Benjamin (1996) on aetiology of personality disorders).

Here I want to emphasise that the therapeutic alliance can be maintained only through a careful analysis and containment of her relational style. In particular: her tendency to move quickly from the position of a punitive Relational Parent (Critical Child of the Relational Parent), the result of her identification with her violent father, to that, complementarily, of a frightened and defensive Child (Critical Child of a Relational Child) stimulates in me the feeling of being attacked without justification or having to take care of a vulnerable child.

At times she seems like an abandoned child who walks away from everyone and walls herself off for days (Rebellious Child of Relational Child), projecting the image of her neglectful mother, who did not understand her pain, on everybody around her. In these cases it is difficult to "reach" her beyond the wall she builds.

She lacks the ability to serenely analyse her needs, wishes, and intentions as well as to properly evaluate how to protect herself in the relationships. In summary, Rita presents one of those pathological ego states profiles (Scilligo, 2009) which represent a challenge for psychotherapists.

My therapeutic proposal requires the constant use of crossed transactions (see later in this paper the concept of antithesis as a therapeutic tool) when the transference processes are active in the session.

I will present a typical exchange in therapy:

P: You do not understand me! You are on the side of my boyfriend and you think I'm a wrong girl. I think it is better if I interrupt therapy …

T: You feel that I have not supported you at this time and I want to understand what made you feel criticised in particular. Do you want to talk about it?

In this brief transactional exchange I understand Rita's behaviour as Rebellious Child of Relational Child: "She goes away full of anger." Also I can recognise, at an implicit level, a tendency to control me with hatred, which is typical of a punitive Relational Parent position: "I take revenge on you because you did not do what I want" and a narrative theme linked to rivalry. Here the transactional antithesis implies that I respond by giving empathic listening (Free Adult of Relational Parent), modelling assertive behaviour (Free Adult of Relational Child) and gently inviting her to open (Protective Adult of Relational Parent).

I described a process that has the goal to create a safe and genuine relational space where Rita can take the risk of opening herself and eventually accepting an interpretation work of her script. Again I want to stress that understanding the psychological positions taken by the patient helps the therapist promote a dynamic context that should facilitate more integrated ego states profiles.

Archaic or complicated destructive experiences that have marked children's lives usually require the reorganisation of developmental passages that become clear in transference processes. The therapeutic regressive work is contemplated in cases like Rita's, if the regression is spontaneous and allows the reorganisation of rigid and destructive relational schemas.

SCTA broadens the concept of transference, highlighting that it is a ubiquitous phenomenon that profoundly influences everyday life (Andersen & Berk, 1998; Scilligo, 2011). In social-cognitive terms transference can be conceptualised as mental representations of significant others that can be activated and applied to new people. The social-cognitive research on transference has shown that "mental representations of significant others serve as storehouses of information about given individuals from one's life, and can be activated (made ready for use) and applied to (used to interpret) other individuals, and that this is especially likely when the new individual in some way resembles a significant other" (Andersen & Berk, 1998, p. 81).

Though the more classical countertransference—the complementary experience evoked in the therapist in reaction to the client's transference—surely occurs, the therapist, just as are the patients, is subject to transference, a word that we can consider more specific to describe the importance of evaluating the effect of such templates also on the psychotherapists (Scilligo, 2009). From my point of view this means that the therapist uses relational "templates" that were formed also during previous significant psychotherapies. Patients do impact therapists with beneficial and less beneficial effects, depending on the therapist's self-reflection capacity.

The complex interplay of transference/countertransference processes has been outlined by authors like Clarkson (1992), by relational transactional analysts (Hargaden & Sills, 2002) and by integrative transactional analysts (Erskine, 1991). It seems to me that social-cognitive studies offer a fresh view of transference as a completely "normal" process. Sometimes transference can be associated with pathology, suffering, and inappropriateness while at other times may be quite appropriate. Usually the transference reactions are automatic and unconscious and, in therapy, they are objects of exploration and understanding if they generate distress in the person's life. Given the social-cognitive vision of transference this point is important because it is not considered useful to analyse "all" manifestations of transference.

All the representations of significant others influence interpersonal perceptions, whether formed in childhood, adolescence, or adulthood. As Andersen notes: "... according to Sullivan, typical patterns of interaction between self and other should be activated when a significant-other representation is activated, which should in turn activate relevant aspects of the self-concept ..." (Andersen & Berk, 1998, p. 85). Some aspects of self-evaluation reflect the tone of the significant other representation, but when these aspects are negative, a defensive or compensatory self-enhancement appears to occur in the working self-concept as a whole (Andersen & Berk, 1998).

The transference process can be examined in terms of process and/or in terms of its content (ibid.). In psychotherapy the most critical transference processes happen as a consequence of very destructive representations (*content*) of important others that are a source of distress and defensiveness, also because these processes are often unconscious and the person is somehow submitted to them. Moreover, when the *process* of transference appears somehow rigid and not open to dealing with new information, it presents problematic issues as well.

In this chapter I do not intend to analyse the complexity of these processes, but I want to highlight some points: the interacting components of the therapeutic relation, highlighted by psychodynamic authors— real relationship, therapeutic alliance, narcissistic alliance, transference (Tosi, 1991)—start to have less pronounced boundaries as transference impacts on each component. Moreover, therapists and patients are at the same level, although in a different role, which implies a great challenge for therapists.

In supervision I often ask two main questions to therapists when I analyse transference processes. The first question is, "What does your affect reaction to this patient tell you *about him/her?*" This is the classical question used to analyse a reactive countertransference in the therapist. It implicitly sees the therapist's affect reaction as empathically depending on the patient.

The second question is: "What does your affect reaction to this patient say about *yourself* in relation to this patient?" I have noticed that this second question can powerfully promote awareness of the therapist's participation in the intersubjective field of the therapeutic relation both in its constructive and destructive aspect, helping the therapist to see what Self is affecting therapeutic work. As a matter of fact both questions are useful in highlighting different aspects of the intersubjective field.

Self and narratives

The ego states model and the social-cognitive perspective suggest a relational view of the Self as composed by several Selves. The Self surface is a system of declarative and procedural memories which represents the person in all its potential manifestations (Scilligo, 2009). It is formed by all potential Selves that each person can activate. Each of them represents a precipitate of the relational/interpersonal experiences characterised by the evolutionary and developmental dimensions (Fig. 5).

From my point of view, each Self has a narrative that includes personal, interpersonal, and cultural levels (Tosi, 2010). Those levels are intertwined and influence each other. As a matter of fact in the narrative and social-cognitive perspective the script of a person can be understood as the dynamic cluster of narratives created by a person with specific sub-scripts related to the different selves (Tosi, 2010). Transference, that for Berne (1961) was at the basis of the script, is conceptualised as conditional patterns of thought and behaviour that occur under special conditions until one can say that personality is made up by a cluster of these conditional patterns that tend to persist in time (Andersen & Berk, 1998). Following this line of thought, I think that in psychotherapy we should examine what Self the patient has developed in given

Self ego states

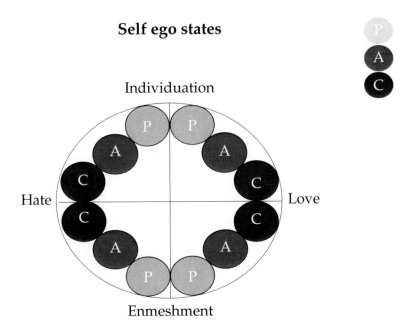

Figure 5. The twelve Self ego states.

contexts and what contexts the patient needs to develop more adaptive or authentic Selves. New Selves need new intrapsychic, interpersonal, and cultural contexts and the construction of new stories.

Clinical example

I will present a brief therapy account as an example of a new story and a new Self that starts to develop in a therapeutic passage.

Sofia is a forty-year-old woman who wants to explore the meaning of violent, intrusive fantasies against her two-year-old beloved son. When she was two years old her family migrated to a village in northern Italy, where they lived in a community formed by other like-minded migrants. In a session, Sofia tells the following memory: she is three years old and she plays with the garbage gathered in containers outdoors, in the garden surrounding the homes of her community members. She describes herself as neglected and abandoned, nobody is with her, and her mother is distracted.

I don't feel empathetic because she seems to be "playing" Victim, which, in the social-cognitive ego states model, would mean that she is adapting angrily to a Critical Relational Parent. I ask Sofia to collect memories and stories related to that period, asking her mother and older sister more information about that life stage. She comes to the following session quite surprised: her relatives gave her a different view of that period because it seems that many children lived in that community; she was not isolated and played often with her peers.

Slowly a new story unfolds: the child playing with the garbage was angrily scolded by her mother who repressed her exploration behaviour. While I feel genuinely close to her, I offer my interpretation that gives new words to that small child: "That baby was curious and creative and needed to be guided when exploring the world." Sofia feels moved by my interpretation and starts to develop a new narrative of herself. The child that starts to explore the physical world needs to be confirmed with love and enthusiasm and contained with protective control while Sofia was angrily controlled by her mother: that means a Relational Parent that "controls and hates". So in that event she was not really "abandoned", a behaviour characterised by "freedom and hate".

That experience lived by Sofia encompasses a personal/developmental level (the exploration-orientation-attachment developmental stage typical of the Free Child), an interpersonal level (with her anxious mother), and a cultural-contextual level linked to the special needs of a community non-integrated in the broader local culture. That event, together with many others of similar tone, is internalised as a prototypical relational pattern characterised by hate and control. Sofia, as an adult, does not feel she has an internal space to live and develop her creative and procreative potential. On the contrary in many situations she tends to activate a Critical Self (she blames and discounts herself not feeling up to situations and identifying with her aggressive mother). My interpretation offers an antithetical view of herself that she is ready and happy to develop.

The well-being system

L. S. Benjamin (1996) suggests that at least five basic processes are at work in the transformation of relational experiences into inner-world experience:

1. *Complementarity*. The person reacts from the complementary position to the others. For example, the child answers with loving dependence to the mother who hugs him with love. It is the same principle of complementary transactions in classical TA.
2. *Introjection*. Treating oneself as one is treated by a significant other. Note that in this model introjection is not opposed to projection as in classical psychoanalysis.
3. *Similarity*. Imitating the significant other.
4. *Opposite*. Adopting behaviours that are on opposite quadrants,for example, rebellious vs. protective, or free vs. critical.
5. *Antithesis*. Adopting behaviours that are the complement of the opposite.

We think that such predictive principles account for the major dynamics of ego states development, if we consider conscious and unconscious levels and the motivational system as theorised by SCTA. At the unconscious level I include the repressed and non-repressed unconscious and the implicit memory phenomena—procedural memory, priming and emotional memory (Tosi, 2008).

The antithesis is especially important for us practitioners because it is related to a special type of crossed transaction.

In the Rita example the therapist could easily react to Rita's accusations, becoming a critical Parent as a consequence of a projective identification process. Answering to Rita's accusations offering empathic understanding promotes a new process that should stimulate Rita to open up with freedom in a safe relational context. The interpretation work of her defence should follow that therapeutic step.

In the Gloria example, the therapist decided to stimulate a complementary use of Gloria's Protective Adult transacting from her Protective Adult of the Relational Parent. If the therapist had reacted complementarily to Gloria's Rebellious Adult with her Rebellious Adult she could have started to forget important contents brought by her in the sessions or to ignore her physical and emotional distress, etc. When the therapist showed her interest for a topic that she knew important for her, Gloria was grateful and touched. As a matter of fact the therapist proposed to Gloria an opposite attitude from that internalised by her distracted mother and stimulated a protective Adult self-reflection towards herself.

In SCTA treatment aims to promote the so called *"well-being system"*, that network of developmental ego states that includes the activation of Free Adult, Free Child, Protective Child, Protective Adult and moderate levels of Free Parent and Protective Parent.

Persons provided with this profile of ego states present a good balance of passivity and activity, a high level of positive affects mirrored in their ability to act from their wishes while accepting the limitations of the situations they are in. Persons with a profile of ego states that we can define as linked to a secure attachment tend to be in contact with their wishes, listen to themselves, and can manage their emotions. They move keeping their values flexibly in mind, having chosen them in an authentic way, and choose protective norms related to the context in which they happen to be. They know how to use the resources they find around them and are able to enjoy (Scilligo, 2009).

From my point of view, this vision of well-being entails that each person has to find her own balance between the dynamic impulses of aspiration and cooperation.

Conclusions

The theories are cognitive processes that help us make sense of and create our reality. Like any cognitive process it is important that they are open to ongoing experiences, to the evaluation of results, and to the awareness that they are affected by our position in the context observed. So I hope to have given the reader some tools of knowledge related to a theory that seeks to explain behaviours taking into account the complexity of human beings and the respect that is due when we work in the helping relationships. At the same time, since we also need simplicity in the communication process, I hope to have used words and examples that allow a dialogue in the community of transactional analysts.

CHAPTER TWELVE

Gender psychopolitics: men becoming, being, and belonging

Karen Minikin & Keith Tudor

The therapeutic work presented in this chapter and our reflections on it represent a contemporary Transactional Analysis that is informed both by radical psychiatry and relational Transactional Analysis. Radical psychiatry (The Radical Therapist Collective, 1971; Roy & Steiner, 1988; Steiner, 1981, 2000; Steiner et al., 1975; Wyckoff, 1976), which, in some ways, is a lost tradition of Transactional Analysis, was based on an analysis of alienation, oppression, and power, and emphasised liberation through contact, consciousness-raising, groups, and action. Relational Transactional Analysis (Cornell & Hargaden, 2005; Fowlie & Sills, 2011; Hargaden & Sills, 2002; Summers & Tudor, 2000; Tudor & Summers, 2014), which, in many ways, reflects the "relational turn" in psychotherapy, emphasises intersubjectivity, and relationality. In doing this we bring together the "old" and the "new" and, looking to the present and the future, question whether oppression and alienation are relevant in contemporary Transactional Analysis (Minikin, 2011) and, more broadly, in contemporary psychotherapy.

We refer to psychopolitics as a term that encompasses both a general reference to a psychotherapy that is informed by the social/political world, and a specific reference to the anti-psychiatry movement of the late 1960s and '70s (Sedgwick, 1982).

We refer to gender as we are both interested in gender politics—and psychopolitics—and because it was a major influence on early radical psychiatry: over a quarter of *The Radical Therapist* (The Radical Therapist Collective, 1971) was devoted to "Women and Men", with another eight chapters on gender in two subsequent publications, *Readings in Radical Psychiatry* (Steiner et al., 1975) and *Love, Therapy and Politics* (Wyckoff, 1976). In this chapter, we focus specifically on therapeutic work with men as, while men are the dominant gender in society, they are in the minority in therapy, both as clients and in some fields as therapists, and we are interested to explore how social identity as a man manifests in therapy.

As part of the first criterion for the Certified Transactional Analysis Oral Examinations in counselling, education, and psychotherapy, candidates are assessed as to their ability to describe the implications of cultural, racial, and social identities and the significance of these on the assessment, the contract, the work, and the relationship (European Association for Transactional Analysis (EATA), 2014; International Transactional Analysis Association (ITAA), 2013). In the organisational field, this criterion is "Understanding the professional context" and refers to "personal and contextual vision" and "awareness of ... cultural, social perspectives" (ITAA & EATA, both Section 12.7.11). In our experience as trainers, supervisors, and examiners, we have observed trainees and candidates (and examiners) struggle with what this criterion means, and part of our motivation to write this chapter is to offer something that does discuss social identity and its relevance for our work.

We are curious that men don't come to therapy (or that they engage with therapy less than women do), and wonder whether it is still the case, as Heppner and Gonzales observed over twenty-five years ago, that for men it is unacceptable to have problems, considered unmanly to seek help, and embarrassing to reveal inadequacies. We wonder, therefore, whether, as Rowan (1997) put it, therapy is an initiation in healing the male psyche; and we are interested in whether instrumental reason is still a defining characteristic of the male psyche, types of which Bennett (1995) identified as: domination, distance, control, and an attitude of success and failure.

The other aspect of gender represented in this chapter is that Karen is the therapist, so we are writing about a woman working with men. As a therapist, Karen has been committed to integrating social identity in her work and these extracts show her approach and her—and our—thinking about her work with some of the men in her practice. Her case examples offer illustrations of how she supports and challenges them to awaken and deepen their connection with their masculinity, including deconstructing their identities through examining their personal histories, social integration, and the relational dynamics within the therapeutic dyad: "out there", "back then", and "in here" (Menninger, 1958). Whilst our focus in this chapter is on gender, we are also mindful of other oppressions and their impact in psychological dynamics, especially those of race and culture. Karen embodies different races, and had a cross-cultural experience in her upbringing; Keith has been involved in cross-cultural work for many years, has written on the subject of being white (Naughton & Tudor, 2006), and is an active member of a bicultural professional group in Aotearoa New Zealand.

We refer to becoming, being, and belonging as a useful framework for describing men's social identity development—in life and in therapy—and one that encompasses the work of writers as diverse as Karl Marx, George Allport, Carl Rogers, Simone de Beauvoir, and Eric Berne. From Marx (1932) we derive a philosophical analysis of alienation and, through the tradition of radical psychiatry, we think in terms of "man", in this instance, men, being alienated from themselves, each other, and women, in various ways. We find the radical psychiatry formula, Alienation = Oppression + Mystification + Isolation, a useful way of thinking about the elements and process of alienation—and its corollary, Liberation = Awareness + Contact + Action, as a helpful way of thinking about "treatment" or psychopolitical therapy. From de Beauvoir (1949) we draw on the constructivist perspective that "one is not born, but rather becomes, a woman" (p. 267), and we think that this is no less true for men. From Allport (1955) we derive the importance of socialisation in the development of personality. From Rogers, we acknowledge the importance of empathy in challenging alienation: "It is one of the most potent aspects of therapy, because it releases, it confirms, it brings even the most frightened client into the human race. If a person can be understood, he or she belongs" (1986, p. 129); in short, "empathy dissolves alienation" (Rogers, 1975, p. 151). From Berne, we value the importance of transacting or relating—and of analysing—in becoming, being, and belonging. Given our constructivist perspective, we should clarify that we are not using "being" as a reference to a fixed, essentialist state, but rather to a continual process of being and integrating being human.

Radical psychiatry and relationality

One of the challenges offered by radical psychiatry was the reclaiming of the term and the practice of "psychiatry", translated from its Greek origins as "soul healing". In this sense, "radical" referred to roots, that is, getting back to the original roots or meaning of the word, although, in terms of its political analysis, radical also signified and reflected its left-wing perspective on and analysis of psychiatry and the medical establishment. With regard to gender, some of the early radical psychiatrists talked and wrote about men's oppression, not in an attempt to negate the differences between women's and men's oppression but, rather, as a way of understanding men's alienation. As DeGolia (1976) put it: "As workers, professionals, and businessmen, we are plugged into competitive, political, social, and economic systems the nature of which reinforces our isolation from each other" (pp. 180–181)

The centrality of alienation to the cause of mental distress provides scope to think about a relational radical psychiatry at individual, interpersonal, institutional, and social/cultural levels (Batts, 2002). At social and cultural levels, people feel recognised or diminished by the degree of acceptance or rejection that is shown to them. Often acceptance is offered in proportion to the degree of conformity to the dominant culture(s). Many groups holding marginalised identities can, therefore, feel alienated from the society or country to which they technically "belong". This has a very contemporary resonance with (as we were completing this chapter) the massacre in Paris on January 7, 2015 of twelve people who worked for the French satirical newspaper *Charlie Hebdo*, in response to which there has been renewed discussion about what it means to be and belong as a French citizen, what are shared national values and ethical principles, and whether such values, and, specifically, free speech, are universal and absolute or relative and relational. Then, within group and organisational dynamics, sometimes as a result of family or organisational/managerial hierarchies, people are provoked into experiences of isolation, disengagement, and other kinds of "dis-stress". People working in organisations can feel alienated from the product of their work and the work itself, and people in living groups can, of course, feel alienated from others and themselves. These alienated experiences are co-created interpersonally, in personal relationships and, of course, within the therapeutic dyad through transference and countertransference. At the level of the individual, we can consider the ways in which unsatisfying and traumatic experiences in context have been internalised and fixated to create alienated aspects of self. We see this as informing the structure of ego states, for example the self-dynamics between different aspects within the Child ego state.

Relational work seeks to understand in depth and breadth (context) how we connect, relate, and co-create together. Having a relational approach in Transactional Analysis means that both therapist and client bring their subjectivity to the work. This includes all conscious, nonconscious, and unconscious dynamics from past and present experience (Summers & Tudor, 2000). Subjectivity also includes our values and political sensibilities. Our view is that, in psychotherapy, the therapist is available to be as present as possible in herself as well as in her attentiveness to clients. By "present", we mean being aware of her feelings, fantasies, bodily sensations, images, thoughts, and so on, as well as her temporary disengagement from the work. In this sense, we see awareness and contact, as articulated by radical psychiatry, as "relational". We see the therapist's task as maintaining a frame of mind that is as open and curious as possible. We think of her level of involvement (Erskine, 1993) as including a willingness also to be uncomfortable in the service of clients. By this we mean that the therapist is willing to notice when she feels threatened or defensive and to stay alive and responsive to the co-creative dynamics in the consulting room. Relational engagement means that the therapist is willing to shift her position at times, exploring alternative frames of reference—and, of course, this includes the way the therapist makes use of the support and challenge of supervision and personal therapy. We think that the therapist's openness to change (Kriegman & Slavin, 1998; Minikin, 2013) is an important dimension in furthering the work.

Introducing the clients

Here we present the four clients that have helped us think about contemporary connections with masculinity. All the men have given permission for their work to be presented in writing, and their identities, including their names and minor historical details have been adjusted in consultation with them to protect their identity. Tony requested a

European name as a name from the country of his origin may have revealed his identity.

Patrick

Patrick is a twenty-five-year-old man. He is white, middle class, and identifies himself as heterosexual. He suffered with depression during his late teens. The youngest son in his family, he experienced emotional and physical abandonment from his father who was ill. His father's illness meant his mother was preoccupied by her husband's health. Patrick struggles to feel established as a man. Despite the evidence of his effectiveness as a football and swimming coach and his popularity with children, he describes feeling unvalued. The therapist feels somewhat protective of him, which she understands in part as a concordant countertransference (Clarkson, 1992; Racker, 1957).

Tony

Tony is a forty-year-old Asian man, who identifies himself as heterosexual. His parents came to England unable to speak English and made a life in southern England. All five children helped in the family business. His father was notably absent in the therapeutic work, until the therapist remarked on it. It seemed his father had spent most of his life in England depressed. Tony shared more about him and it seemed his father had shrunk to a "shell of a man". Having lost the status and respect he had in his home country, it seemed hard for him to recover and find a place in this foreign community. Also like Patrick, Tony had been clinically depressed since he left home at eighteen to go to university.

Freddie

Freddie is a white forty-one-year-old man, who came to therapy because he was struggling in his relationship with his wife and was considering separation. He has two children of primary school age and he is a devoted and involved father. Freddie is a "self-made" man. He had humble beginnings and as an adult has started up and worked in different businesses. He has managed to accumulate some wealth and has been a classical provider for his family. Freddie presents as dominant and self-assured. He expresses his authority freely with others, including with the therapist. Freddie was the third child of six and his parents separated when he was a baby. He does not know why and has never met his birth father. He shows no curiosity about this.

George

George is approaching sixty, the oldest son of a northern working class family. He identifies as a father figure in both his professional and personal lives. At the time of him starting his therapy, he was separated from his wife, though he was hoping they would be reconciled. George said he focused on his education as his escape from his family and social group. He was the first in his family to go to university. He has expressed enjoying the opportunity to speak privately in therapy about subjects he hasn't been able to voice before.

Having introduced our themes and the clients, we now explore aspects of their stories in order to illustrate the development of male social identity in terms of becoming, being, and belonging.

A deficit of fathering: oppression + mystification in becoming a man

This section explores the impact of an absent father on a growing boy, and considers how such an absence can be oppressive. One of the core difficulties both Patrick and Tony presented was of it being very hard, a real struggle to launch themselves into the adult world of men. They brought many stories to Karen that spoke to this theme, as well as envy and anger towards other men who seemed to find it easy. In this first extract we consider Patrick, the younger of the two men:

PATRICK: So I said to my girlfriend can we please not see these folk for a couple of weeks at least. They are lovely but they also annoy the hell out of me.

KAREN: You are telling me that it sometimes feels like your nose is being rubbed in it.

PATRICK: Yeah …

KAREN: So when you talk about the other twenty-six year olds, I feel you are letting me know you are comparing yourself and you want to know what the measure is of yourself as a man coming up for twenty-six.

PATRICK: Yeah I just don't feel twenty-six.

We think of this as an emerging theme in gender scripting: there seemed to be a particular way in which Patrick and Tony both felt themselves lacking in comparison to others. Patrick saw other men as more capable, more resourced, a view that echoes DeGolia's point about competition. At the same time, I (Karen) thought of this as a developmental deficit, a particular kind of oppression that was born from the absence of a vital father. Hargaden (2013) wrote about the importance of a father figure, as a "third" person in facilitating movement out of symbiosis. In describing this dynamic, she also pointed to the consulting room, as well as the influence of society and culture, all of which create a "third" position. The therapist sought to raise consciousness of the oppression Patrick felt, both from his internalised incapacitated father and from a cultural and society pressure to acquire some material wealth, to show explicitly the measure of his masculinity.

We suggest that an internalised absent, passive, or incapacitated father makes the oppression more mystifying than an aggressive or bullying father. In the latter the child knows how he is wounded, whereas in the former, the child only knows that he struggles to feel alive and well. The deadening, even violent internal process is not visible. Put this together with the modern Western constructs of masculinity (for example, Gregory, 2001; Shadbolt, 2009; Wieland, 2015), and it is no wonder these men thought they were fundamentally lacking.

As these themes were explored, turned over, reviewed, the work touched back on his father again. Patrick's grief was usually expressed with anger and contempt towards his father. This time, Patrick felt more connected to his sense of loss and sadness in his life.

KAREN: I keep thinking about what your father modelled to you as a grown man. He had aptitude, potential. But in becoming destructive and then ill he created havoc for all those around him … destroyed your family, your group.

PATRICK: Yeah I think it is fair to say that he came across so regretful and talked of the opportunities he missed. I would hate to look back on my life with such regret …

KAREN: You saw his torment …

PATRICK: Yeah, he did achieve some things and then regretted what he lost over a six, seven year period … umm … but I don't think I will do the destructive things he did.

KAREN: Yes, you are different from him. But you seem to be putting your finger on something important about your father's relationship to success that you can relate to. There is a longing in you to have something you can be proud of without fearing you are going to lose it.

PATRICK: Hmm … [pause] … this is quite sad [cries].

KAREN: Your sadness feels connected to you and your father?

PATRICK: I think missed opportunity and regretful feelings are familiar.

As Patrick contacted his feelings of loss including the loss of a present and vibrant father, he recovered some of his own vitality in his young life. As the therapist I (Karen) was aware of how both my masculine and feminine sides were evoked by Patrick. I noticed feeling both maternal and paternal at times and could relate to some of his experiences as I remembered the challenges in my twenties of meeting demands of independent adult life. Whilst, as a woman, I can never know what it is like to be in a man's body and have Patrick's experiences, for some of my life I worked in the world of men, including authoritative men. I wondered how my witness and knowledge of these experiences facilitated some rapport with Patrick and Tony. Also, as a woman, I thought—and think—that it is important that both men find themselves other men that they could respect and feel supported by in the social world. This is a reflection of the ways in which our identity and experiences bring resources to the work, but are always inevitably limited and that "thirds" other than the one created in the consulting room are important.

Patrick described feeling "young" and I was aware of the losses in his adolescence. This was different from the experience I had with Tony. My earlier work with him had the feel of being in the presence of an ever-hungry baby that longed for comfort and mothering. He could not hold or retain the comfort that talking with me brought beyond the consulting room. I often felt that I ceased to exist as soon as he shut the door as he left. This disconnect had a flavour of an internally violent process, which is common when people have experienced early trauma. It was as if the more alive self-in-contact could not be retained, and was an alienated part of himself.

This capacity for an alienated self-experience came partly from a traumatic loss, including abandonment when he was very young. It seemed to have hardened his heart in relation to himself. This was an oppressive and mystifying process that seemed unconscious, but which could be accessed through my experience of ceasing to exist. In becoming aware of this, which I understood as a transformational transference (Hargaden & Sills, 2002), I could then bring this into the work later.

These transferential experiences were held and then spoken about in time and eventually Tony developed more awareness and confidence to acknowledge when he was angry with the therapist. As the work progressed, Tony reported feeling very provoked by some of the more "strutting" men in his workplace. We understood this as his rejection of aggression, particularly the kind expressed as arrogance. Interestingly, he soon became friends with one of these characters and as he started to look to other men around him as role models, he became livelier, more sexually charged, and his interest in women changed. From having seen them as objects providing or withholding maternal gratification, they became potential friends and partners for him. For the past year, Tony has taken up dance lessons. These have provided a great opportunity for him to move his body (he has a natural aptitude for dance) and to touch women. In this extract, he shares his attraction to one of the women in his class.

TONY: I was thinking … the other thing is … when I was messaging Rebecca yesterday, I felt really excited. Whereas normally I don't …

KAREN: There is a charge in you.

TONY: Like the first time I felt emotional … about her … really weird.

KAREN: There is something about her you find very attractive.

TONY: Hmm.

KAREN: Do you know what it is?

TONY: She's very pretty, but she can dance as well …

KAREN: Your body likes hers.

Radical psychiatry was very influenced by the work of Reich and in the books on radical therapy and the issues of the magazine *Radical Therapy* (1969–1972), there are many references to the body and bodywork:

> Men have been taught to relate to their surrounding world from
> an almost entirely intellectual perspective … [that] ignores feelings

and fears emotions. Our sex-role training discounts not only our feelings, but those of others as well ... . In order to reclaim our feelings—and it *is* a process of reclaiming—we must start to reclaim our *bodies*. (DeGolia, 1976, p. 188)

As Tony recovered from his depression, the heavy oppression he had lived under started to lift. The life was pouring back into him and this was especially marked by his capacity to joke and laugh with his therapist. Their relationship took on a new, more vital feel that included different perspectives and ways of relating.

This work also shows how therapeutic work on a developmental deficit may be done in a way that reflects a two-person psychology (Stark, 1999), as distinct from a one-and-a-half-person corrective or reparative emotional experience—and by a female therapist. Whilst it is sometimes necessary and, indeed, desirable for men to work with men, both individually and in groups (Heppner & Gonzales, 1987; Tudor, 1999), such "matching" is not necessarily sufficient or always appropriate, and in any case can be challenging (Tremblay & L'Heureux, 2005). In our experience men can do good therapeutic work with men and with women, just as women can do good therapeutic work with women and with men (Johnson, 2005). As with all therapy, what is important is that gender dynamics, in and out of the therapeutic relationship, are reflected upon, and discussed—in therapy, supervision, and training (Rowan, 1997). The example with Tony illustrates an expansion from maternal longing to engaging with his sexual desire in his relations with women. The following cases continue the theme of how oppression operates in masculinity, how this is embodied, and how demystifying this and raising awareness helps men in themselves as well as in relating to women.

Deconstructing the Fascist within: from oppression to liberation (awareness) in being a man

Freddie had a sculptured and athletic physique, which belied a hidden fallibility of a vulnerable heart. We say this both metaphorically and literally as he has something wrong with his heartbeat. In the first session I (Karen) became transfixed by his stony physical exterior. His body was perfectly contoured, yet, at that meeting, seemed without animation or sexual charge. I gazed at this man and found myself unable to speak. He broke the silence with a contemptuous comment:

FREDDIE: You are going to have to do more than just sit there.

His aggression woke me from my trance; I welcomed the opportunity to recover and responded with honesty:

KAREN: I was struck by your stillness … I find myself reflecting now that you look quite traumatised.

In response Freddie's face and body softened and, in my eyes, he seemed more human. Outside he presented as a success: a man who had it all. Focused and competitive, he took charge. He was a product of modern-day capitalism and proud of his achievements. He was the man in her practice most aligned with the Western cultural fit of representations of the masculine. Yet he seemed lost in his soul connection to himself and others.

Reflecting on Freddie's presentation brought to mind some psychopolitical ideas, firstly, about capitalism and masculinity: "Capitalism replaces notions of 'self fulfilment' with ideas of 'getting on' and 'proving yourself' which turn out to be endless tasks, because we are always proving ourselves against others" (Seidler, 1991, p. 76); and, secondly, about masculine constructs:

> Men who could be described as numb may have, but repress, an inner rage at how they were treated as children … . They may develop an extreme vulnerability and lash out when they feel they are being shamed, hurt, rejected, or disrespected. (Gregory, 2001, p. 174)

Gregory's research of masculine constructs was based on a survey of Australian men, research that highlighted the many ways in which white Australian men felt entitled to their authority in their families and in society. Such entitlement also entails a subjugation of all that is considered vulnerable and emotional, and associated with the feminine. We understand this as a particular form of self-oppression—and mystification, in that such entitlement is based on the coercion of others in interpersonal and social settings to conform to the same ideology in order to maintain or conserve psychic and social homeostasis. This echoes the concern—and focus—that radical psychiatrists had regarding the oppressive power of the internal Critical Parent. As Wieland (2015) has commented on the effect of introjecting such constructs: "Fascism within the mind and within society is the alienated child of this broken marriage" (p. 12). Here Wieland was referring to the loss of the social and cultural context, an aspect of the "third" also described by Hargaden (2013).

I (Karen) listened to Freddie's story of his actual broken marriage, and his anxiety about living separately from his children. I heard the rage that his wife was expressing and thought it seemed to stem from her developing awareness of oppression in this relationship. I reflected this back along with my sense of how he had been affected by his recent relationship difficulties and the terrible distressing loss he felt in missing his children.

Confronting Freddie to raise his awareness of the impact he had on others, especially women, was sensitive work. I recognised the need both to expose his capacity to oppress, and to treat him with utmost respect and sensitivity given his predisposition to shame. An example of this is a discussion that followed an incident during dinner. One of his daughters had been defiant and Freddie had made an impulsive physical move towards her. His fist accidentally caught the side of her plate, sending it flying, along with her dinner. His daughter burst into tears and fled from the room.

FREDDIE: So my question is, what is it that we can be doing to make it a bit easier for her?

KAREN: You are working hard at this ... for your daughter's sake. I suppose there is also something for us to understand about what happens for you when people block your authority.

FREDDIE: I do feel a little bit of "Arrrgh! Goodness me ... grr! ... anger!!"

KAREN: What do you think that is about?

FREDDIE: Just ahhh ... [pause] ... losing control I suppose ... for me ... my thought is ... . Like she said, "Daddy when you shout at me, you scare me. Errr ... I am scared of you." [Pause]

KAREN: She is scared and she is angry.

Freddie's initial impetus, and stimulus/invitation to me, was to merge together so that we could metaphorically parent his daughter. I understood this as an example of unconscious oppression and mystification in the interpersonal dynamics between us. In other words, Freddie sought to suppress his awareness of his rage because he felt ashamed about it. If he could avoid his shame, he might stabilise himself, maintain his OK-ness, and deflect blame. If he could recruit me into a joint project, he may feel safe. In this incident, and his recounting of it, he tried to shift the focus of "badness" onto his daughter, and define what happened as "only an accident", thereby discounting his responsibility for his actions and options. This was an unconscious attempt to mystify both himself and me by showing how keen he was to help and support his child. That is not to say that he was or is lying. He has a genuine wish to behave in ways that are supportive and emotionally facilitative for his child. Yet, if he and I had focused attention on his goodness, and his desire to help his child, without acknowledging his anger, something important would have been missed. His impulsive rage would continue to be an alienated part of himself, and, in being alienated from himself, may continue to erupt and thus cause alienation in his relationship with others.

In the 1970s, it seemed like there was an awakening of political consciousness, particularly with regard to sexual and racial oppression and overt discrimination (for writings on which with regard to men, see Seidler, 1992). The emphasis in radical psychiatry was on emancipating aspects of humanity that were oppressed in the real world and fighting the oppressor, which was socially and culturally fixed. While this is relevant today, particularly in challenging oppressive systems (including our own Internal Oppressor/Critical Parent), we do not think that anger is the only feeling that needs to be contacted for liberation. In terms of our internal world, there are all sorts of losses, trauma, and ruptures that need to be grieved. Of course, from a relational perspective, all loss is grounded in relationship, as is grieving and recovery. Contact with another or others is essential and that includes sharing the sadness, rage, and fears all associated with grief. Echoing the radical psychiatry formulae, we frame this as: Emotional Life $\rightarrow$ Emotional Literacy + Relationship(s) = Liberation.

Recognising Freddie's struggle with difference meant that I as the therapist usually felt some level of anxiety when confronting him. Yet more and more I saw and felt his relief when I stepped in with authority.

It was as if in taking her authority, I could relieve him of fiercely needing to hold on to his. He seemed relieved in sharing aspects of his identity about which he felt ashamed, relief that they could be looked at and explored without fear of being humiliated by being metaphorically castrated (Monick, 1991). We agree with and appreciate Shadbolt's (2009) linking of sexuality and shame: "The treatment of issues related to sexuality often involves the 'treatment' of shame and the recovery of excitement, vitality, and aliveness as well as a resolution of the 'me versus not-me' impasse" (p. 170). This last point is an(other) example of where, for some male clients, working with a female therapist, who is clearly "not me", may be therapeutically helpful.

Contact with self and others: belonging as a man

In our final example, we reflect on George and an aspect of his journey towards recognising his vulnerability. He has begun to find a way in which the feminine and the masculine need not be so split inside him. George is learning to be a mediator and, just before this extract, he had expressed feeling very disturbed whilst away on his training. He described dropping rather suddenly into his vulnerability, because he and his peers were inadvertently back late from lunch:

GEORGE: Four of us went to lunch and I felt responsible for everyone … despite the others being capable people. I felt guilty we were late, though I wasn't controlling when we left, nor was I doing the driving, but I still felt guilty. The other three were females.

KAREN: How interesting …

GEORGE: Yeah, it is interesting …
[PAUSE]

At this point, I held my reaction to the word "females", which to me seemed a strange term, given these were his friends and peers. I also caught his emerging awareness of the gender politics in this peer group.

KAREN: So, you were the leader and the others were the followers in your mind?

GEORGE: Yeah, I hadn't thought about it till now …

George went on to describe the strong somatic response he had to "getting it wrong". He had started to shake physically and he had lost his ability to speak.

KAREN: What do you imagine will happen to you if you had a moment like that here?

GEORGE: Here?

KAREN: Hmm.

GEORGE: Umm … I would probably ask you for help.

KAREN: What would you fear would happen in your more irrational self?

GEORGE: I don't … I think quite honestly, Karen, I think I have got past being scared of you. Um … I think I would consciously say, "Karen, I need help."

KAREN: Do you think I wouldn't see that?

GEORGE: I think you would [quietly] … and that is why that trust is there.

I worked directly with our relationship at this point to explore where he was in the transferential dynamics with me. I had been aware of a developing trust and also wanted to see if he was ready to talk more deeply. It seemed that for now, he needed to feel he was safe with me.

KAREN: And we are learning, it is very frightening for you to feel dependent.

GEORGE: Yeah and it comes down to not trusting others … I have transferred mistrust to everyone in my life … and the realisation I've had is how I tend to be more intimate with people I haven't known for that long.

KAREN: And you haven't had something bad happen to test the trust?

GEORGE: Yes, exactly.

KAREN: So what I am hearing is that with the longer term relationships, like us … when things go wrong, it becomes really tough.

GEORGE: I have often said I will trust you 100% until you screw me; once you screw me, you are dead; and of course there are always going to be times when ruptures occur …

KAREN: … when you feel screwed, which is your experience of what happened last week.

GEORGE: Hmm, uh huh … that is exactly what happened.

KAREN: And it is exactly your *experience* of what happened.
GEORGE: [Laughs] Yeah, I will take that …

This was a playful challenge on my part to point out George's subjectivity. We then went back to explore what had happened within his small peer group. What had also shocked George was that when he became vulnerable, it was the seemingly more vulnerable member in the group that had offered him the opportunity to recover.

KAREN: So a powerful experience for you to come to realise you could abandon your position and rely on a woman's capacity to attune to you and take the lead.
GEORGE: Yeah well … I was not expecting her to take control the way she did.
KAREN: No. I had a sense of her seeing something and she was able to hold herself together and respond.
GEORGE: She said afterwards, that she is at her best when the pressure is on.
KAREN: When others can hold vulnerability, she has space for something different.
GEORGE: Yeah … she is a very vulnerable individual usually.
KAREN: But not in that moment.
GEORGE: No! She saw a side of me she had not seen before and I saw a side of her I had not seen before.
KAREN: So it seems something is possible to be shared: that leadership and vulnerability can be shared between the men and women in the group, between the vulnerable and the apparent strong ones. I sense this might open up all sorts of creative possibilities of dynamics in the group.
GEORGE: I think our group needs a shake-up.

It is no coincidence that radical psychiatrists did—and still do—most of their work in groups, as groups (families, tribes, neighbourhoods, communities, organisations, etc.) are the site both of alienation and, through contact, relationship(s), and a sense of belonging, of "cure" or liberation. As Wieland (2015) has put it recently: "We are born within a group and we acquire our identity within a group" (p. 94), and, in terms of men's sense of belonging as men, there is, of course, an argument for therapeutic groups for and of men (Rabinowitz, 2005). While Transactional Analysis has, traditionally, focused on autonomy (self-determination) (Berne, 1964), we also advocate its corollary, that is, homonomy (Angyal, 1941; Tudor, 2011a, 2011b), or a sense of belonging, as an equal if not more fundamental aspect of the human condition—and the outcome of psychotherapy, counselling, education, and organisational TA. Groups also provide greater opportunity for the "third", or what Wieland (2015) has referred to as "triangular space" which:

> leads to the recognition and acceptance of a multiplicity of relationships that include both sameness and difference, both being inside and outside a relationship, both observing and being observed and culminates in a composite self in which different identifications are integrated including the identification with mother, that is it includes the integration of femininity within the male self. We call this the democratic self which can recognise and accept plurality but is nevertheless rooted in its own identification with its parental figures. (p. 86)

George went on to say how he was beginning to understand how unconsciously oppressive and distant he had been in his marriage by needing to be the man in charge in his family. Potentially, this denied other people's minds, and denied other people an opportunity to know his internal and more emotional world. He began to use his therapy to slowly believe others might be interested in his emotional state without needing to judge him on whether or not he was a decent enough man. As Mazzetti (2010) put it: "Only when we are aware of the relativism of our constructs can we take the risk to really open our minds to others. The result can be the co-creation of a common, culturally mixed, relational space" (p. 191). Only when, in this case, men can deconstruct masculinity, what it means to be a man, a guy, a boy, or a "bloke" (Bailey, 2001), can they really be, continue to become, and to belong as men.

Conclusion

The therapeutic work which we have presented in this chapter shows aspects of men's relationship with themselves (intrapsychic level), with other men and women in their lives, including Karen as their therapist (interpersonal, and social/cultural levels), and with the impact of gender, through their own development and experience as well as its social construction (institutional/social/cultural level).

While the particular experience of alienation may have changed from the mid nineteenth century when Marx (1867) wrote his critique of capitalism in the context of industrialisation, we think that the concept of alienation and its translation by radical therapists is still a useful concept with which to understand and work with alienated relationships, that is, from ourselves, with each other, from our social/cultural context, and, indeed, from the land and the Earth. Radical therapists translated Marx's taxonomy of alienation as that from our hearts, or love; from our minds, or our capacity to think; from our bodies, or feelings; and from our hands, or work (Steiner, 2000).

In terms of providing or co-creating a therapy that is demystifying and liberating, we agree with Shadbolt (2009) who, writing about sexuality, commented on the importance of the therapeutic space:

> When space is provided in which the awareness of difference and the experience of existing separately is accepted, integration and recovery of the "not-me" aspect of the self becomes possible, and clients can celebrate their excitement, vitality, or whatever they wish. (pp. 170–171)

With regard to Patrick, Tony, Freddie, and George, the therapy continues to evolve; and it has been moving and informative for Karen to share the relevant vignettes and reflections with each of her clients.

Our final reflection concerns the word "radical". As we have suggested, we find both meanings of radical—as roots, and as a left-wing political/social analysis—useful. There is, however, a danger in the way in which a return to roots or what is considered fundamental has been and is being used as a justification for fundamentalism (Tudor, 2007). It appears that, currently, we need to protect our love of the radical from the hate that is being directed against a version of it, that is, for example, the radical Islamic State. Fear and hate drive people apart: men against women, white against black, the West against the Orient, Muslims against Jews, Muslims against Muslims, and so on. We do terrible things to each other because, it appears, we cannot tolerate difference(s): perhaps because of our "Fascist states of mind". In response, we suggest that, through the couch and the ballot box (Tudor & Hargaden, 2002), through personal therapeutic work informed by psychopolitics (Minikin, 2011, 2013), and through political activity informed by psychology, we need to emancipate ourselves from our internal fascists and develop expansive, integrating, and pluralistic democratic minds—and hearts.

REFERENCES

Ainsworth, M. D. S., Blehar, M. C., Waters, E., & Wall, S. (1978). *Patterns of Attachment: A Psychological Study of the Strange Situation*. Oxford: Lawrence Erlbaum.

Allen, J. R. (2003). Biological underpinnings of treatment approaches. *Transactional Analysis Journal, 33*: 23–31.

Allen, J. R. (2010). Redecision therapy: Underappreciated developmental, relational, and neuroconstructive processes. *Transactional Analysis Journal, 40*: 149–158.

Allen, J. R. (2011). The experienced self as a developmental line and its use in script work. *Transactional Analysis Journal, 41*: 58–68.

Allen, J. R., & Allen, B. A. (1972). Scripts: The role of permission. *Transactional Analysis Journal, 2*: 72–74.

Allport, G. (1955). *Becoming: Basic Considerations for a Psychology of Personality*. New Haven, CT: Yale University Press.

American Psychiatric Association (1994). *Diagnostic and Statistical Manual of Mental Disorders (4th ed., text rev.)*. Washington, DC: American Psychiatric Association, 2000.

American Psychiatric Association (2013). *Diagnostic Statistic Manual. Reference to the Diagnostic Criteria from DSM-5*. Arlington, VA: American Psychiatric Publishing, pp. 646–649.

Andersen, S. M., & Berk, M. S. (1998). Transference in everyday experience: Implications of experimental research for relevant clinical phenomena. *Review of General Psychology, 2*: 81–120.

Andersen, S. M., & Chen, S. (2002). The relational self: An interpersonal social-cognitive theory. *Psychological Review, 109*: 619–645.

Angyal, A. (1941). *Foundations for a Science of Personality*. New York: Commonwealth Fund.

Apprey, M. (2006). Difference and the awakening of wounds in intercultural psychoanalysis. *Psychoanalytic Quarterly, 75*: 73–93.

Aron, L. (1996). *A Meeting of Minds: Mutuality in Psychoanalysis*. Hillsdale, NJ: Analytic Press.

Aron, L. (2003). The paradoxical place of enactment in psychoanalysis. *Psychoanalytic Dialogues, 13*: 623–631.

Aron, L., & Harris, A. (2005). *Relational Psychoanalysis: Volume II, Innovation and Expansion*. Hillsdale, NJ: Analytic Press.

Bailey, B. (2001). *Bewilderness* (J. K. Cooper, director). London: United International Pictures.

Baird, B., Smallwood, J., Mrazek, M. D., Karn, J. W. Y., Franklin, M. S., & Schooler, J. W. (2012). Inspired by distraction: Mind wandering facilitates creative incubation. *Psychological Science, 23*(10): 1117–1122.

Baldwin, M. W. (1997). Relational schemas as a source of if-then self inference procedures. *Review of General Psychology, 1*: 326–335.

Barr, J. (1987). Therapeutic relation model. *Transactional Analysis Journal, 17*: 134–140.

Bary, B. B., & Hufford, F. M. (1990). The six advantages to games and their use in treatment. *Transactional Analysis Journal, 20*: 214–220.

Batts, V. (2002). Is reconciliation possible? Lessons from combating "modern racism". In: I. T. Douglas (Ed.), *Waging Reconciliation: God's Mission in a Time of Globalization and Crisis* (pp. 35–76). New York: Church Publishing.

Baumeister, R., Dale, K., & Sommer, K. (1998). Freudian defense mechanisms and empirical findings in modern social psychology: Reaction formation, projection, displacement, undoing, isolation, sublimation, and denial. *Journal of Personality, 66*: 1081–1144.

Beebe, B., & Lachmann, F. M. (1988). The contribution of mother-infant mutual influence to the origins of self—and object relationships. *Psychoanalytic Psychology, 5*: 305–337.

Beisser, A. (1971). The paradoxical theory of change. In: J. Fagan & I. L. Shepherd (Eds.), *Gestalt Therapy Now: Theory,Techniques, Applications* (pp. 77–80). New York: Harper & Row.

Benjamin, J. (1995). *Like Subjects, Love Objects: Essays on Recognition and Sexual Difference*. New Haven, CT: Yale University Press.

Benjamin, J. (2004). Beyond doer and done to: An intersubjective view of thirdness. *Psychoanalytic Quarterly, 73*: 5–46.

Benjamin, L. S. (1974). Structural analysis of social behavior (SASB). *Psychological Review, 81*: 392–425.

Benjamin, L. S. (1996). *Interpersonal Diagnosis and Treatment of Personality Disorders (2nd ed.)*. New York: Guilford Press.

Bennett, M. (1995). Why don't men come to counselling? Some speculative theories. *Counselling, 6*: 310–313.

Berne, E. (1955) Intuition IV: Primal Images and Primal Judgment, in P. McCormick, (Ed). (1977) *Intuition and ego states: A series of papers by Eric Berne*, San Francisco: TA Press.

Berne, E. (1957) Intuition V: The ego image, in P. McCormick, (Ed) (1977) *Intuition and ego states: A series of papers by Eric Berne*, San Francisco: TA Press.

Berne, E. (1961). *Transactional Analysis in Psychotherapy: A Systematic Individual and Social Psychiatry*. New York: Grove Press.

Berne, E. (1963). *The Structure and Dynamics of Organizations and Groups*. Philadelphia, PA: J. B. Lippincott.

Berne, E. (1964). *Games People Play: The Psychology of Human Relationships*. New York: Grove Press.

Berne, E. (1966). *Principles of Group Treatment*. New York: Oxford University Press.

Berne, E. (1970). *Sex in Human Loving*. New York: Simon & Schuster.

Berne, E. (1972). *What Do You Say After You Say Hello? The Psychology of Human Destiny*. New York: Grove Press.

Bion, W. R. (1962). *Learning from Experience*. London: Heinemann.

Bion, W. R. (1963). *Elements of psychoanalysis*. London: Karnac.

Bollas, C. (1987). *The Shadow of the Object: Psychoanalysis of the Unthought Known*. New York: Columbia University Press.

Bollas, C. (1989). *Forces of Destiny: Psychoanalysis and Human Idiom*. Northvale, NJ: Jason Aronson.

Bollas, C. (1999). *The Mystery of Things*. London: Routledge.

Boszormenyi-Nagy, I., & Spark, G. (1973). *Invisible Loyalties: Reciprocity in Intergenerational Family Therapy*. New York: Harper & Row.

Bowlby, J. (1969). *Attachment. Volume I of Attachment and Loss*. New York: Basic Books.

Bowlby, J. (1973). *Separation: Anxiety and Anger. Volume II of Attachment and Loss*. New York: Basic Books.

Bowlby, J. (1979). *The Making and Breaking of Affectional Bonds*. London: Tavistock.

Bowlby, J. (1980). *Loss: Sadness and Depression. Volume III of Attachment and Loss*. New York: Basic Books.

Bowlby, J. (1988). *A secure base*. New York: Basic Books.

Boyd, H. S. (1972). Suicidal decisions. *Transactional Analysis Journal*, 2: 87–88.

Boyd, L. (1986). Closing escape hatches: Decisions for healthy living. *Transactional Analysis Journal*, 16: 247–249.

Britton, R. (2007). From analysis of children's play to enactment in adult psychoanalysis. Paper presented at the International Psychoanalytical Association conference, July 27, Berlin, Germany.

Bromberg, P. M. (1996). Standing in the spaces: The multiplicity of self and the psychoanalytic relationship. In: P. M. Bromberg (Ed). *Standing in the Spaces: Essays on Clinical Process, Trauma and Dissociation* (pp. 267–290). New York: Psychology Press.

Bromberg, P. M. (2006). *Awakening the Dreamer: Clinical Journeys*. Mahwah, NJ: Analytic Press.

Brown, L. (2011). *Intersubjective Processes and the Unconscious*. Hove, UK: Routledge.

Bucci, W. (2001). Pathways to emotional communication. *Psychoanalytic Inquiry*, 21: 40–70.

Buckner, R. L., Andrews-Hanna, J. R., & Schacter, D. L. (2008). The brain's default network: Anatomy, function, and relevance to disease. In: A. Kingstone & M. D. Miller (Eds.), *The Year in Cognitive Neuroscience* (pp. 1–38). Malden, UK: Blackwell.

Burke, W., & Tansy, M. (1991), Countertransference disclosure and models of therapeutic action. *Contemporary Psychoanalysis*, 27: 351–384.

Campos, L. P. (1986). Empowering children: Primary prevention of script formation. *Transactional Analysis Journal*, 16: 18–23.

Campos, L. P. (1995). Redecision therapy with incarcerated disturbed youth.*Transactional Analysis Journal*, 25: 361–366.

Carver, C. S. (2004). Self-regulation of action and affect. In: R. F. Baumeister & K. D. Vohs (Eds.), *Handbook of Self-regulation: Research, Theory and Applications* (pp. 13–39). New York: Guilford Press.

Cassius, J. (1977). Bioenergetics and TA. In: M. James (Ed.), *Techniques in Transactional Analysis for Psychotherapists and Counselors* (pp. 272–282). Reading, MA: Addison-Wesley.

Cassius, J. (1980). Bodyscript release: How to use bioenergetics and transactional analysis. In: J. Cassius (Ed.), *Horizons in Bioenergetics: New Dimensions in Mind/Body Psychotherapy* (pp. 212–244). Memphis, TN: Promethean Publications.

Ceridono, D., Gubinelli, M., & Scilligo, P. (2009). Gli stati dellon of action and affect. Into access and change (Ego states in social-cognitive Transactional Analysis). *Idee in Psicoterapia*, 2: 85–100.

Chambless, D. L. (2005). Compendium of empirically supported therapies. In: G. P. Koocher, J. C. Norcross, & S. S. Hill (Eds.), *Psychologists' Desk Reference*. New York: Oxford University Press.

Childs-Gowell, E. (2000). *Regression and Protection*. Seattle, WA: Sudden Printing.

Childs-Gowell, E., & Kinnaman, P. (1978). *Bodyscript Blockbusting: A Transactional Analysis Approach to Body Awareness*. San Francisco, CA: Transactional Publications.

Choy, A. (1990). The winner's triangle. *Transactional Analysis Journal, 20*(1): 40–46.

Clark, B. D. (1991). Empathetic transactions in the deconfusion of Child ego states. *Transactional Analysis Journal, 21*: 92–98.

Clark, F. (2011). Psychotherapy as a mourning process. *Transactional Analysis Journal, 31*: 156–160.

Clarkson, P. (1992) *Transactional Analysis Psychotherapy—an Integrated Approach*. Hove, UK: Routledge.

Clarkson, P. (2003). *The Therapeutic Relationship*. London: Whurr.

Clarkson, P., & Fish, S. (1988). Rechilding: Creating a new past in the present as a support for the future. *Transactional Analysis Journal, 18*: 51–59.

Cooper, S. H. (2010). *A Disturbance in the Field: Essays in Transference-Countertransference Engagement (Relational Perspectives Book Series)*. London: Routledge.

Cooper, S. H., & Levit, D. B. (1998). Old and new objects in Fairbairnian and American relational theory. *Psychoanalytic Dialogues, 8*: 603–624.

Cornell, W. F. (1975). Wake up "Sleepy": Reichian techniques and script intervention. *Transactional Analysis Journal, 5*: 144–147.

Cornell, W. F. (1997). Touch and boundaries in Transactional Analysis: Ethical and transferential considerations.*Transactional Analysis Journal, 27*: 30–37.

Cornell, W. F. (2000). Transference, desire and vulnerability in body-centered psychotherapy. *Energy & Character, 30*: 29–37.

Cornell, W. F. (2003). The impassioned body: Erotic vitality and disturbance in psychotherapy. *British Gestalt Journal, 12*: 92–104.

Cornell, W. F. (2005). In the terrain of the unconscious: The evolution of a transactional analysis therapist. *Transactional Analysis Journal, 35*: 119–131.

Cornell, W. F. (2008a). What do you say if you don't say unconscious? *Transactional Analysis Journal, 38*: 93–100.

Cornell, W. F. (2008b). Self in action: The bodily basis of self-organization. In: F. S. Anderson (Ed.), *Bodies in Treatment: The Unspoken Dimension* (pp. 29–49). Hillsdale, NJ: Analytic Press.

Cornell, W. F. (2008c). *Explorations in Transactional Analysis: The Meech Lake Papers*. San Francisco, CA: TA Press.

Cornell, W. F. (2009a). A stranger to desire: Entering the erotic field. *Studies in Gender and Sexuality, 10*: 75–92.

Cornell, W. F. (2009b). Why have sex?: A case study in character, perversion and free choice. *Transactional Analysis Journal, 39*: 136–148.

Cornell, W. F. (2010). Aspirations or adaptation?: An unresolved tension in Eric Berne's basic beliefs. *Transactional Analysis Journal, 40*: 243–253.

Cornell, W. F. (2011). SAMBA, TANGO, PUNK: Commentary on paper by Steven H. Knoblauch. *Psychoanalytic Dialogues, 21*: 428–436.

Cornell, W. F. (2014). The intricate intimacies of psychotherapy and questions of self-disclosure. In: D. Loewenthal & A. Samuels (Eds.), *Relational Psychotherapy, Psychoanalysis and Counselling: Appraisals and Reappraisals*. London: Routledge.

Cornell, W. F. (2015a). *Somatic Experience in Psychoanalysis and Psychotherapy: In the Expressive Language of the Living*. London: Routledge.

Cornell, W. F. (2015b). Play at your own risk: Games, play and intimacy. *Transactional Analysis Journal, 45*: 70–90.

Cornell, W. F., & Hargaden, H. (2005). *From Transactions to Relations: The Emergence of a Relational Tradition in Transactional Analysis*. Chadlington, UK: Haddon Press.

Cornell, W. F., & Landaiche III, N. M. (2006). Impasse and intimacy: Applying Berne's concept of script protocol. *Transactional Analysis Journal, 36*:196–213.

Cornell, W. F., & Landaiche, N. M. (2007). Why body psychotherapy?: A conversation. *Transactional Analysis Journal, 37*: 256–262.

Cornell, W. F., & Landaiche III, N. M. (2008). Nonconscious processes and self-development: Key concepts from Eric Berne and Christopher Bollas. *Transactional Analysis Journal, 38*: 200–217.

Cornell, W. F., & Olio, K. A. (1992). Consequences of childhood bodily abuse: A clinical model for affective interventions. *Transactional Analysis Journal, 22*: 131–143.

Cornell, W. F., & Olio, K. A. (1993). Therapeutic relationship as the foundation for treatment of adult survivors of sexual abuse. *Psychotherapy: Theory, Practice and Research, 30*: 512–523.

Cowles-Boyd, L., & Boyd, H. (1980). Playing with games: The game/play shift. *Transactional Analysis Journal, 10*: 8–11.

Craig, J. M., & Wong, N. C. (Eds.) (2011). *Epigenetics: A reference manual*. Wymondham, UK: Caister Academic Press.

Crossman, P. (1966). Permission and protection. *Transactional Analysis Bulletin, 5*: 152–154.

Damasio, A. (1999). *The Feeling of What Happens: Body and Emotion in the Making of Consciousness*. New York: Harcourt Brace.

Dashiell, S. R. (1978). The parent resolution process: Reprogramming psychic incorporations in the parent. *Transactional Analysis Journal, 8*: 289–294.

Davies, J. M. (1994). Love in the afternoon: A relational reconsideration of desire and dread in the countertransference. *Psychoanalytic Dialogues, 4*: 153–170.

Davies, J. M. (1997). Dissociation, therapeutic enactment, and transference-countertransference processes: A discussion of papers on childhood sexual abuse by S. Grand and J. Sarnat. *Gender and Psychoanalysis, 2*: 241–257.

Davies, J. M. (1998). Between the disclosure and foreclosure of erotic transference-countertransference: Can psychoanalysis find a place for adult sexuality? *Psychoanalytic. Dialogues, 8*: 747–766.

Davies, J. M. (2004). Whose bad objects are we anyway?: Repetition and our elusive love affair with evil. *Psychoanalytic Dialogues, 14*: 711–732.

Davies, J. M., & Frawley, M. J. (1994). *Treating the Adult Survivor of Childhood Sexual Abuse*. New York: Basic Books.

Deaconu, D. & Stuthridge, J. (Eds.) (2015). Theme issue: Games and Enactment. *Transactional Analysis Journal, 45*: 2.

De Beauvoir, S. (1949). *The Second Sex*. H. M. Parshley (Trans.). London: Penguin, 1972.

DeGolia, R. (1976). Thoughts on men. In: H. Wyckoff (Ed.), *Love, Therapy and Politics* (pp. 180–194). New York: Grove Press.

De Luca, M. L., & Tosi, M. T. (2011). Social-cognitive Transactional Analysis: An introduction to Pio Scilligo's model of ego states. *Transactional Analysis Journal, 41*: 206–220.

Dictionary.com (2014). http://dictionary.reference.com/browse/psychopathology, accessed September 2014.

Dimen, M. (2003). *Sexuality, Intimacy, Power*. Hillsdale, NJ: Analytic Press.

Dimen, M. (2005). Sexuality and suffering, or the Eew! factor. *Studies in Gender and Sexuality, 6*: 1–18.

Dimen, M. (2011). Lapsus linguae, or a slip of the tongue?: A sexual violation in an analytic treatment and its personal and professional aftermath. *Contemporary Psychoanalysis, 47*: 35–79.

Drye, L. C., Goulding, R. L., & Goulding, M. M. (1973). No-suicide decisions: Patient monitoring of suicidal risk. *American Journal of Psychiatry, 18*: 17–23.

Dusay, J. M. (1966). Responses to games in therapy. *Transactional Analysis Bulletin, 5*: 136–137.

Eagle, M. (2011). *From Classical to Contemporary Psychoanalysis: A Critique and Integration*. London: Routledge.

Edwards, S. J., & Pfaff, J. J. (1997). *Managing Youth Suicidal Behaviour*. Perth, Australia: Scott Four Colour Print.

English, F. (1969). Episcripts and the "hot potato" game. *Transactional Analysis Bulletin, 8*: 77–82.

English, F. (1971). The substitution factor: Rackets and real feelings: Part I. *Transactional Analysis Journal, 1*: 27–32.

English, F. (1972). Rackets and real feelings: Part II. *Transactional Analysis Journal, 2*: 23–25.

English, F. (1977). Let's not claim it's script when it ain't. *Transactional Analysis Journal, 7*: 130–138.

English, F. (1998). On receiving the 1997 Eric Berne memorial award for hot potato transmissions and episcripts. *Transactional Analysis Journal, 28*: 10–15.

Erskine, R. G. (1974). Therapeutic intervention: Disconnecting rubberbands. *Transactional Analysis Journal, 4*: 7–8. Republished 1997 in: R. G. Erskine (Ed.), *Theories and Methods of an Integrative Transactional Analysis: A Volume of Selected Articles* (pp. 172–173). San Francisco, CA: TA Press.

Erskine, R. G. (1980). Script cure: Behavioral, intrapsychic, and physiological. *Transactional Analysis Journal, 10*:102–106. Republished 1997 in: R. G. Erskine (Ed.), *Theories and Methods of an Integrative Transactional Analysis: A Volume of Selected Articles* (pp. 151–155). San Francisco, CA: TA Press.

Erskine, R. G. (1991). Transference and transactions: Critique from an intrapsychic and integrative perspective. Transactional Analysis Journal, 21: 63–76. Republished 1997 in: R. G. Erskine (Ed.), *Theories and Methods of an Integrative Transactional Analysis: A Volume of Selected Articles* (pp. 129–146). San Francisco, CA: TA Press.

Erskine, R. G. (1993). Inquiry, attunement, and involvement in the psychotherapy of dissociation. *Transactional Analysis Journal, 23*: 184–190. Republished 1997 in R. G. Erskine (Ed.), *Theories and Methods of an Integrative Transactional Analysis: A Volume of Selected Articles* (pp. 37–45). San Francisco, CA: TA Press.

Erskine, R .G. (1994). Shame and self-righteousness: Transactional Analysis perspectives and clinical interventions. *Transactional Analysis Journal, 24*: 86–102. Republished 1997 in: R. G. Erskine (Ed.), *Theories and Methods of an Integrative Transactional Analysis: A Volume of Selected Articles* (pp. 46–67). San Francisco, CA: TA Press.

Erskine, R. G. (1997). The therapeutic relationship: Integrating motivation and personality theory. Republished 1997 in R. G. Erskine (Ed.), *Theories and Methods of an Integrative Transactional Analysis: A Volume of Selected Articles* (pp. 7–19). San Francisco, CA: TA Press.

Erskine, R. G. (2001). Psychological function, relational needs and transferential resolution: Psychotherapy of an obsession. *Transactional Analysis Journal, 31*: 220–226.

Erskine, R. G. (2003a). Bonding in relationship: A solution to violence? *Transactional Analysis Journal, 32*: 256–260.

Erskine, R. G. (2003b). Introjection, psychic presence and Parent ego states: Considerations for psychotherapy. In: C. Sills & H. Hargaden (Eds.), *Ego States: Key Concepts in Transactional Analysis, Contemporary Views* (pp. 83–108) London: Worth.

Erskine, R. G. (2008). Psychotherapy of unconscious experience. *Transactional Analysis Journal, 38*: 128–138.

Erskine, R. G. (2009). Life scripts and attachment patterns: Theoretical integration and therapeutic involvement. *Transactional Analysis Journal, 39*: 207–218.

Erskine, R. G. (2010a). Integrating expressive methods in a relational psychotherapy. *International Journal of Integrative Psychotherapy, 1*: 55–80.

Erskine, R. G. (2010b). Life scripts: Unconscious relational patterns and psychotherapeutic involvement. In: R. G. Erskine (Ed.), *Life Scripts: A Transactional Analysis of Unconscious Relational Patterns* (pp. 1–28). London: Karnac.

Erskine, R. G. (2011). Therapeutic involvement. In: H. Fowlie & C. Sills (Eds.), *Relational Transactional Analysis: Principles in Practice* (pp. 29–45). London: Karnac.

Erskine, R. G. (2013). Relational group process: Developments in a Transactional Analysis model of group psychotherapy. *Transactional Analysis Journal, 43*: 262–275.

Erskine, R. G. (2014a). What do you say before you say good-bye? The psychotherapy of grief. *Transactional Analysis Journal, 44*: 279–290.

Erskine, R. G. (2014b). Nonverbal stories: The body in psychotherapy. *International Journal of Integrative Psychotherapy, 5*: 21–33.

Erskine, R. G. (2015). *Relational Patterns,Therapeutic Presence: Concepts and Practice of Integrative Psychotherapy.* London: Karnac.

Erskine, R. G., D'Amico, J., King, E., Markevitch, J., Nack, C., & Reiser, I. (2001). Investigation of effective methods in the psychotherapy of obsession. [Unpublished raw data.] Institute for Integrative Psychotherapy, New York.

Erskine, R. G., & Moursund, J. P. (1988). *Integrative Psychotherapy in Action.* London: Karnac.

Erskine, R. G., Moursund, J. P., & Trautmann R. L. (1999). *BeyondEmpathy: A Therapy of Contact-in-Relationship.* New York: Brunner/Mazel.

Erskine, R. G., & Trautmann, R. L. (1996). Methods of an integrative psychotherapy. *Transactional Analysis Journal, 26*: 316–328. Republished 1997 in: R. G. Erskine (Ed.), *Theories and Methods of an Integrative Transactional*

Analysis: A Volume of Selected Articles (pp. 20–36). San Francisco, CA: TA Press.

Erskine, R. G., & Trautmann, R. L. (2003). Resolving intrapsychic conflict: Psychotherapy of Parent ego states. In: C. Sills & H. Hargaden (Eds.), *Ego States: Key Concepts in Transactional Analysis, Contemporary Views* (pp. 109–134). London: Worth.

Erskine, R. G., & Zalcman, M. J. (1979). The racket system: A model for racket analysis. *Transactional Analysis Journal, 9*: 51–59. Republished 1997 in R. G. Erskine (Ed.), *Theories and Methods of an Integrative Transactional Analysis: A Volume of Selected Articles* (pp. 156–165). San Francisco, CA: TA Press.

European Association for Transactional Analysis (2014). *Training and Examination Handbook*. Retrieved December 30, 2014, from http://www.eatanews.org/training-manuals-and-supplements.

Eusden, S. (2011). Relational transactional analysis and ethics—minding the gap. In: H. Fowlie & C. Sills (Eds.), *Relational Transactional Analysis: Principles in Practice* (pp. 269–277). London: Karnac.

Fairbairn, W. R. D. (1952). *Psychoanalytic Studies of the Personality*. London: Routledge.

Fisher, S., & Greenberg, R. P. (1985). *The Scientific Credibility of Freud: Analysis and Ethics*. New York: Columbia University Press.

Fonagy, P., Gergely, G., Jurist, E., & Target, M. (2002). *Affect Regulation, Mentalization, and the Development of the Self*. New York: Other Press.

Fowlie, H., & Sills, C. (2011). *Relational Transactional Analysis: Principles in Practice*. London: Karnac.

Frankl, V. (1962). *Man's Search for Meaning. An Introduction to Logotherapy*. Boston, MA: Beacon, 2006.

Freud, A. (1965). *Normality and Pathology in Childhood: Assessments of Development*. New York: International Universities Press.

Freud, A. (1968). *The Ego and the Mechanisms of Defence*. London: Hogarth.

Freud, S. (1912b). The dynamics of transference. *S. E., 12*: 97–108. London: Hogarth.

Freud, S. (1912e). Recommendations to physicians practising psychoanalysis. *S. E., 12*: 109–120. London: Hogarth.

Freud, S. (1913i). The disposition to obsessional neurosis. *S. E., 12*: 311–326. London: Hogarth.

Freud, S. (1915e). The unconscious. *S. E., 14*: 166–204. London: Hogarth.

Freud, S. (1920g). *Beyond the Pleasure Principle. S. E., 18*: 3–64. London: Hogarth.

Gabbard, G. O., & Ogden, T. (2009). On becoming a psychoanalyst. *International Journal of Psychoanalysis, 90*: 311–327.

Gildenbrand, K., & Shivanath, S. (2011). Rackets and racket feelings: Breaking through the racket system, a case of transformation of experience in short-term therapy. In: H. Fowlie & C. Sills (Eds.), *Relational Transactional Analysis: Principles in Practice* (pp. 109–116). London: Karnac.

Gill, M. M. (1982). *Analysis of Transference: Theory and Technique (Vol. 1)*. Madison, CT: International Universities Press.

Gleick, J. (1987). *Chaos: Making a New Science*. New York: Viking.

Goldstein, J., & Kornfield, J. (1987). *Vipassana. El camino de la meditación interior (Seeking the Heart of Wisdom)*. D. González Raga & F. Mora (Trans). Barcelona, Spain: Kairos, 1996.

Gomez, L. (2004). Humanistic or psychodynamic—what is the difference, and do we have to make a choice? *Self & Society, 31*(6): 5–19.

Goulding, R. L. (1972). New directions in transactional analysis: Creating an environment for redecision and change. In: C. J. Sager & H. S. Kaplan (Eds.), *Progress in Group and Family Therapy* (pp. 105–134). New York: Brunner/Mazel.

Goulding, R. L. (1985). Group therapy: Mainline or side line? In: J. K. Zeig (Ed.), *The Evolution of Psychotherapy* (pp. 300–306). New York: Brunner/Mazel.

Goulding, R. L., & Goulding, M. M. (1978). *The Power Is in the Patient: A TA/Gestalt Approach to Psychotherapy*. San Francisco, CA: TA Press.

Goulding, R. L., & Goulding, M. M. (1979). *Changing Life through Redecision Therapy*. New York: Brunner/Mazel.

Green, A. (1996). Has sexuality anything to do with psychoanalysis? *International Journal of Psychoanalysis, 77*: 345–350.

Greenberg, J. (1986). Theoretical models and the analyst's neutrality. *Contemporary Psychoanalysis, 22*: 87–106.

Greenson, R. R. (1965). The problem of working through. In: M. Schur (Ed.), *Drives, Affects, Behaviour* (pp. 277–314). New York: International Universities Press.

Gregory, L. (2001). Gender scripting as a factor in domestic violence. *Transactional Analysis Journal, 31*: 172–181.

Grotstein, J. (2005). Projective transidentification: an extension of the concept of projective identification. *International Journal of Psychoanalysis, 86*: 1051–1069.

Guistolise, P. G. (1996). Failures in the therapeutic relationship: Inevitable *and* necessary. *Transactional Analysis Journal, 26*: 284–288.

Gurdjieff, G. I. (1963). *Meetings with Remarkable Men*. London: Routledge & Kegan Paul.

Harris, T. (1967). *I'm OK—You're OK: A Practical Guide to Transactional Analysis*. New York: Grove Press.

Hargaden, H. (2013). Building resilience: The role of firm boundaries andthe third in relational group therapy. *Transactional Analysis Journal,* 43: 284–290.

Hargaden, H., & Sills, C. (2001). Deconfusion of the Child ego state. *Transactional Analysis Journal, 31*: 55–70.

Hargaden, H., & Sills, C. (2002). *Transactional Analysis: A Relational Perspective.* Hove, UK: Brunner-Routledge.

Hellinga, G. (2004). *Lastige lieden* (Difficult People). Meppel, Netherlands: Boom.

Heppner, P. P., & Gonzales, D. S. (1987). Men counseling men. In: M. Schur, M. Stevens, G. Good, & G. A. Eichenfield (Eds.), *Handbook of Counseling and Psychotherapy with Men* (pp. 30–38). Newbury Park, CA: Sage.

Hine, J. (1990). The bilateral and ongoing nature of games. *Transactional Analysis Journal, 20*: 28–39.

Hoffman, I. Z. (1983). The patient as interpreter of the analyst's experience. *Contemporary Psychoanalysis, 19*: 389–422.

Horowitz, L. M., Rosenberg, S. E., & Bartholomew, K. (1993). Interpersonal problems, attachment styles and outcome in brief dynamic psychotherapy. *Journal of Consulting and Clinical Psychology, 61*: 549–560.

Horowitz, M. J. (Ed.) (1991). *Person Schemas and Maladaptive Interpersonal Patterns.* Chicago, IL: University of Chicago Press.

Hunt, J. (2011). Exploring the relational meaning of formulae G in supervision and self-supervision. In: H. Fowlie & C. Sills (Eds.), *Relational Transactional Analysis* (pp. 287–303). London: Karnac.

Ikonen, P., & Rechardt, E. (2010). *Thanatos, Shame, and Other Essays. On the Psychology of Destructiveness.* London: Karnac.

International Transactional Analysis Association (2013). *Training and Examination Handbook.* Retrieved December 30, 2014, from https://www.itaaworld.org/itaa-training-examinations-handbook.

Jacobs, T. J. (1986). On countertransference enactments. *Journal of American Psychoanalytic Association, 34*: 289–307.

Jacobs, T. J. (2013). *The Possible Profession: The Analytic Process of Change.* New York: Routledge.

James, M. (1981). *Breaking Free: Self Reparenting for a New Life.* Reading, MA: Addison Wesley.

James, M., & James, J. (1991). *Passion for Life. Psychology and the Human Spirit.* New York: Penguin.

James, M., & Jongeward, D. (1978). *Born To Win—Transactional Analysis with Gestalt Experiments.* New York: Addison-Wesley.

Janzing, C., & Kerstens, J. (2012). *Werken in een therapeutisch milieu* (Working in a Therapeutic Milieu). Houten, Netherlands: Bohn, Stafleu, & van Loghum.

Jenkins, P., & Teachworth, A. (2010). Psychogenetics in redecision therapy: The next generation of couples work. *Transactional Analysis Journal*, 40: 121–129.

Johnson, N. G. (2005). Women helping men: Strengths of and barriers to women therapists working with male clients. In: G. E. Good & G. R. Brooks (Eds.), *The New Handbook of Counseling and Psychotherapy with Men* (pp. 291–307). San Francisco, CA: Wiley.

Joines, V. (1977). An integrative systems perspective. In: G. Barnes (Ed.), *Transactional Analysis after Eric Berne: Teaching and Practices of Three TA Schools* (pp. 257–272. New York: Harper & Row.

Joines, V., & Stewart, I. (2002). *Personality Adaptations*. Chapel Hill, NC: Lifespace Publishing.

Joseph, B. (1985). Transference: The total situation. *International Journal of Psychoanalysis*, 66: 447–454.

Kadis, L. (Ed.) (1985). *Redecision Therapy: Expanded Perspectives*. Watsonville, CA: Western Institute for Group and Family Therapy.

Kahler, T., & Capers, H. (1974). The miniscript. *Transactional Analysis Journal*, 4: 26–42.

Karpman, S. (1968). Fairy tales and script drama analysis. *Transactional Analysis Bulletin*, 7: 39–43.

Kelley, C. R. (1988). *Body Contact in Radix Work*. Vancouver, WA: Kelley/Radix.

Kelley, C. R. (2004). *Life Force … the Creative Process in Man and in Nature*. Victoria, BC: Trafford.

Kenny, D. (2014). *From Id to Intersubjectivity. Talking about the Talking Cure with Master Clinicians*. London: Karnac.

Kihlstrom, J. F. (1984). Conscious, subconscious, unconscious: A cognitive perspective. In: K. S. Bowers & D. Meichenbaum (Eds.), *The Unconscious Reconsidered* (pp. 149–210). New York: Wiley.

Klein, M. (1957). *Envidia y Gratitud y otros trabajos* (*Envy and Gratitude and Other Works*). V. S. de Campo, S. Dubcovsky, V. Fischman, H. Friedenthal, A. Koremblit, D. Liberman, R. Malflm, H. A. Murray, & D. M. Schneider (Eds. & Trans.). Barcelona, Spain: Paidos, 1994.

Klein, M. (1987). The selected Melanie Klein. J. Mitchell (Ed.). New York: Free Press.

Kluckholm, C., & Murray, H. A. (1953). Personality formation: The determinants. In: C. Kluckholm, H. A. Murray, & D. M. Schneider (Eds.), *Personality in Nature, Society, and Culture* (pp. 53–67). New York: Knopf.

Kobak, R. R., & Sceery, A. (1988). Attachment in late adolescence: Working models, affect regulation, and representation of self and others. *Child Development*, 59: 135–146.

Kohut, H. (1977). *The Restoration of the Self: A Systematic Approach to the Psychoanalytic Treatment of Narcissistic Personality Disorder.* New York: International Universities Press.

Kriegman, D., & Slavin, M. (1998). Why the analyst needs to change: Toward a theory of conflict, negotiation, and mutual influence in the therapeutic process. *Psychoanalytic Dialogues, 8*: 247–284.

Kristeva, J. (1997). *The Portable Kristeva.* New York: Columbia University Press.

Landaiche, N. M. (2012). Learning and hating in groups. *Transactional Analysis Journal, 42*: 186–198.

Landaiche, N. M. (2013). Looking for trouble in groups developing the professional's capacity. *Transactional Analysis Journal, 43*: 296–310.

Lange, C. (2013). *Letting Go.* Washington, DC: Orca Music Publishing.

Laplanche, J., & Pontalis, J. B. (1968). *Diccionario de psicoanálisis (Vocabulaire de la Psychanalyse).* F. Cervantes Gimeno (Trans.). Barcelona, Spain: Labor, 1987.

Latner, J. (2000). The theory of Gestalt therapy. In: E. Nevis (Ed.), *Gestalt Therapy: Perspectives and Applications* (pp. 13–56). Cambridge, MA: Gestalt Press.

Leigh, E. (2011). The censorship process—from destillation to essence. In: H. Fowlie & C. Sills (Eds.), *Relational Transactional Analysis: Principles in Practice* (pp. 327–336). London: Karnac.

Levine, S. B. (2003). The nature of sexual desire: A clinician's perspective. In: *Archives of Sexual Behavior, 32*: 279–285.

Lieberman, M. A., Yalom, I. D., & Miles, M. B. (1973). *Encounter Groups: First Facts.* New York: Basic Books.

Ligabue, S. (1991). The Somatic component of the script in early development. *Transactional Analysis Journal, 21*: 21–30.

Little, M. I. (1981). *Transference Neurosis and Transference Psychosis.* New York: Jason Aronson.

Little, M. I. (1990). *Psychotic Anxieties and Containment.* New York: Jason Aronson.

Little, R. (1999). Working within transference—countertransference transactions. In: K. Leach (Ed.), *ITA Conference Papers.* London: Institute of Transactional Analysis.

Little, R. (2001). Schizoid processes: Working with the defences of the withdrawn Child ego state. *Transactional Analysis Journal, 31*: 33–43.

Little, R. (2005). Integrating psychoanalytic understanding in the deconfusion of primitive ego states. *Transactional Analysis Journal, 35*: 132–146.

Little, R. (2006). Ego state relational units and resistance to change. *Transactional Analysis Journal, 36*: 7–19.

Little, R. (2011a). Countertransference self-disclosure. In: H. Fowlie & C. Sills (Eds.), *Relational Transactional Analysis: Principles in Practice* (pp. 47–56). London: Karnac.

Little, R. (2011b). Impasse clarification within the transference-countertransference matrix.*Transactional Analysis Journal, 41*: 22–38.

Little, R. (2013). The new emerges out of the old: An integrated relational perspective on psychological development, psychopathology, and therapeutic action.*Transactional Analysis Journal, 43*: 106–121.

Loewald, H. W. (1970). Psychoanalytic theory and psychoanalytic process. *Psychoanalytic Study of the Child, 25*: 45–68.

Luborsky, L., & Crits-Christoph, P. (1990). *Understanding Transference: The CCRT (Core Conflictual Relational Theme) Method.* New York: Basic Books.

Lyons-Ruth, K. (2000). "I sense that you sense that I sense … ": Sander's recognition process and the specificity of relational moves in the psychotherapeutic setting. *Infant Mental Health Journal, 21*: 85–98.

Mahler, M. S., & Furer, M. (1968). *On Human Symbiosis and the Vicissitudes of Individuation.* New York: International Universities Press.

Main, M. (1990). Cross-cultural studies of attachment organization: Recent studies, changing methodologies, and the concept of conditional strategies. *Human Development, 33*: 48–61.

Main, M. (1995). Recent studies in attachment: Overview with selected implications for clinical work. In: S. Goldberg, R. Muir, & J. Kerr (Eds.), *Attachment Theory: Social, Developmental and Clinical Perspectives* (pp. 407–474). Hillsdale, NJ: Analytic Press.

Marcus, E. (2010). *Why Suicide?* New York: Harper Collins.

Maroda, K. J. (1999). *Seduction, Surrender, and Transformation.* Hillsdale, NJ: Analytic Press.

Maroda, K. J. (2004). *The Power of Countertransference: Innovations in Analytic Technique.* Hillsdale, NJ: Analytic Press.

Marx, K. (1867). *Capital. Vol. 1.* F. Engels (Ed.); S. Moore & E. Aveling (Trans.). Moscow: Progress Publishers, 1967.

Marx, K. (1932). *Economic and Philosophical Manuscripts of 1844.* Moscow: Progress Publishers, 1959.

Masse, V. (1995). The treatment of post-traumatic stress disorder using redecision therapy. *Transactional Analysis Journal, 25*: 356–360.

Massey, R. (1985). TA as a family systems therapy. *Transactional Analysis Journal, 15*: 120–141.

Massey, R. (1989). Script theory synthesized systemically. *Transactional Analysis Journal, 19*: 14–25.

Massey, R., Corney, S., & Just, R. L. (1988). Integrating genograms and script matrices. *Transactional Analysis Journal, 18*: 325–335.

Mazzetti, M. (2010). Eric Berne and cultural script. *Transactional Analysis Journal, 40*: 187–195.

Mazzetti, M. (2013). Being there: Plunging into relationship in transactional analysis supervision. *Transactional Analysis Journal, 43*: 95–102.

McAdams, D. P., & Pals, J. L. (2006). Fundamental principles for an integrative science of personality. *American Psychologist, 61*: 204–217.

McClelland, J. L., Rumelhart, D. E., & the PDP Research Group (1986). *Parallel Distributed Processing: Explorations in the Microstructure of Cognition (Vol. 2)*. Cambridge, MA: MIT Press.

McLaughlin, J. T. (1991). Clinical and theoretical aspects of enactment. *Journal of American Psychoanalytic Association, 39*: 595–614.

McLaughlin, J. T. (1995). Touching limits in the analytic dyad. *Psychoanalytic Quarterly, 64*: 433–465.

McLaughlin, J. T. (2005). *The Healer's Bent: Solitude and Dialogue in the Clinical Encounter*. Hillsdale, NJ: Analytic Press.

McNeel, J. R. (1975). Redecisions in psychotherapy: A study of the effects of an intensive weekend group workshop. Unpublished doctoral dissertation, California School of Professional Psychology, San Francisco, CA.

McNeel, J. R. (1976). The parent interview. *Transactional Analysis Journal, 6*: 61–68.

McNeel, J. R. (1977). The seven components of redecision therapy. In: G. Barnes (Ed.), *Transactional Analysis after Eric Berne: Teachings and Practices of Three TA Schools* (pp. 425–441). New York: Harper's College Press.

McNeel, J. R. (1999). Redecision therapy as a process of new belief acquisition. *Journal of Redecision Therapy, 1*: 103–115.

McNeel, J. R. (2002a) Redecision therapy as a process of new belief acquisition: The attachment injunctions. *Journal of Redecision Therapy, 2*: 108–122.

McNeel, J. R. (2002b). Redecision therapy as a process of new belief acquisition: The identity injunctions. *Journal of Redecision Therapy, 2*: 123–134.

McNeel, J. R. (2010). Understanding the power of injunctive messages and how they are resolved in redecision therapy. *Transactional Analysis Journal, 40*: 159–169.

McQuillin, J., & Welford, E. (2013). How many people are gathered here? Group work and family constellation theory. *Transactional Analysis Journal, 43*: 352–365.

Mellor, K. (1979). "Being killed, killing, and dying." *Transactional Analysis Journal, 9*: 182–188.

Mellor, K., & Andrewartha, G. (1980). Reparenting the parent in support of redecisions. *Transactional Analysis Journal, 10*: 197–203.

Menninger, K. (1958). *Theory of Psychoanalytic Technique*. New York: Basic Books.

Migone, P. (2006). Breve storia della ricerca in psicoterapia (Brief history of psychotherapy research). In: N. Dazzi, V. Lingiardi, & A. Colli (Eds.), *La ricerca in psicoterapia (Research in Psychotherapy)* (pp. 31–48). Milan, Italy: Raffaello Cortina.

Mikulincer, M. (2007). *Attachment in Adulthood. Structure, Dynamics, and Change.* New York: Guilford Press.

Mikulincer, M., & Shaver, P. R. (2003). The attachment behavioural system in adulthood: Activations, psychodynamics and interpersonal processes. In: M. P. Zanna (Ed.), *Advances in Experimental Social Psychology, Vol. 35* (pp. 53–152). New York: Academic Press.

Mills, J. (2005). *Treating Attachment Pathology.* New York: Jason Aronson.

Mills, J. (2012). *Conundrums—A Critique of Contemporary Psychoanalysis.* New York: Routledge.

Minikin, K. (2011). TA in the wider world: The politics and psychology of alienation. In: H. Fowlie & C. Sills (Eds.), *Relational Transactional Analysis: Principles in Practice* (pp. 211–219). London: Karnac.

Minikin, K. (2013). Conflict and change in therapeutic relating. *The Transactional Analyst, 3*: 39–42.

Mischel, W., & Shoda, Y. (1995). A cognitive-affective system theory of personality: Reconceptualizing situations, dispositions, dynamics, and invariance in personality structure. *Psychological Review, 102*: 246–268.

Mitchell, S. (1988). *Relational Concepts in Psychoanalysis.* Cambridge, MA: Harvard University Press.

Moiso, C. (1985). Ego states and transference. *Transactional Analysis Journal, 15*: 194–201.

Monick, E. (1991). *Castration and Male Rage.* Toronto, Canada: Inner City Books.

Moursund, J. P., & Erskine, R. G. (2003). *Integrative Psychotherapy: The Art and Science of Relationship.* Pacific Grove, CA: Brooks/Cole-Thomson Learning.

Mucci, C. (2013). *Beyond Individual and Collective Trauma: Intergenerational Transmission, Psychoanalytic Treatment, and the Dynamics of Forgiveness.* London: Karnac.

Naughton, M., & Tudor, K. (2006). Being white. *Transactional Analysis Journal, 36*: 159–171.

Nichol, M. P., & Schwartz, R. C. (2008). *Family Therapy: Concepts and Methods (8th ed.).* New York: Pearson Education.

Nitsun, M. (1996). *The Anti-group: Destructive Forces in the Group and Their Creative Potential.* London: Routledge.

Nolan, K. (2008). Understanding obsessive-compulsive disorder: An integration of transactional analysis and psychoanalysis. *Transactional Analysis Journal, 38*: 72–86.

Noriega Gayol, G. (1995). Self-reparenting with female delinquents in jail. *Transactional Analysis Journal, 25*: 208–210.

Noriega Gayol, G. (2004). Codependence: A transgenerational script. *Transactional Analysis Journal, 34*: 312–322.

Noriega Gayol, G. (2009). On receiving the 2008 Eric Berne Memorial Award for Mechanisms of Transgenerational Script Transmission. *Transactional Analysis Journal, 39*: 8–13.

Noriega Gayol, G. (2010). Transgenerational scripts: The unknown knowledge. In: R. G. Erskine (Ed.), *Life Scripts: A Transactional Analysis of Unconscious Relational Patterns* (pp. 269–290). London: Karnac.

Noriega Gayol, G., Ramos, L., Medina-Mora, M. E., & Villa, A. R. (2008). Prevalence of codependence in young women seeking primary health care and associated risk factors. *American Journal of Orthopsychiatry, 78*: 199–210.

Novak, E. T. (2013). Combining traditional ego state theory and relational approaches to transactional analysis in working with trauma and dissociation. *Transactional Analysis Journal, 43*: 186–196.

Novak, E. T. (2014). When relief replaces loss: Parental hatred that forecloses loving attachment. *Transactional Analysis Journal, 44*: 255–267.

Novellino, M. (1984). Self-analysis of countertransference in integrative transactional analysis. *Transactional Analysis Journal, 14*: 63–67.

Novellino, M. (1985). Redecision analysis of transference: A TA approach to transference neurosis. *Transactional Analysis Journal, 15*: 202–206.

Novellino, M. (1990). Unconscious communication and interpretation in Transactional Analysis. *Transactional Analysis Journal, 20*: 168–172.

Novellino, M. (2004). *Psicoanalisi Transazionale (Transactional Psychoanalysis)*. Milan, Italy: Franco Angeli.

Novellino, M. (2006). The Don Juan syndrome: The script of the great losing lover. *Transactional Analysis Journal, 36*: 33–43.

Novey, T. B. (1998). A proposal for an integrated self. [Letter to the editor.] *The Script, 28*: 6.

Novey, T. B., Porter-Steele, N., Gobes, L., & Massey, R. F. (1993). Ego states and the self-concept: A panel presentation and discussion. *Transactional Analysis Journal, 23*: 123–138.

Ogden, P., Minton, K., & Pain, C. (2006). *Trauma and the Body*. New York: W. W. Norton.

Ogden, T. (1982). *Projective Identification and Psychotherapeutic Technique*. Northvale, NJ: Jason Aronson.

Ogden, T. (1992). *The Matrix of the Mind: Object Relations and the Psychoanalytic Dialogue*. London: Karnac.

Ogden, T. (1994). *Subjects of Analysis*. Lanham, MD: Rowman & Littlefield.

Ohlsson,T. (1998). Two ways of doing regressive therapy: Using TA proper and using expressive techniques. *Transactional Analysis Journal, 28*: 83–87.

O'Reilly-Knapp, M. (2001). Between two worlds: The encapsulated self. *Transactional Analysis Journal, 31*: 44–54.

O'Reilly-Knapp, M., & Erskine, R. G. (2010). The script system: An unconscious organization of experience. In: R. G. Erskine (Ed.), *Life Scripts: A Transactional Analysis of Unconscious Relational Patterns* (pp. 291–308). London: Karnac.

Panksepp, J. (1998). *Affective Neuroscience: The Foundations of Human and Animal Emotions.* Oxford: Oxford University Press.

PDM Task Force (2006). *Psychodynamic Diagnostic Manual.* Silverspring, MD: Alliance of Psychoanalytic Organizations.

Perls, F. S. (1969). *Gestalt Therapy Verbatim.* Lafayette, CA: Real People Press.

Perls, F. S., Hefferline, R., & Goodman, P. (1951). *Gestalt Therapy: Excitement and Growth in the Human Personality.* New York: Julian Press.

Piaget, J. (1952). *The Origins of Intelligence in Children.* New York: International Universities Press.

Poland, W. S. (1996). *Melting the Darkness: The Dyad and Principles of Clinical Practice.* Northvale, NJ: Jason Aronson.

Poland, W. S. (2006). The analyst's fears. *American Imago, 63*: 201–217.

Poland, W. S. (2013). The analyst's witnessing and otherness. *Journal of the American Psychoanalytic Association, 48*: 17–36.

Porges, S. W. (1995). Orienting in a defensive world: Mammalian modifications of our evolutionary heritage: A Polyvagal Theory. *Psychophysiology, 32*: 301–318.

Price, L. (2014). Back to the beginning: An exploration of the treatment and effects of therapeutic regression to dependence in psychotherapeutic practice. [Unpublished doctoral dissertation, De Montfort University, UK.]

Rabinowitz, F. E. (2005). Group therapy for men. In: G. E. Good & G. R. Brooks (Eds.), *The New Handbook of Counseling and Psychotherapy with Men* (pp. 264–327). San Francisco, CA: Wiley.

Racker, H. (1957). The meanings and uses of countertransference. *Psychoanalytic Quarterly, 26*: 303–357.

Racker, H. (1968). *Transference and Countertransference.* London: Karnac.

Radical Therapist Collective, The (1971). *The Radical Therapist* . J. Agel (Ed.). New York: Ballantine.

Reich, W. (1933). *Character Analysis.* New York: Farrar, Straus, & Giroux.

Renik, O. (1998). The role of countertransference enactment in a successful clinical psychoanalysis. In: S. Ellman & M. Moskowitz (Eds.), *Enactment: Toward a New Approach to the Therapeutic Relationship* (pp. 111–128). Northvale, NJ: Jason Aronson.

Riesenberg Malcolm, R. (1986). Interpretation: The past in the present. *International Review of Psycho-Analysis, 13*: 433–443.

Rogers, C. R. (1975). Empathic: An unappreciated way of being. In: *A Way of Being* (pp. 137–163). Boston, MA: Houghton Mifflin, 1980.

Rogers, C. R. (1986). Rogers, Kohut, and Erickson: A personal perspective on some similarities and differences. *Person-Centred Review, 1*: 125–140.

Rowan, J. (1997). *Healing the Male Psyche: Therapy as Initiation*. London: Routledge.

Roy, B., & Steiner, C. (Eds.) (1988). *Radical Psychiatry: The Second Decade*. Unpublished manuscript, retrieved December 30, 2014 from www. emotional-literacy.com/rp0.htm.

Rycroft, C. (1968). *A Critical Dictionary of Psychoanalysis*. London: Nelson.

Said, E., & Noriega, G. (1983). Some Mexican cultural scripts. *Transactional Analysis Journal, 13*: 241–242.

Salters, D. (2013). Sandplay and family constellation: An integration with transactional analysis theory and practice. *Transactional Analysis Journal, 43*: 224–239.

Salzman, L. (1980). *Treatment of the Obsessive Personality*. New York: Jason Aronson.

Sartre, J. -P. (1976). *Sartre on Theatre*. M. Contat & M. Rybalka (Eds.) London: Quartet.

Satir, V. (1983). *Conjoint Family Therapy*. Palo Alto, CA: Science and Behavior Books.

Satir, V. (1991). *The Satir Model: Family Therapy and Beyond*. Palo Alto, CA: Science and Behavior Books.

Schacter, D. L., & Buckner, R. L. (1998). Priming and the brain. *Nevron, 20*: 185–195.

Schacter, D. L., Gilbert, D. T., & Wegner, D. M. (2011). *Psychology (2nd ed.)*. New York: Worth.

Schaeffer, B. (2009). Sexual addiction. *Transactional Analysis Journal, 39*: 153–162.

Schiff, J. L. (1977). One hundred children generate of a lot of TA. In: G. Barnes (Ed.), *Transactional Analysis after Eric Berne* (pp. 52–76). New York: Harper & Row.

Schiff, J. L., Schiff, A. W., Mellor, K., Schiff, E., Schiff, S., Richman, D., Fishman, J., Wolz, L., Fishman, C., & Momb, D. (1975). *Cathexis Reader: Transactional Analysis Treatment of Psychosis*. New York: Harper & Row.

Schore, A. N. (1994). *Affect Regulation and the Origin of the Self: The Neurobiology of Emotional Development*. Hillsdale, NJ: Lawrence Erlbaum.

Schore, A. N. (1997). A century after Freud's project: Is a rapprochement between psychoanalysis and neurobiology at hand? *Journal of the American Psychoanalytic Association, 45*: 807–840.

Schore, A. N. (2003). Early relational trauma, disorganised attachment and the development of a predisposition to violence. In: M. F. Solomon & D. J. Siegel (Eds.), *Healing Trauma, Attachment, Mind, Body and Brain*. New York: W. W. Norton.

Scilligo, P. (1986). *La sinfonia dei molti Sé* (The Symphony of Many Selves). Rome: LAS.

Scilligo, P. (1998). Gli stati dell'io definiti in termini dimensionali (The ego states dimensionally defined). *Psicologia Psicoterapia e Salute, 4*: 89–116.

Scilligo, P. (2004). Tra scienza ed ermeneutica nella psicoterapia: un'analisi critica del naturalismo scientifico e vie d'uscita (Between science and hermeneutic: a critical analysis of scientific naturalism and way out). *Psicologia Psicoterapia e Salute, 9*: 107–124.

Scilligo, P. (2009). *Analisi transazionale socio-cognitiva (The Social-cognitive Transactional Analysis)*. Rome: LAS.

Scilligo, P. (2011). Transference as a measurable social-cognitive process: An application of Scilligo's ego states model. *Transactional Analysis Journal, 41*: 196–205.

Sedgwick, P. (1982). *Psychopolitics*. London: Pluto Press.

Seidler, V. (1991). *Recreating Sexual Politics: Men, Feminism and Politics*. London: Routledge.

Seidler, V. (Ed.) (1992). *Men, Sex, & Relationships: Writings from Achilles Heel*. London: Routledge.

Shadbolt, C. (2009). Sexuality and shame. *Transactional Analysis Journal, 39*: 163–172.

Shadbolt, C. (2012). The place of failure and rupture in psychotherapy. *Transactional Analysis Journal, 42*: 5–16.

Shapiro, D. (1965). *Neurotic Styles*. New York: Basic Books.

Shmueli, A. (2014). Let's call the whole thing off. By Aida Edemariam. *The Guardian Magazine*, December 20.

Siebert, A. (2007). La resiliencia: Construir en la adversidad (Resilience: Build in adversity). Barcelona, Spain: Aliena.

Siegel, D. (1999). *The Developing Mind: How Relationships and the Brain Interact to Shape Who We Are (Second edition)*. New York: Guilford Press, 2012.

Siegel, D. (2007). *The Mindful Brain: Reflection and Attunement in the Cultivation of Well-Being*. New York: W. W. Norton.

Sills, C. (2007). *Critical Moments in Psychotherapy*. Seminar presentation in Wellington, New Zealand, November.

Sills, C., & Hargaden, H. (Eds.) (2003). *Ego States: Key Concepts in Transactional Analysis, Contemporary Views* (pp. 109–134). London: Worth.

Simon, P. (1966). I am a rock. In: P. Simon & A. Garfunkel, *Sounds of Silence*. CBS Records.

Slavin, J. (2003). The innocence of sexuality. *Psychoanalytic Quarterly*, 72: 51–80.

Slavin, J. (2007). The imprisonment and liberation of love: The dangers and possibilities of love in the psychoanalytic relationship. *Psychoanalytic Inquiry*, 27: 197–218.

Spencer, J., Balter, L., & Lothane, Z. (1992). Otto Isakower and the analyzing instrument. *Journal of Clinical Psychoanalysis*, 6: 246–260.

Stark, M. (1999). *Modes of Therapeutic Action*. Northvale, NJ: Jason Aronson.

Stein, R. (1998a). The poignant, the excessive and the enigmatic in sexuality. *International Journal of Psychoanalysis*, 79: 253–268.

Stein, R. (1998b). The enigmatic dimension of sexual experience: The "otherness" of sexuality and primal seduction. *Psychoanalytic Quarterly*, 67: 594–625.

Stein, R. (2008). The otherness of sexuality: Excess. *Journal of the American Psychoanalytic Association*, 56: 43–71.

Steiner, C. (1974). *Scripts People Live: Transactional Analysis of Life Scripts*. New York: Grove Press.

Steiner, C. (1981). *The Other Side of Power*. New York: Grove Press.

Steiner, C. (2000). Radical psychiatry. In: R. J. Corsini (Ed.), *Handbook of Innovative Therapy* (pp. 578–586). Chichester, UK: Wiley.

Steiner, C., Wyckoff, H., Golstine, D., Lariviere, P., Schwebel, R., Marcus, J., & Members of the Radical Psychiatry Center (Eds.) (1975). *Readings in Radical Psychiatry*. New York: Grove Press.

Stern, D. B. (2003). *Unformulated Experience: From Dissociation to Imagination in Psychoanalysis*. New York: Taylor & Francis.Stern, D. B. (2010). *Partners in Thought: Working with Unformulated Experience, Dissociation and Enactment*. London: Routledge.

Stern, D. B. (2013). Relational freedom and therapeutic action. *Journal of the American Psychoanalytic Association*, 61: 227–255.

Stern, S. (1994). Needed relationships and repeated relationships: An integrated relational perspective. *Psychoanalytic Dialogues*, 4: 317–345.

Stewart, I., & Joines, V. (1987a). *TA today: A New Introduction to Transactional Analysis*. Chapel Hill, NC: Lifespace Publishing.

Stewart, I., & Joines, V. (1987b). *TA today: A New Introduction to Transactional Analysis. Second edition*. Chapel Hill, NC: Lifespace Publishing, 2012.

Stolorow, R. (1994). The nature and therapeutic action of psychoanalytic interpretation. In: R. D. Stolorow, G. E. Atwood, & B. Brandchaft (Eds.), *The Intersubjective Perspective* (pp. 43–55). Northvale, NJ: Jason Aronson.

Stolorow, R., Brandchaft, B., & Atwood, G. (1987). *Psychoanalytic Treatment: An Intersubjective Approach*. Hillsdale, NJ: Analytic Press.

Stuntz, E. (1973). Multiple chairs technique. *Transactional Analysis Journal,* 3: 29–32.

Stuthridge, J. (2006). Inside out: A transactional analysis model of trauma. *Transactional Analysis Journal, 36*: 270–283.

Stuthridge, J. (2012). Traversing the fault lines: Trauma and enactment. *Transactional Analysis Journal, 42*(4): 238–251.

Stuthridge, J. (2015). All the world's a stage: Games, enactment and countertransference. *Transactional Analysis Journal, 45*: 104–116.

Stuthridge, J. (2015b). Countertransference as a pathway to understanding script. In: W. Cornell, A. de Graaf, T. Newton, & M. M. Thunnissen (Eds.), *Into TA: A Comprehensive Textbook of Transactional Analysis.*

Summers, G. (2011). Dynamic ego states: The significance of nonconscious and unconscious patterns, as well as conscious patterns. In: H. Fowlie & C. Sills (Eds.), *Relational Transactional Analysis: Principles in Practice* (pp. 59–67). London: Karnac.

Summers, G., & Tudor, K. (2000). Cocreative transactional analysis. *Transactional Analysis Journal, 30*: 23–40.

Symington, N. (1986). *The Analytic Experience, Lectures from the Tavistock.* London: Free Association.

Tholenaar de Borbon, A. (1983). Cultural scripts in the Dominican Republic. *Transactional Analysis Journal, 13*: 243–245.

Thunnissen, M. (2015). Transactional analysis in a hospital setting with patients with personality disorders. In: Cornell, W., de Graaf, A., Newton, T., & Thunnissen, M. (Eds.) *Into TA: A Comprehensive Textbook on Transactional Analysis.* London: Karnac, pp. 305–309.

Thunnissen, M. M. (2001). It's all in the game! *Transactional Analysis Journal, 31*: 262–267.

Thunnissen, M. M. (2009). *Een persoonlijkheidsstoornis en nu? (A Personality Disorder—and Now What?).* Koog aan de Zaan, Netherlands: Poiesz Uitgevers Spreekuur thuis.

Thunnissen, M. M. (2010). Redecision therapy with personality disorders: How does it work and what are the results? *Transactional Analysis Journal, 40*: 114–120.

Thunnissen, M. M., Duivenvoorden, H. J., & Trijsburg, R. W. (2001). Experiences of patients after short-term inpatient Transactional Analysis psychotherapy. *Transactional Analysis Journal, 31*(2): 121–128.

Tosi, M. T. (1991). L'alleanza narcisistica nella relazione terapeutica (The narcisistic alliance in the therapeutic relationship). *Atti del Convegno Nazionale di Analisi Transazionale (Proceedings of the National Conference of Transactional Analysis).* April 12–13, Venice, Italy.

Tosi, M. T. (2008). The many faces of the unconscious: A new unconscious for a phenomenological Transactional Analysis. *Transactional Analysis Journal, 38*: 119–127.

Tosi, M. T. (2010). The lived and narrated script: an ongoing narrative construction. In: R. G. Erskine (Ed.), *Life Scripts: a Transactional Analysis of Unconscious Relational Patterns* (pp. 29–54). London: Karnac.

Tosi, M. T. (2011). The challenges of the narrative script. In: R. G. Erskine (Ed.), Life scripts: Definitions and points of view. *Transactional Analysis Journal, 41*: 256–258.

Trautmann, R. L. (1985). Letter from the editor. *Transactional Analysis Journal, 15*: 188–191.

Trautmann, R. L. (2003). Psychotherapy and spirituality. *Transactional Analysis Journal, 33*: 32–36.

Trautmann, R. L., & Erskine, R. G. (1981). Ego states analysis: A comparative view. *Transactional Analysis Journal, 11*: 178–185.

Trautmann, R. L., & Erskine, R. G. (1999). A matrix of relationships: Acceptance speech for the 1998 Eric Berne Memorial Award. *Transactional Analysis Journal, 29*: 14–17.

Tremblay, G., & L'Heureux, P. (2005). Psychosocial interventions with men. *International Journal of Men's Health, 4*: 55–71.

Trevarthen, C., & Aitken, K. (2001). Infant intersubjectivity: Research, theory and clinical applications. *Journal of Child Psychology and Psychiatry, 42*: 3–48.

Tudor, K. (1999). Men in therapy: Opportunity and change. In: J. Wild (Ed.), *Working with Men for Change* (pp. 73–97). London: UCL Press.

Tudor, K. (2003) The neopsyche: The integrating Adult ego state. In C. Sills & H. Hargaden (Eds.), Ego states (pp. 201–231). London, UK: Worth Reading.

Tudor, K. (2007, January 26). Person-centred therapy: Foundations, fundamentals and fundamentalism. Keynote speech at the Annual Congress of the Vereniging voor Cliëntgerichte Psychotherapie (VCgP) (Dutch Society of Client-Centred Therapy), Amersfoort, Holland.

Tudor, K. (2011a). Understanding empathy. *Transactional Analysis Journal, 41*: 39–57.

Tudor, K. (2011b). Empathy: A cocreative perspective. *Transactional Analysis Journal, 41*: 322–335.

Tudor, K., & Hargaden, H. (2002). The couch and the ballot box: The contribution and potential of psychotherapy in enhancing citizenship. In: C. Feltham (Ed.), *What's the Good of Counselling and Psychotherapy? The Benefits Explained* (pp. 156–178). London: Sage.

Tudor, K., & Summers, G. (2014). *Co-creative Transactional Analysis: Papers, Dialogues, Responses, and Developments*. London: Karnac.

Uma Priya, R. (2007). Transactional Analysis and the mind/body connection. *Transactional Analysis Journal, 37*: 286–293.

Van Beekum, S. (2012). Connecting with the undertow: The methodology of the relational consultant. *Transactional Analysis Journal, 42*: 126–133.

Verney, J. (2009). Mindfulness and the Adult ego state. *Transactional Analysis Journal*, *39*: 247–255.

Waldekranz-Piselli, K. C. (1999). What do we do before we say Hello? The body as the stage setting for the script. *Transactional Analysis Journal*, *29*: 31–48.

Wallin, D. (2007). *Attachment in Psychotherapy*. New York: Guilford Press.

Welford, E. (2014). Giving the dead their rightful place: Grief work with the family system. *Transactional Analysis Journal*, *44*: 320–333.

White, T. (2008). The no suicide contract: A relational process. *European Association of Transactional Analysis Newsletter*, October: 7–13.

White, T. (2011). *Working with Suicidal Individuals: a Guide to Providing Understanding, Assessment and Support*. London: Jessica Kingsley.

White, T. (2013). *Working with Drug and Alcohol Users: a Guide to Providing Understanding, Assessment and Support*. London: Jessica Kingsley.

Widdowson, M. (2014). Avoidance, vicious cycles, and experiential disconfirmation of script: Two new theoretical concepts and one mechanism of change in the psychotherapy of depression and anxiety. *Transactional Analysis Journal*, *44*: 194–207.

Wieland, C. (2015). *The Fascist State of Mind and the Manufacturing of Masculinity*. London: Routledge.

Winnicott, D. W. (1949). Mind and its relation to the psyche-soma. In: D. W. Winnicott (Ed.), *Through Paediatrics to Psycho-Analysis: Collected Papers* (pp. 243–254). London: Karnac, 2004.

Winnicott, D. W. (1965). Ego distortions in terms of true and false self. In: *The Maturational Processes and the Facilitating Environment: Studies in the Theory of Emotional Development* (pp. 140–152). London: Karnac.

Winnicott, D. W. (1968). The use of an object. In: *Playing and Reality*. London: Tavistock, 1971.

Winnicott, D. W. (1971). *Playing and Reality*. London: Tavistock.

Winnicott, D. W. (1974). Fear of breakdown. *International Review of Psychoanalysis*, *1*: 103–107.

Winnicott, D. W. (1984). *Deprivation and Delinquency*. C. Winnicott, R. Shepherd, & M. Davis (Eds.). London: Tavistock/Routledge.

Winnicott, D. W. (1989). *Psychoanalytic Explorations*. C. Winnicott, R. Shepherd, & M. Davis (Eds.). Cambridge, MA: Harvard University Press.

Wolf, E. S. (1988). *Treating the Self: Elements of Clinical Self Psychology*. New York: Guilford Press.

Woods, K. (1996). Projective identification and game analysis. *Transactional Analysis Journal*, *26*: 228–231.

Woods, K. (2000). The defensive function of the game scenario. *Transactional Analysis Journal*, *30*: 94–97.

302 REFERENCES

Woods, K. (2001). A case presentation using game theory and levels of defense. *Transactional Analysis Journal, 31*: 268–273.
Woods, K. (2002). Primary and secondary gains from games. *Transactional Analysis Journal, 32*: 190–192.
Woollams, S., & Brown, M. (1978). *Transactional Analysis*. Ann Arbor, MI: Huron Valley Institute Press.
Wyckoff, H. (Ed.) (1976). *Love, Therapy and Politics*. New York: Grove Press.
Zalcman, M. (1990). Game analysis and racket analysis: Overview, critique and future developments. *Transactional Analysis Journal, 20*: 4–19.
Zelazo, P. D., Hong Gao, H., & Todd, R. (2007). The development of consciousness. In: P. D. Zelazo, M. Moscovitch, & E. Thompson (Eds.), *The Cambridge Handbook of Consciousness* (pp. 405–432). Cambridge: Cambridge University Press.
Žvelc, G. (2009). Between self and others: Relational schemas as an integrating construct in psychotherapy. *Transactional Analysis Journal, 39*: 22–38.
Žvelc, G. (2010). Relational schemas theory and transactional analysis. *Transactional Analysis Journal, 40*: 8–22.
Žvelc, G., Černeti , M., & Košak, M. (2011). Mindfulness-based Transactional Analysis. *Transactional Analysis Journal, 41*: 241–254.

INDEX

Mucci, C. 124–125
Murray, H. A. 2
mutual enactment 188

narcissism 111
natural child ego state 161
Naughton, M. 259
new bad object 51–53
Nichol, M. P. 179
Nicotine 176
Nitsun, M. 97
No Exit 37
Nolan, K. 2
nonconscious 125
non-verbal symbol 203
non-verbal therapies 213, 216
Noriega Gayol, G. xiii, 20, 119–120,
    122, 129, 135
normal person suicide 166
Novak, E. T. 13, 120
Novellino, M. 2, 5, 13, 45, 123, 141,
    194, 247
Novey, T. B. 233

obsession, transactional analysis of
    1–25
    and overactivity of mental
        functioning 12
    avoidance 5
    avoidant attachment pattern 14–15
    awareness 8–9
    confrontation 15–16
    definition of 2–3
    elaborative case 9–24
    homeostatic functions 7–8
    intrapsychic reorganisation 6–7
    life script in 5–6
    overview 1–3
    present moment and 8–9
    relational inquiry 22–23
    relational psychotherapy 15
    script system in 5–6, 21

therapeutic errors 13–14
therapeutic relationship 5
Ogden, P. 205
Ogden, T. 43, 51, 188, 192, 199
Ohlsson, T. 28
Olio, K. A. 81
optimal neutrality 44–45
O'Reilly-Knapp, M. 6, 16, 35, 146
original introjected transaction 123

painful sensations 157
palimpsests 155
Pals, J. L. 1
Panksepp, J. 186
parent ego state 25, 124, 149
perfect child 246
Perls, F. S. 58, 142, 146, 148
personality disorder 210
personality theory 162
personality 173, 211
Pfaff, J. J. 166
phase of psychotherapy 148
phenomenological enquiry 193
physis 126–127, 141
Piaget, J. 31, 243
Piaget's formal operations 243
Poland, W. 81
Poland, W. S. 81
Pontalis, J. B. 124
Porges, S. W. x
Porter-Steele, N. 233
Power Is In the Patient, The 58
powerless 196
Price, L. 156
primal image 198
primal judgement 198
procedural memories 140
process of *symbolisation* 242
programme 213
programme therapies 213
projective identification 123–124,
    188, 218